Borges and the Politics of Form

LATIN AMERICAN STUDIES
VOLUME 11
GARLAND REFERENCE LIBRARY OF THE HUMANITIES
VOLUME 1158

LATIN AMERICAN STUDIES
DAVID WILLIAM FOSTER, *Series Editor*

THE CONTEMPORARY PRAXIS
OF THE FANTASTIC
Borges and Cortázar
by Julio Rodríguez-Luis

TROPICAL PATHS
*Essays on Modern
Brazilian Literature*
edited by Randal Johnson

THE POSTMODERN IN LATIN
AND LATINO AMERICAN
CULTURAL NARRATIVES
Collected Essays and Interviews
edited by Claudia Ferman

READERS AND LABYRINTHS
*Detective Fiction in Borges,
Bustos Domecq, and Eco*
by Jorge Hernández Martín

MAGIC REALISM
Social Context and Discourse
by María-Elena Angulo

RESISTING BOUNDARIES
*The Subject of
Naturalism in Brazil*
by Eva Paulino Bueno

LESBIAN VOICES
FROM LATIN AMERICA
Breaking Ground
by Elena M. Martínez

THE JEWISH DIASPORA
IN LATIN AMERICA
*New Studies on
History and Literature*
edited by David Sheinin
and Lois Baer Barr

JEWISH WRITERS
OF LATIN AMERICA
A Dictionary
edited by Darrell B. Lockhart

READERS AND
WRITERS IN CUBA
*A Social History
of Print Culture,
1830s–1990s*
by Pamela Maria Smorkaloff

BORGES AND THE
POLITICS OF FORM
by José Eduardo González

VOICES OF THE SURVIVORS
*Testimony, Mourning, and Memory
in Post-Dictatorship Argentina
(1983–1995)*
by Liria Evangelista

BORGES AND THE POLITICS OF FORM

José Eduardo González

GARLAND PUBLISHING, INC.
A MEMBER OF THE TAYLOR & FRANCIS GROUP
NEW YORK AND LONDON
1998

Copyright © 1998 by José Eduardo González
All rights reserved

Library of Congress Cataloging-in-Publication Data

González, José Eduardo.
    Borges and the politics of form / by José Eduardo González.
       p.   cm. — (Garland reference library of the humanities ; v. 1158.
  Latin American studies ; v. 11)
     Includes index.
     ISBN 0-8153-2803-6 (hc : alk. paper)
    1. Borges, Jorge Luis, 1899– —Political and social views.
2. Politics in literature. I. Title. II. Series: Garland reference library
of the humanities ; vol. 1158. III. Series: Garland reference library
of the humanities. Latin American studies ; vol. 11.
PQ7797.B635Z7273 1998
868—dc21   98-5254
                                                                                                         CIP

Printed on acid-free, 250-year-life paper
Manufactured in the United States of America

CONTENTS

Acknowledgments   vii

Introduction   3

In Search of a Different Modernism   11

Thinking as Pleasure: Borges and the Culture Industry   57

Between Krazy Kat and *Battleship Potemkin*   97

La peinture de la pensée   143

The Other Face of Modernity: Borges as an Antifascist   169

Works Cited   201

Index   209

ACKNOWLEDGMENTS

I would like to thank a number of people for their assistance and support. To Julio Rodríguez-Luis, who was the director of the dissertation from which most of the chapters of my book came from. I am also indebted to David William Foster for his useful editorial comments. Thanks to my family and my friends for their support. I dedicate this book to them, and, especially, to Mildred.

Borges and the Politics of Form

INTRODUCTION

> There were not always novels in the past, and there will not always have to be; not always tragedies, not always great epics; not always were the forms of commentary, translation, indeed, even so-called plagiarism, playthings in the margins of literature; they had a place not only in the philosophical but also in the literary writings of Arabia and China. Rhetoric has not always been a minor form, but set its stamp in antiquity on large provinces of literature–Walter Benjamin, *Reflections*

For years critics have refused to address the question of politics in Borges. With a few exceptions, most critics still see Borges's fiction as "apolitical" or "ahistorical." Those who defend this position argue that Borges was not interested in local but in universal topics. On the other side, we have those who attack Borges because he has withdrawn himself from the "real" world and constructed a fictional world of his own. They accuse Borges of Byzantinism, of failing to address in his literary work contemporary social problems.

In both cases, whether it is to defend or attack Borges, the supposition is that any types of political or historical concerns are entirely absent from his work (or, at least, from his fantastic stories). There are, in fact, very few studies about the political aspects of Borges's writings (see the articles by Franco, "Utopia"; Ruffinelli; Rodríguez-Luis; and Rodríguez Monegal, "Borges and Politics"). Many of those available are simply personal attacks directed at the author and not serious analyses of his work (for example some of the articles in Fló's anthology, *Contra Borges*). But even serious studies of politics in Borges are largely ignored by Borges criticism. The few valuable articles about the topic are never reprinted or included in anthologies of criticism on Borges.[1]

There are two reasons that might help explain the general attitude of Borges critics toward the issue of politics in Borges. One is that Borges himself was against the notion of politically committed art. In his numerous interviews he helped to promote the idea that his stories were "apolitical." The other is the fact that Borges often set his fictions in "exotic" places and that his topics seem to deal with philosophical problems, not with social ones. In fact, one has to admit that the content of Borges's stories tell us very little about the problems and changes that the Argentine society was experiencing at the time he wrote them or about Borges's political ideology. My approach is going to be different. Instead of looking at the *content* of Borges's fiction I will primarily analyze its *form*. To be exact, I will analyze the origins and development of fictional form in Borges's writings. I hope to show that the changes that Borges makes in his style of writing are not arbitrary ones. On the contrary, these formal changes reflect Borges's reaction to the social changes that the Argentine society was undergoing.

I subscribe to Benjamin's statement that "there were not always novels," that literary forms do not appear and disappear without any reason. Although I see formal changes as closely related to social and historical ones, I have tried to stay away from the type of interpretation (*à la* Jameson) that is sometimes too quick to attribute fixed historical meanings to literary forms. In the belief that this kind of generalization limits the use of literary forms for the study of literature, I have chosen to emphasize that a certain literary form might acquire a personal meaning for an author and that he or she might reject or accept that form based on his or her interpretation. Thus, besides trying to understand the historical and traditional meaning of the forms employed by Borges, I also will look for his personal analysis of them. For exam-

---

[1] In an anthology edited by Alazraki (*Critical Essays on Jorge Luis Borges*) there is not a single article dealing with the political aspect of Borges's writings. Only recently, critics like Beatriz Sarlo have begun to pay attention to the historical circumstances under which Borges created his literary work.

ple, what did the fantastic tale or the novel of adventure represent for Borges? Why did he decide to use these forms for his stories? Or why did he have to create a hybrid half-essay/half-short story form for his prose writings? Answering these questions, as I said before, will allow us to see the political meaning of Borges's stories.

I want to use "politics" in this study in the most general sense of the term. I am not referring to any political position taken by Borges on specific issues (even though I will also be addressing that aspect of Borges's politics) but to his attitude in general toward the social changes taking place in Argentina and the problems caused by modernization. The term "modernization" refers to a series of social changes that began to be felt in the West as early as the sixteenth century, but had their greatest impact on the arts toward the end of last century and the beginning of this one. The main changes brought about by modernization were the industrialization of Anglo-European societies, that is, the transition from a precapitalist economy to a capitalist one, and the replacement of a traditional society by one in which all established ideas are challenged and the traditional hierarchical structures dismantled. In his book *All That Is Solid Melts into Air*, Marshall Berman briefly summarizes the incredible amount of changes that were taking place and modifying everyday life:

> The maelstrom of modern life has been fed from so many sources: great discoveries in the physical sciences, changing our images of the universe and our place in it; the industrialization of production, which transforms scientific knowledge into technology, creates new human environments and destroys old ones, speeds up the whole tempo of life, generates new forms of corporate power and class struggle; immense demographic upheavals, severing millions of people from their ancestral habitats, hurtling them half-way across the world into new lives; rapid and often cataclysmic urban growth; systems of mass communication, dynamic in their development, enveloping and binding together the most diverse people and societies; increasingly powerful national states, bureaucratically structured and operated, constantly striving to expand their

powers; mass social movements of people, and peoples, challenging their political and economic rulers, striving to gain some control over their lives; finally, bearing and driving all these people and institutions along, an ever-expanding, drastically fluctuating capitalist world market. (16)

Because of the maelstrom of changes produced by social modernization, modern life is usually characterized by ephemerality and fragmentation. The modern world, as opposed to a traditional one in which everything and everyone had a place assigned beforehand, is one of constant change and uncertainty. Modernity did not break traditional rules and ways of thinking to replace them with new ones for everyone but to allow the coexistence of multiple ideas, to give individuals the freedom to explore different possibilities. Tradition was "replaced" by different, often incompatible, world views. The result of this plurality of points of view was, of course, an overwhelming sense of fragmentation and chaos. The immediate consequence of this fragmentation of modern life is that all sense of historical continuity is lost:

> [M]odernity can have no respect even for its own past, let alone that of any premodern social order. The transitoriness of things makes it difficult to preserve any sense of historical continuity. If there is any meaning to history, then that meaning has to be discovered and defined from within the maelstrom of change, a maelstrom that affects the terms of discussion as well as whatever it is that it is being discussed. Modernity, therefore, not only entails a ruthless break with any or all preceding historical conditions, but it is characterized by a never ending process of internal ruptures and fragmentations within itself. (11-12)

Modernization, as I will use the term in this study, refers to the spread of modern technology as well as social and cultural norms throughout the world. Modernism, on the other hand, is the main cultural manifestation of modernity. Modern culture is the result of the unprecedented social developments produced by modernization, and it is usually considered a representation of them. The main characteristics of Modernism are consequently related to the effects of modernization discussed above: the distrust of history, the rejection of a linear conception of time, the representation of multiple points of views. But the main characteristic, as in the case of social modernization, was an undermining of authority and tradition. Modernist writers rebelled against the arbitrariness of established artistic rules. Modernism, however, is not only a reflection of modernization; as we will see, it also reacts to and rejects many of the changes created by social modernization.

Modernism was a cultural movement that started toward 1880 and lasted until the Second World War. It is usually divided into two periods, the first one ending in the 1930s and usually known by the name of High Modernism. The second one, which lasted approximately until the 1950s, included movements like Surrealism and was both a reaction and a continuation of the first Modernism. Modernism was more than a "movement;" it was several movements. Defining the relationship between Modernism and social modernization has always presented several problems, especially because of the absence of artistic rules that would apply to all modernist movements. Modernism, for example, expresses the same distrust of history and tradition that I have mentioned above as the result of social modernization. But not all modernist writers reacted in a similar way to the fragmentation of history. Some authors tried to order the chaos and fragmentation of modern life by using myth. Myth became a structuring device that helped writers to put contemporary history in order. But there were also writers, especially after the 1930s, who rejected any idea of order and embraced the total chaos of modern life (an attitude also found in earlier movements like Dadaism). Modernism is full of this type of contradictions as can be seen from another controversial characteristic that should be mentioned here. I am referring to the general modernist view of the relation between art and society. Some modernist artists, especially high-modernist ones, proclaimed the autonomy of the work of art. That is, they saw their art as detached from society, as a self-sufficient object. Art for them existed in a world of its own and bore no relation to society. But again not everyone agreed with the idea of aesthetic autonomy. For other writers Modernism's challenging of tradition and history, its disposition to break all the rules, made it the perfect vehicle to subvert the established social order (see Bürger, *Theory of the Avant-Garde*). By subverting the artistic and communicative norms of society, Modernism was attacking "the bourgeois social structure" and the capitalist economical system in general. This characteristic is perhaps more evident in late modernist movements like Surrealism, but, again, it can also be found in some high-modernist works. There are other characteristics of Modernism, such as emphasis on originality, the idea of will-to-style, the rejection of popular culture that will be introduced in the following chapters. I am particularly interested, then, in two manifestations of modernity to which Borges reacts. One is the modernist literary movement mentioned above and the other is the economic and social modernization of Argentina. Borges's evaluation of these two events is determined by the difference in how the modernization process occurred in the most industrialized countries and in Latin America: as I will explain in my first chapter, social modernization was not a homogeneous process in the Anglo-European world or in Latin America. The main difference was, of course, Latin America's economic and cultural situation of dependency on the industrialized world. The nature of the modernization process in Latin America is in great part determined by this dependency.

Each one of my chapters deals with a specific aspect of the form of Borges's short stories—i.e., his solution to the perennial Modernism/Realism opposition, his adaptation of popular literature elements—but in many cases the reader will discover that in every new chapter I keep going back to issues discussed in the previous ones. For example, my analysis of Borges's style begins in my first chapter, when I try to interpret the meaning of the several stylistic stages that his prose goes through. However, since the group of texts that I am most interested in analyzing in this book are the *ficciones* that he wrote during the decades of the 1940s and 1950s, my third and fourth chapters are devoted to discovering the origin and ideological meaning of the paratactic style in which he wrote them (which is also the style that is most commonly associated with Borges, partly because it is to the stories from this period that he owes his fame). Thus, in my third chapter I disprove the theory that this paratactic style is the result of an imitation of cinematic montage techniques. But it is not until the fourth chapter that I finally offer a theory about his distinctive fragmentary prose as having its origin in his studies of Spanish and English baroque literature and British Empiricism. This does not mean that the chapters cannot be read individually. The book has been written in a way that allows its chapters to be studied non-sequentially.

My first chapter focuses on Borges's reaction to the social and cultural modernization that Argentina was undergoing during the first decades of this century. The argument centers on Borges's recognition of Argentina's condition of cultural and economic "dependence" that became evident to everyone after the 1929 crash, and his artistic responses to those problems. Borges saw the two possible economic options, dependency or nationalism (a rejection of foreign influence), as represented by the two competing artistic models of Modernism and Realism, respectively. This led him to search for an alternative to both of them and to use the fantastic genre as an artistic or imaginary solution to the condition of "dependency."

The second chapter, "Thinking as Pleasure," is concerned with the influence of the culture industry, another aftereffect of the early modernization of Argentina, on Borges's work. I try to prove in this chapter that the precarious economic situation in which the Borgeses found themselves during the 1930s brought an abrupt end to the artificial separation of "work" and literature (writing as the opposite of working, of making money) that Borges had always taken for granted as a young man. The paradoxical result of Borges having to work to support his family is that the Anglo-European modernist notion of *writing as work* is banished from his fictional texts. Curiously, the structural organization that is required in order to eliminate "work" from his fictions is also what allows him to incorporate as part of his narrations elements from popular literature and erase the boundary between "highbrow" (modernist) art and "lowbrow" commercial products.

The third chapter, entitled "Between Krazy Kat and *Battleship Potemkin*," is a continuation of the investigation initiated in the previous one about the relation between Borges's fictional texts and the culture industry. In these two chapters I have tried to show how the structure of Borges's fictions allows (and encourages) the reader to derive "intellectual" pleasure from them. More importantly, however, is that by analyzing the influence of commercial art on Borges we can notice the amazing ability of the Borgesean discourse to appropriate and neutralize other discourses—something that I find strikingly similar to the strategies employed by the American classical film to appropriate alternative modes of filmmaking.

My fourth chapter, "*La peinture de la pensée*," was initially intended to be a correction of most studies of Borges's style, which have usually ignored the importance of the baroque style for Borges's creation of his "estilo entrecortado." The entire chapter is devoted to an interpretation of his style as a reaction to the overspecialization brought about by social modernization. It also argues that what is normally taken to be an example of Postmodernism in his texts—the "death of the subject"—could also be read as a nostalgia for a pre-modern time.

My last chapter focuses on the evolution of Borges's political ideology during the last three decades of his life. The key to understand this period of his life and work, I believe, is found in his experience with fascism and Peronism. Thus, I try to find in his anti-fascist and anti-Peronist writings an explanation for the distrust in democratic politics that he repeatedly expressed later in life.

IN SEARCH OF A DIFFERENT MODERNISM

One of the most widely accepted theories about the origin of artistic Modernism is based on the idea that, in Europe, the modernization and industrialization of society created the feeling that a new age either had begun or was going to arrive soon:

> Modernity's specific orientation toward the future is shaped precisely to the extent that societal modernization tears apart the old European experiential space of the peasant's and craftsman's lifeworlds, mobilizes it, and devalues it into directives guiding expectations. These traditional experiences of previous generations are then replaced by the kind of progress that lends to our horizon of expectation (till then anchored fixedly in the past) a "historically new quality, constantly subject to being overlaid with utopian conceptions." (Habermas 12)

The idea of modernity draws its power from a material experience of progress that offers modern subjects the possibility of Utopia: the belief that the world can be radically transformed in all its aspects. It is this modern and highly optimistic dream of Utopia that is represented in the arts as the desire for the New and for originality (Adorno 47; Jameson, *Postmodernism* 312-13). The formal innovations, as well as the creation of new literary movements or "isms," were the unavoidable after-effects of the spirit of modernity. Modernization, which in this account of modernity seems to mean primarily economic development, acted as a powerful catalyst for the new cultural movement that appeared in Europe toward the end of last century. Most historians of modernity admit that, on the one hand, the capitalist economic development during the nineteenth century tore down the ancient feudal world in Europe and, as a consequence, slowly turned organic communities into alienated and atomized societies and that, on the other, the same development also brought positive changes to the material and spiritual world. Modernization, for example, transformed the individual lives and personalities of the people living directly under its influence. There was, in the modern European world, "a tremendous emancipation of the possibility and sensibility of the individual self, now increasingly released from the fixed social status and rigid role-hierarchy of the precapitalist past, with its narrow morality and cramped imaginative range" (Anderson 98). It is this positive aspect of modernity that gave rise to Utopian expectations.[1] To measure the importance of this Utopian feeling for European Modernism one has to remember that the European world during the high-modernist period was still largely premodern. It is exactly that dream of a new society that "encouraged" modernist writers to emphasize in their writings the modern side (modern technology and behavior) of their social environment and to suppress its very strong premodern elements. In an excellent critique of Marshall Berman's book on Modernism, *All That Is Solid Melts into Air*, Perry Anderson argues that one of the decisive socioeconomic "coordinates" in relation to which one must understand the emergence of that cultural movement was the "imaginative proximity of social revolution" (see Perry Anderson's article, "Modernity and Revolution"). In 1914 the economies of the European countries were still mostly run by agrarian and aristocratic classes. During this time, Anderson tells us, industrialization was rapidly dismantling the forms of the *ancient régime*. However, there was not yet a single capitalist democracy fully formed. Whether a capitalist or a socialist new order would follow the disappearance of the old regime was still uncertain. Thus, Anderson argues that the prospect of a revolution during this epoch helped to foment the hope for change that lies at the base of artistic Modernism. In the following pages I will contend that the evolution of Borges as a writer can only be explained by the tension between his early utopian feelings and a pessimistic attitude that kept growing throughout his life. Moreover,

---

[1]For an excellent account of the social changes brought about by modernity and their effects on the artistic world, see Berman's *All That Is Solid Melts Into Air* and Harvey's *The Condition of Postmodernity*.

Borges's relation to artistic Modernism can only be understood in relation to the modification of his utopian dreams. After the preceding reflections on the importance that the search for the New had on the origin and development of modernist literature, the obvious first step should be to interpret the meaning of Borges's well-known rejection of originality in literature. The idea that writers are unable to create anything new or that everything has already been written, appears time and again in Borges's texts. However, one should not yield to the temptation of thinking that this characteristic automatically turns Borges into a postmodern writer. It is more fruitful to look for the origin of Borges's rejection of the New in the meaning that this concept acquires within his particular historical situation.

Borges was not always opposed to modernist aesthetics. In fact, the young Borges was an avid reader and an enthusiastic promoter of modernist literature. He was a member of an avant-garde group called "Ultraism" (*Ultraísmo*) while residing in Spain during the 1920s, and later he was responsible for taking the main ideas of that movement to Argentina. Ultraism was a literary movement that, like many other "isms" during the modernist period, tried to express a new perception of literature. Its most distinctive characteristic was that it saw metaphor as the essential element of poetry. The purpose of the Ultraist poets was to transcend or go beyond (ultra) everyday reality through the creation of extremely original metaphors. As it happened with other avant-garde movements during this period (the first two decades of the century), social and political justice were important issues for Ultraism.

One of the most interesting aspects of Borges's Ultraist work are the first poems that he wrote as a member of the movement, some of which were dedicated to Russia and to the Russian Revolution.[2]

---

[2]Borges collected these early poems in a book that he never published. Borges says that he destroyed the manuscript (entitled either *The Red Psalms* or *The Red Rhythms*) before he left Spain (March 1921) (see Borges, "Autobiographical Essay" 223; Rodríguez Monegal, *Literary Biography* 165-66). Some of the poems, however, were published between 1919 and 1921 in several literary magazines (*Ultra*, *Grecia*, *Cosmópolis*). They all have been collected by Carlos Meneses (Borges,

Given the antagonistic attitude that Borges developed later in his life toward politically committed art, some literary critics are still at pains trying to explain Borges's early attitude in favor of this revolutionary movement. While some critics have chosen to use those poems—and other writings—to defend Borges from those who criticize him because of his political opinions (Rodríguez Monegal, "Borges and Politics"), others have suggested that Borges's attitude was a "concession" to his friends and other members of the Ultraist movement (Ruffinelli). What Perry Anderson's theory suggests to us, however, is that Borges's enthusiasm for the Revolution seems to have been, at least at some point, genuine and that it was, if not the origin, an essential part of the young Borges's artistic project. Originality in poetry, for Borges at the time, went hand in hand with social change.

An important element in the connection that Borges saw between poetry and politics came from his readings of Expressionist poetry. Rodríguez Monegal has pointed out that from the very beginning this artistic movement became associated in Borges's mind with World War I.[3] Borges and his familiy were traveling through Europe when that war broke out and for the duration of the conflict they safely lived in Switzerland, which was neutral. One of the ways in which Borges "experienced" this war was through the eyes of the German Expressionist poets. Expressionism was a movement that flourished be-

---

Poesía juvenil).

[3]Rodríguez Monegal devotes an entire chapter of his *Literary Biography* to the influence of Expressionism on the young Borges (144-49). Expressionism, as defined by R.S. Furness, was "the expression of a subjective vision regardless of mimesis, a concern for human life, a concern for man crushed by pitiless machinery and ruthless cities which was far more intense and poignant than the naturalist's description of social conditions" (63). One should notice that the Expressionist emphasis on subjectivity deeply influenced Borges and became, in fact, a determinant element in his future aesthetic and political positions (see my chapter "The Other Face"). Espressionist poetry also influenced the Ultraist movement in general, especially with the concept of the metaphor as "expressive rather than imititative" (Furness 20).

tween 1906 and the early 1920s and that extended over visual arts, music, and literature. Even though by some accounts the movement survived until the early 1930s, the First World War can be mentioned as one of the events that put an end to it because, among many reasons, some of the leading artists of the movement died during the conflict. Curiously, Borges attributes the intensity of the Expressionist poetry to the fact that the poets experienced the war first hand (*Inquisiciones* 147-48). His Ultraist poetry was greatly influenced by the extremely unusual Expressionist images but also by the denunciation of the war and by the idea of a world brotherhood that he found there. These were elements that contributed to his view of an interrelationship between art and politics.[4] Perhaps it is more important to notice, however, that in Borges's evaluation of Expressionism, he finds a close tie between "real life" or experiences in the real world and literature. This is exactly the type of connection that is going to progressively disappear from Borges's view of literature and that will be in the end replaced by the idea that literature comes out of literature, not life.

But the fact that at one point in his life Borges saw as interrelated literary innovations and revolutionary social movements is in reality less interesting than how Borges redefined his conception of Ultraism once he abandoned his early politically committed attitude. Jorge Ruffinelli shows that, after Borges returned to Argentina, he "purified" the Ultraist movement by excluding from it any type of political concerns and rhetoric. Borges turned Ultraism into a movement preoccupied only with an aesthetic revolution. One could suggest that Borges's early poetry, which looked like an imitation of Futurism, was a positive response to the modern society that he was experiencing in Europe: "Spanish ultraism," Borges would say years later, "was overburdened . . . with modernity and gadgets" ("Autobiographical Essay" 225). Obviously the very different social conditions that he found in his

---

[4]The political aspect of Expressionism was the center of a debate between Ernst Bloch and Georg Lukács during the mid 1930s. See Bloch's "Discussing Expressionism" and Lukács's response, "Realism in the Balance." Lukács's defense of Realism was one of the first serious challenges to modernist aesthetics.

native Argentina will force him to revalue his literary project. In *Inquisiciones* (1925), Borges already notices that the idea of the New, so important for Spanish Ultraism, does not attract him anymore:

> El ultraísmo de Sevilla y Madrid fue la voluntad de renuevo, fue la voluntad de ceñir el tiempo del arte con un ciclo novel, fue la lírica escrita como con grandes letras coloradas en las hojas del calendario y cuyos más preclaros emblemas—el avión, las antenas y la hélice—son decidores de una actualidad cronológica. El ultraísmo en Buenos Aires fue el anhelo de recabar un arte absoluto que no dependiese del prestigio infiel de las voces y que durase en la perennidad del idioma como una certidumbre de la hermosura. Bajo la enérgica claridad de las lámparas fueron frecuentes, en los cenáculos españoles, los nombres de Huidobro y de Apollinaire. Nosotros, mientras tanto, sopesábamos líneas de Garcilaso, andariegos y graves a lo largo de las estrellas del suburbio, solicitando un límpido arte que fuese tan intemporal como las estrellas de siempre.[5]

This regression to premodern aesthetics of beauty and the eternal in art (the "universal"), as we will see, is mainly a projection of Borges's de-

---

[5]"Ultraism in Seville and Madrid was a desire for renewal; it was a desire to define a new cycle in the arts; it was a poetry written as if with big red letters on the leaves of a calendar and whose proudest emblems—airplanes, antennae, and propellers—plainly state a chronological nowness. Ultraism in Buenos Aires was the ambition to obtain an absolute art which did not depend on the uncertain prestige of words, and which lasted in the eternity of language as a conviction of beauty. Under the powerful brightness of the lamps, the names of Huidobro and Apollinaire were usually mentioned in Spanish gatherings. We, in the meantime, tested lines from Garcilaso [a Spanish Renaissance poet], wandering ponderously under the stars on the outskirts of the town, asking for an art which was as atemporal as the stars." (*Inquisiciones* 96-97; Rodríguez Monegal's translation, *Literary Biography* 173)

sire to "elevate" Argentine culture to the level of what he considers to be great [European] cultures.

It must be emphasized, however, that the celebration of the New did not disappear completely from Borges's writings after his return to Argentina but that he modified it. The factor that kept the idea of the New alive in his mind was the extraordinary economic development that transformed Argentina during the first two decades of this century (see Sarlo, *Una modernidad periférica* and the first chapter of her book *Jorge Luis Borges*; also Rodríguez Monegal, *Literary Biography* 167-68). Borges was able to contrast the small town that he left with the growing metropolis that he found when he came back. Buenos Aires was becoming a city comparable to the most prosperous European cities at that time. However, Buenos Aires was not fully developed yet (Sarlo, *Jorge Luis Borges* 9-19), and, furthermore, the rest of the country was still living in a eighteenth- or early nineteenth-century world. It is interesting that upon his return to Argentina, Borges does not seem to be preoccupied any longer with some abstract future society but with the possibility of real development within Argentine society. It is no surprise then that

> Argentine *ultraísmo* quickly evolved into another more nationalistically inspired movement now usually termed *martinfierrismo* . . . in which Borges also figured prominently. Now his futuristic vision ("futuristic" in the literal sense) also embraced a desire for a more lucid and authentic national literature, centered (for him) on images of the old quarters of his beloved Buenos Aires. (Irby, "Borges and the Idea" 39)

The City fulfills a double function in these early poems. On the one hand, Borges's reminiscence of the "old quarters," the old Buenos Aires, was part of a general tendency at the time to recover a lost urban past. With the great influx of immigrants coming to Buenos Aires from Europe and from the countryside, and with the economic development of the country in general, the urban landscape acquired a different shape. The City changed to the point that its old inhabitants (who had sentimental ties to it that the "foreigners" did not share) could no longer recognize it:

> [By] the early thirties the cables of electric wires had replaced the old systems of gas and kerosene. The sky of Buenos Aires was already criss-crossed by telephone wires and the roofs were full of radio aerials, for radio came to Buenos Aires as early as it did to the United States. Motorized transport, in particular the trams and the trains, had expanded and diversified. The inhabitants of the city lived at an unprecedented pace: the experience of speed, the experience of artificial light—and of long-distance communications, which would soon give rise to a powerful culture industry—provided a new set of images and perceptions. Those who, like Borges, were older than twenty in 1925 could remember with nostalgia the city at the turn of the century, and could confirm the difference.... The impact of these transformations, which took place in a relatively short period of time, had a subjective dimension: in reality men and women could remember a city that was different from the one in which they were now living. Furthermore, that earlier city was again different to that of their childhood or adolescence. These people's past underlined what had been lost (or what had been gained) in the modern city of the present. (Sarlo, *Jorge Luis Borges* 11-12)

Trying to heal the psychological effects of the alienation that resulted from those changes, books about the old Buenos Aires, old Mexico, or Rio de Janeiro proliferated during the end of last century and the first decades of this one (Rama, *La ciudad* 95-101). On the other hand, the City always symbolized progress for the modernist artists. And in Borges's first books Buenos Aires seems to be fulfilling a similar inspirational function. The difference is that, now, the aim of Borges's utopian view of the future is not linked to any transformation of the social relations prevalent in the modern (European) world, nor is the search for originality and innovation in literature really important for his aesthetics any more. His notion of progress is apparently limited to seeing Buenos Aires reach the level of economic development of the more industrialized societies: "If the providential rain and the providential Italian do not fail us, we will become the Chicago of this side of the planet and even its bakery."[6] Borges's Utopia is a Buenos Aires transformed by a collective effort that, as Irby correctly notices, anticipates that other collective (but fictional) effort to create the Utopia of "Tlön" ("Borges and the Idea" 39). The mission of the Argentine artist at that historical junction, as Borges saw it, was to lay down the foundations for the creation of a future culture with its own distinctive character. That is to say, the creation of a culture that could compete with the old European cultures. A cultural enterprise had to match the economic one that was already underway:

> ya Buenos Aires, más que una ciudá, es un país y hay que encontrarle la poesía y la música y la pintura y la religión y la metafísica que con su grandeza se avienen. Ese es el tamaño de mi esperanza, que a todos nos invita a ser dioses y a trabajar en su encarnación. (Borges, *El tamaño de mi esperanza* 9)[7]

Borges's vision of Argentina's future was utopian in more than one sense: it was impossible for Argentina to achieve real development since its economy was dependent on the markets of what are now called First World countries. One has to be careful when using the expression "First World" as a shorthand for the societies that have been industrialized most rapidly or successfully. One of the prevailing misconceptions about modernization is that whereas in the "First World" it was a homogeneous process, in Latin America, and perhaps in other areas of the

---

[6]Borges's "Afterword" to Pereda Valdés' *Anthology of Modern Uruguayan Poetry* (1927), qtd. in Rodríguez Monegal (*Literary Biography*, 59).

[7]"Now Buenos Aires, more than a city, is a country, and we must find the poetry and the music and the painting and the religion and the metaphysics that correspond to its greatness. That is the magnitude of my hope, which invites all of us to be gods and work toward . . . its incantation." (trans. in Irby, "Borges and the Idea" 39)

Third World, the process was a very uneven one. Not only did all the countries in the so-called First World develop at the same pace, but the modernization that took place in those societies was by no means a homogeneous one. Toward the first decades of this century, as I mentioned above quoting Anderson, even the most industrialized societies were still largely premodern, and in that respect perhaps not very different from the Argentine society of the 1920s. Even today it is impossible to talk about societies that are totally homogeneous (see Jameson, *The Political Unconscious* 95; Raymond Williams 121-27).

One of the elements that affected the different directions that modernization was going to take in Europe and Latin America was the condition of dependency. Like many other Latin American countries, Argentina's integration into the world market economy occurred during the late nineteenth century as part of the establishment of international specialization (or international "division of labor" as it is sometimes called). The nation oriented its economy toward the exportation of raw materials needed by the rapidly industrializing European countries. The economic "boom" at the beginning of the century was the result, not of real industrialization as it happened in some parts of Europe but of an extensive and effective use of land for the production of agrarian exports (such as wheat, wool, and meat), sometimes at the expense of subsistence economic activities (Furtado 27-34). The situation is symptomatic of what was happening all over Latin America.

When all the emphasis was put on exportation, local industries were neglected and a situation of dependence quickly followed. Peripheral countries not only needed the Center to sell their products but also needed to buy from it essential materials that were no longer produced locally, or that, because of the advanced technology necessary for their production, had to be imported. In Argentina's case, its condition of dependence on the European centers (especially and almost exclusively England), which later was going to be the main cause of Argentina's underdevelopment, became evident with the 1929 economic crisis. Although the national economy had been weakening in the years previous to the crisis, 1929 seems to constitute a sort of "border line" after which Borges began to question the equation modernism = economic progress,[8] and would slowly convince himself that Argentina would never escape what he used to call its "South American destiny," meaning by this that his native land would never reach the stage of development of the most advanced European societies (see Rodríguez-Luis, "La intención política"; Jean Franco, "Utopia of a Tired Man"). Obviously, these changes in his way of thinking did not take place overnight. It was a process whose evolution one can follow in Borges's ambiguous attitude toward modernity. And also in the way that Borges redefines his artistic work after he recognized that Argentina was not going to be modernized at the same pace or in the same way as the industrialized countries in Europe. This realization resulted in turning the modernization of Argentine cultural production into a questionable project. Borges's disappointment with the possibilities of social modernization for Argentina, was quickly followed by a revaluation of "cultural progress," which for him was previously symbolized by modernist artistic forms. In a few years the project of social and cultural renovation that he so enthusiastically embraced in the 1920s had partially vanished for Borges. We will see that after an initial rejection of literary Modernism both in its European and Latin American versions, the first half of the

---

[8]"In 1929 dies Beatriz Viterbo, the woman that the main character of 'The Aleph' was in love with. . . . It is also the date engraved on one of the coin's sides in 'The Zahir' and also the date the immortal finally dies; a year later [1930] the events of 'El evangelio según Marcos' take place (*Doctor Brodie's Report*). The role that 1929 seems to play in these stories is that of the ending of a period and the beginning of a revelation. . . . In 1929 Borges is thirty years old and this coincides with a social crisis in Argentina and with his first fictional writings" (Rodríguez-Luis 184). It should be added that in 1929 Otto Dietrich zur Linde (the main character in "Deutsches Requiem") joined the Nazi party, and in "La señora mayor" this is the year when the old lady loses contact with reality.

1930s becomes for Borges a period of transition in which he will look for an alternative to literary Modernism.[9]

A significant change in Borges's style takes place during this epoch. The style that Borges practiced during his avant-garde years was one characterized by daring metaphors and long sentences often linked together by loose conjunctions. He used to put a great emphasis on local slang and on the creation of neologisms. During the early 1930s Borges begins to change his style to what is commonly known as *style coupé*, a style that was frequently practiced by Baroque writers in the sixteenth and seventeenth centuries. Although I will attempt a fuller analysis of the origin, structure, and ideological meaning of the style chosen by Borges in another chapter (see *La peinture*), it will be helpful for our present purpose to give a brief description of the *style coupé*. Also known as curt period or curt style, the *style coupé* distinguishes itself for the briefness of its periods and the absence of causative links that normally connect the sentences in a paragraph. The sentences and paragraphs are broken into very small units, usually separated from each other by a semicolon or a period. The result is a style that is, at times,

---

[9]In an interview with Rosalba Campra, Borges talked about the possibility that Argentina's history may have influenced his writings. One should, of course, notice that he divides this history in two parts, one composed by the first two decades of the century and the other by the rest.

> I believe that even if one would not like to admit it, I believe that there is one [i.e., there is a relationship between historical reality and literature]. I am not particularly interested in politics. But it is obvious that this country was a rapidly developing country towards 1910, towards 1920, and that now [1973] it is falling apart. I suppose that this might influence literature, but not necessarily. Perhaps a country's decline is beneficial for literature. (Campra 128)

The last sentence is an allusion to the quality of his post-1930 writings. After 1929—the beginning of Argentina's "decline"—Borges wrote the stories that made him famous.

very difficult to read because of the absence of transitions. One can already see in *Discusión* (1932) an overlapping of both ways of writing.

As significant as that change of style is the fact that Borges began to write fiction during this time. As an avant-garde writer he only wrote poetry and essays, but as soon as he became discontented with Modernism, Borges started to write fictional prose. It seems that he wanted to reject everything related to his avant-garde years. Borges will only return to poetry years later, but he will never write avant-garde poems again. Obviously, the transition from poetry to narrative cannot be summarized as a simple change from one style to another. When Borges began to write prose he developed two "narrative systems" whose formal structures express two possible alternatives to Modernism (and to his own avant-garde poetry). Both "systems" employ the new *style coupé*, but with different aims. The origin of one of these systems appears in the half-essay/half-short stories of *A Universal History of Infamy* (1935). I am referring, of course, to the disjointed narrative construction and broken style that, after it was refined, became the central form of his fantastic fiction. Fantastic fiction will be in fact the second narrative system employed by Borges, and we will later see how it was constructed as an alternative to Modernism. But first, I will focus my attention on the other system developed by Borges.

The system that I am talking about was used only once, for the story "Street Corner Man" ("El hombre de la esquina rosada"), and, after that, it was constantly, almost obsessively, rejected by Borges. But it was also remembered through each one of those rejections. In many of his numerous interviews Borges mentions "Street Corner Man," even if it is only to call it a "bad," or badly written story, or one of his youthful "mistakes."[10] It is interesting to notice at the same time that

---

[10] For an example of Borges's typical comments about "Street Corner Man" see the following interviews, Burgin 48, Sorrentino 48; in his interviews with Charbonnier he keeps mentioning the story, even though Charbonnier is obviously not interested in talking about it (Charbonnier 5 and 8). In his "Autobiographical Essay," Borges says about the story: "It took me some six years, from 1927 to 1933, to go from the all too

Borges never prohibited its republication as he did with so many of his early poems and books of essays. This text was Borges's first short story and one of his most reworked ones. In it a narrator tells us the story of Rosendo Juárez, a man admired and respected in the slums of Buenos Aires. Rosendo is said to have killed at least two men and, apparently for that reason, he is considered to be a brave man. He has become a sort of local hero. The night the story takes place, Francisco Real, a "foreigner," that is, a person from another part of Buenos Aires, comes to the bar where Rosendo is drinking. Francisco has heard of Rosendo's fame and challenges him to a fight. But inexplicably to everyone present in the bar, Rosendo refuses to fight and leaves the place. Francisco makes fun of him and everyone in the bar thinks that Rosendo is a coward. Later that night, however, Francisco Real is found dead, after apparently having fought with someone. Everyone simply assumes that Rosendo has killed Francisco. But in the last couple of sentences, the reader learns that it is the narrator of the story himself, who up to this moment has been presented to us as a coward, who has killed Real. We discover that the narrator fought with Real because, like everybody else, he admired Rosendo and felt ashamed of Rosendo's behavior that night.

In an interview Borges hinted at the political meaning of this story:

> I had the misfortune of writing a completely unrealistic [*falso*] short story: "Street Corner Man." In my preface to *A Universal History of Infamy* I stated that it was deliberately unrealis-

---

self-conscious sketch 'Hombres pelearon' to my first outright story, 'Hombre de la esquina rosada' (Street Corner Man). . . . Originally titled 'Hombres de las orillas' (Men from the Edge of Town), the story appeared in the Saturday supplement, which was a bit beneath me, I signed with a pen-name, the name of one of my great-grandfathers, Francisco Bustos. Although the story became popular to the point of embarrassment (today I find it stagy and mannered and the characters bogus), I never regarded it as a starting point. It simply stands there as a kind of freak" (*The Aleph* 238).

tic. I knew that the story was impossible. It was more fantastic than any other tale that I have intentionally written as a fantastic short story, and yet I owe the little fame I have to that story. . . . And even though later on I wrote another story, "Rosendo's Tale" ["Historia de Rosendo Juárez"], as a sort of antidote to the other one, it was not taken seriously by anyone. I do not know if people read it, or pretended not to have read it, or maybe they took it as the result of a bad mood of mine. The fact is that I wanted to retell the same story as it could have happened, as I knew it could have happened when I wrote "Street Corner Man" in 1930, in Androgué. The scene of the challenge is unrealistic; the fact that the narrator hides that he is the murderer until the end of the story is unrealistic and it is not justified by anything [in the short story]; the language is so full of local slang that it sounds like a caricature. But may be one needs the kind of unreality that this story features. Also, the story lent itself to nationalistic vanities, like the idea that we were (or we had been) very courageous; may be that is why people liked it. When I was rereading it for a new edition I felt very ashamed of it and I tried to erase words or expressions that were obviously a bad imitation of local speech, in other words, that looked unrealistic. Curiously, those who admire this short story call it "Hombre de la Casa Rosada" ["Man from the Pink House"] (Audience laughs) and assume that I am talking about the President. (María Esther Vázquez 47)

The Casa Rosada (Pink House) is the seat of the government in Argentina. Borges was no doubt scorning Roger Callois' French translation of his story. Callois gave it the title "L'Homme au coin de la maison rose," which literally means "The man on the corner of the Pink House." According to Borges, pink corner refers to "the painted walls of the street-corner *almacenes*, [which] were both groceries and saloons, where men drank and played cards" (*The Aleph* 266). However, there is no mention in the story of the bar being at a corner nor of the color of its walls.[11] The president that Borges is referring to is Hipólito Irigoyen, for whom Borges actively campaigned in 1927. It is difficult not to see the parallel that Borges's contemporaries noticed between the story plot and what happened during the Irigoyen administration. An extremely popular president when he was elected, Irigoyen, like Rosendo Juárez in the story, did not know how to react when he had to face the country's economic problems, especially the 1929 crisis already mentioned. Toward 1930 Irigoyen became extremely isolated, losing contact not only with the Argentine people but also with the other members of his party. He was easily overthrown that year by a military *coup d'état*. Against this background it is easy to see why the readers of this story saw it as symbolic of the country's situation: Juárez's popularity, and the isolation he is in after his refusal to fight, and the shame felt by the narrator and other members of the neighborhood stand for Irigoyen's amazing popularity, for his inability to face the country's problems, and for the feeling of shame that his behavior might have provoked among the Argentine people.[12] Within this context, the meaning of the narra-

---

[11]See Bernès, "Notes et variantes." 1498. Bernès also makes a very interesting analysis of three words of the title (*hombre*, *esquina* and *rosada*). These "notes" appear in Bernès's French edition of Borges's complete works, which is, by far, the best one that has been published in any language.

[12]In a letter to Alfonso Reyes explaining the reasons for the *coup d'état*, Borges said:

> About the supression of the *Doctor* [i.e., Irigoyen], I can assure you that, in spite of the fact that it was needed, it was necessary, it was just, it has created a very disagreeable atmosphere. The revolution (or army coup supported by the people) is a victory of common sense against the usual dishonesty and the arbitrariness, but all these bad things corresponded to a mythology, to a tenderness, to a happiness, to an extravagant image of the Doctor conspiring from the presidential palace itself. Buenos Aires had to repudiate his domestic mythology and build very quickly some enthusiasm for *acts of heroism* in which nobody really believes, on the basis (insignificant for the

tor's behavior in "Street Corner Man" (he overcomes his fear and kills Real) is clearly that of a call for the Argentine people to act heroically in a moment of crisis. Borges seems to be asking the Argentine people to do something to get out of the crisis. The story promotes a nationalistically inspired rejection of foreign influence. In relation to that, the word "rosada" in the title (as well as the name of the main character, "Rosendo") suggests the name of Juan Manuel Rosas, Argentina's nineteenth-century strongman. In one of his early writings Borges sees similarities between Irigoyen and Rosas, both seen as symbols of nationalism:

> El silencio arrimado al fatalismo tiene eficaz encarnación en los dos caudillos mayores que abrazaron el alma de Buenos Aires: en Rosas e Irigoyen. Don Juan Manuel, pese a sus fechorías e inútil sangre derramada, fue queridísimo del pueblo. Irigoyen, pese a las mojigangas oficiales, nos está siempre gobernando. La significación que el pueblo apreció en Rosas,

---

> spirit) that these soldiers are not thieves. To sacrifice Myth to Lucidity, what do you think? Bernard Shaw, undoubtedly, would approve. . . . [B]efore (I repeat) we had stupidity but with it the noisy opposition newspapers, the "Long Live" and "Death To" which flourished on the walls, in the tangos and milongas; now we have *Independence Under Martial Law*, a fawning press . . . an the established myth that the former regime was cruel and tyrannical (qtd. in Rodríguez Monegal, *Literary Biography* 231-32).

Rodríguez Monegal adds, after quoting the letter, that the letter "shows that Georgie [Borges] had finally come to believe all that a corrupted press had said about Irigoyen and his friends. But Georgie was right about the Irigoyen myth, and that was what really mattered" (232). Obviously, the acts of heroism that he was expecting to see were of a different kind. But at least until he believed in the necessity to create a mythology for Buenos Aires.

entendió en Roca y admira en Irigoyen, es el escarnio de la teatralidad, o ejercerla con sentido burlesco.[13]

"Street Corner Man," then, can be seen as a reaction to both the social and the artistic situation in Argentina at the moment the story was written. On the one hand, Borges seems to suggest the necessity to adopt a nationalistic attitude to solve the problems brought about by a modernization based on Argentina's dependence on foreign markets. On the other, he opposes the realism of "Street Corner Man" to the modernist aesthetics that at the time were being copied by Argentine writers. However, this nationalistic and conservative reaction was short lived. As Borges became more pessimistic, this initial nationalist outburst appeared useless to him, a mistake. Thus, when in his interview with Vázquez Borges calls the story unreal (*cuento falso*: false, unreal), he is not only referring to the mimetic pretensions of the style employed but also to the political and artistic position expressed in it. As Borges himself says in the interview, he rewrote "Street Corner Man" years later and published it as "Rosendo's Tale" (in *Doctor Brodie's Report* [1970]). If in the first story the narrator turns out to be more courageous than Juárez, in this new version Rosendo Juárez describes the cowardly fashion in which the narrator of "Street Corner Man" really killed Francisco Real. The narrator's act was thus not one of heroism but of cowardice. If previously the courageous act of the narrator in "Street Corner Man" was intended to show Borges's faith in Argentina's capacity to move forward, it is obvious that by the time he writes "Rosendo's Tale" that faith has completely disappeared.

---

[13]"Silence combined with fatalism is effectively embodied in the major caudillos who have captured Buenos Aires' soul: Rosas and Irigoyen. Don Juan Manuel, in spite of his misdeeds and all the blood he uselessly spilled, was much loved by the people. Irigoyen, in spite of the official masquerades, governs us still. What the people loved in Rosas, understood in Roca, and now admire in Irigoyen is the scorn of theatricals, or the fact that if they use some, they do it with comic sense." (*Inquisiciones* 32; translated by Rodríguez Monegal in his *Literary Biography* 229)

In contrast to the other stories collected in *A Universal History of Infamy*, "Street Corner Man" distinguishes itself for its realistic tone, excellent characterization and the effective use of "Argentinisms" (or local slang). Also by the "easy flow" of the narration, that is to say, the seamless concatenation of events. One can notice as well the presence of elements that will reappear in Borges's later fictions: a well-made plot, the "geometrization" of the story (that is, the introduction of parallelisms and symmetries among events [see *The Aleph* 265]), the use of a final twist that gives a whole new meaning to the narration. Amado Alonso, in a now well-known review of the first edition of *A Universal History of Infamy*, noticed the difference that I mentioned earlier between Borges's style in this book and that of his previous works. Alonso also praised "Street Corner Man" as superior to the other pieces in the collection, in that way setting a precedent for future favorable critiques of the story (Alonso 372-74). At the time, Alonso was the best known literary critic writing in Argentina and a good friend of Borges. Also since he probably exerted a great influence on him, it is surprising that Borges did not follow Alonso's implied advice (to continue using the narrative strategies employed in "Street Corner Man"), and that he went on instead to employ a totally different narrative system or style.

I have explained that in "Street Corner Man" Borges was looking for an alternative to Modernism. This second narrative system, which is the one used for the other stories included in *A Universal History of Infamy* does not seem to have been initially intended as an alternative to Modernism, but it will be developed into one when Borges takes it as a model for his fantastic fiction. The narrative system of "Street Corner Man" was realistic and based on local topics. Borges also employed for it local slang and a traditional short story structure. The new narrative system will be not only unrealistic (fantastic), but also based on "universal" topics, written in a standard (and even a bit latinized) Spanish language and with a hybrid half-story/half-essay structure. This system also employs parataxis, like "Street Corner Man," but the disjunction of sentences and scenes has been exacerbated to a greater degree. The reader is forced to supply the missing transitions, and the narrative flow is constantly interrupted by the absence of linking phrases and causative conjunctions. So unusual for a narrative work was this paratactic style that the first translators of Borges's work into English used to add causative links between sentences to help the readers follow the narration. The form of this second narrative system, as I said, is a combination of the essay and the short story. The essay/short story form is evident in some of Borges's most famous stories like "Pierre Menard" and "Tlön, Uqbar, Orbis Tertius." Like all the other characteristics of this narrative style, this structure has its origin in the other tales included in *A Universal History of Infamy* with "Street Corner Man." These tales have appropriately been called "proto-fictions" by Silvia Molloy because they are not completely original narrations. Yet they are already written in the form and style in which Borges will write his fantastic tales of 1940s and 50s. The "tales of infamy" were written and published in *Crítica* almost immediately after Borges finished "Street Corner Man." Borges borrowed the topics for these stories from diverse (and disparate) sources. In them, he speculates about the reasons behind the actions of minor historical figures (pirates, impostors, gangsters, hoodlums) while at the same time narrating the story of their lives. After calling "Street Corner Man" a "freak" in his "Autobiographical Essay," Borges says about the other stories in the collection: "The real beginning of my career as a story writer starts with a series of sketches entitled *Historia universal de la infamia* (A Universal History of Infamy). . . . The irony of this is that "Street Corner Man" really was a story but that these sketches and several of the fictional pieces which followed them, and which very slowly led me to legitimate stories, were in the nature of hoaxes and pseudo-essays" (Borges, 239). The texts look like short essays, each one divided into a few "scenes," and each scene preceded by a subheading.

The extremely paratactical style that Borges chose for his "tales of infamy" (and that he will continue using from then on), was a style that until then he had only used in essays. This style begins to appear with *Evaristo Carriego* (1930), and by the time he writes the essays included in *Discusión* (1932), it has been almost perfected. It was apparently not a style that Borges had conceived of as a narrative tool (for that he was developing the style of "Street Corner Man"). It could be argued then that Borges's initial adoption of the essayistic form is not the result of a need for innovation—against which he had turned—but rather of a "narrative deficiency." Let us explain this briefly. If the action in his other stories in *A Universal History of Infamy* does not "flow," like that of "Street Corner Man," it is because Borges was trying to turn his essayistic style into a narrative one—and the attempt was not entirely successful. Put another way, Borges was looking for a narrative style other than the one used in "Street Corner Man." The only one available to him was then the one that he had been using to write essays, but he first had to adapt it for fiction writing. If the tales of infamy have an essay-like structure, it is not because they were intentionally written in that form but because Borges was not able to translate effectively the style of his essays to his narrative work. The problem with the "tales of infamy," the reason why they do not make for a very enjoyable reading experience, is that one can never tell whether they are short stories or essays. The fictional elements present in them tell us that they are not essays. But as stories, they are very difficult to follow because of their disjointed structure. Borges found the solution to this narrative problem in 1936, when he wrote an "essay" on a nonexistent book ("The Approach to Al'mu-tasim" [*Ficciones* 37-44; *Obras* 1.414-18]) as a sort of joke that he wanted to play on his friends. He then discovered a literary form that allowed him to narrate without being actually narrating: the fictional essay. Unable to accept the style of "Street Corner Man," when Borges started to write fiction again in 1938/39, he decided to exploit the possibilities of the essay form in his fantastic tales. After that, even the most "straight-forward" of his future stories kept an essay-like structure. It is no surprise that many of his stories start as a transcription of an "unpublished manuscript."

We have then two different narrative systems: one found in "Street Corner Man," which is essentially realistic, and the other one developed using the structure of the "tales of infamy." The coexistence of these two narrative systems in the same collection of short stories underlines the fact that Borges made an extremely conscious decision regarding the writing of fiction. Two narrative modes were simultaneously available to Borges, at some point during the mid-thirties he decided to choose one narrative system and ignore the other. The system that Borges chose would become the literary form of his fantastic stories. It is then the rejection of a particular narrative model that we see as one of the most important movements on the part of Borges that affected his career as a writer. It was not merely an innocent "shift" from an early prose style to a one developed later, as most critics would have it (see Alazraki, *La prosa narrativa*). In fact, one could tentatively define Borges's choice as a rejection of the realistic narrative mode seen as an alternative to modernist aesthetics. Modernity (the avant-garde aesthetics), as we saw, had already been rejected by Borges when he realized that a direct imitation of European cultural models was not possible in Latin America. Borges then tried to find an "alternative" to Modernism in "Street Corner Man" by going back to Realism.

Peter Bürger has raised the question of whether it is necessary to use modern artistic forms in order to be a modern artist. In his article "The Decline of the Modern Age," Bürger starts by criticizing T.W. Adorno's theory of art, which among other things says that an artist must always use the most advanced artistic techniques available and should not employ artistic materials that are "outdated." For the cultural period that concerns us here (Modernism), this means that only avant-garde or "modern" art is possible and that any attempt to return to previous modes of artistic expression (such as Realism) must be rejected. For Adorno it is not merely a question of change in artistic taste; it is also related to the quality of the art one wishes to create. A truly relevant work of art (the one that will survive the test of time) can only be achieved by using the most advanced techniques:

> Today a huge store of past art, which in its own time was highly rated, turns out to be inadequate in terms of immanent artistic criteria. Its deficiencies are uncovered by the progression of time, which is not to say that they are deficiencies in relation to changing tastes only: on the contrary, they are faults in the objective quality of much past art. Only the most advanced art has a chance against the decay wrought by time. (*Aesthetic Theory* 60)

Adorno would have condemned Borges's return to a realistic style of writing. For Adorno, realism could only produce works that were unable to capture the truth of the modern world (Zuidervaart 40).[14] But Peter Bürger explains that the tendency of going back to premodern artistic techniques is a practice that one can find even in the works of some of the best-known modern artists of this century:

> As early as 1917 Picasso had abruptly broken off his cubist phase with his portrait of his wife ("Olga in the Reclining Chair") that smacked of Ingres. In subsequent years, he alternatively painted cubist and "realistic" pictures. In 1919, Stravinsky, who just two years earlier had written the avantgarde *Histoire du soldat*, returned to the 18th century music with the ballet *Pulcinella*. And in 1922 Paul Valéry, with his collection of poems *Charmes*, sought to re-establish the ideal of a strict, formal classicism. Not only second-rate artists rejecting their own age oriented themselves by the classical model, but with Picasso and Stravinsky (Valéry's case is somewhat different) it came to include precisely those who had contributed decisively to the development of modern art. (*Decline* 118)

Bürger challenges in his article Adorno's thesis that only one artistic material (the most advanced one) can be recognized in a given epoch. He explains that since the avant-garde movements, artists have begun to employ artistic techniques from previous cultural periods and that, in fact, one of the characteristics of postmodern art is the juxtaposition of different stocks of material (Bürger first explained these ideas in *Theory of the Avant-Garde* [17-20, 63]). This suggests the possibility that Borges's "Street Corner Man" is the equivalent of the return to past artistic techniques by Picasso or Stravinsky. It was an attempt to create a modern work of art but employing traditional literary techniques. No doubt Borges saw realism as an alternative style of writ-

---

[14]For an excellent account of Adorno's theories about art, see Zuidervaart's book *Adorno's Aesthetic Theory: The Redemption of Illusion*. The last chapter is particularly interesting because it also presents a critique of Bürger's writings. Also, a good general introduction to Adorno's thinking is Jay Martin, *Adorno*.

ing. Coincidentally, it is precisely during the 1930s when critics such as Lukács started to look at realistic writing as an alternative to Modernism.[15] But from Borges's critical comments on realism one can infer that this was a technique that he considered "artificial." His constant attacks on realistic literature let us know that for him traditional realistic writing was inadequate to represent reality.[16]

It is easy to understand how the model practiced in "Street Corner Man" could be considered later a mistake by Borges. His earlier nationalism (expressed in avant-garde literary forms) was justified because its aim was to modernize Argentina, to turn it into a Latin American equivalent of an European country. But a story centered on a local topic and employing "outdated" literary forms was only a step backwards because it implied an "exaggerated" nationalism, probably hostile to foreign influences. However, given the 1930s economic crisis, that a temporary nationalistic turn in Borges's ideology might have taken place is not unconceivable. But the belief that economic and cultural dependency cannot be overcome by turning one's back to Europe and its forms of social organization made him reject the realistic style of "Street Corner Man" as a literary mode and look for an alternative to Modernism other than Realism.

The double rejection of Modernism and Realism and the necessity to find an alternative to both of them, expresses perfectly, at the level of literary forms, what Borges saw as his country's real dilemma.

---

[15]One of Lukács's best-known attacks on Modernism can be found in *The Meaning of Contemporary Realism*. Even if Lukács's reasons for prescribing Realism (and proscribing Modernism) are difficult to accept today, an interesting way of looking at his debates with Bretch first and later with Adorno (which were a continuation of the debate with Bloch about Expressionism; see note 4) is to understand them as a challenge to the idea that only modern artistic forms can be used to express a modern reality. As an introduction to these aesthetics debates, see Ronald Taylor's anthology *Aesthetics and Politics*.

[16]The classic example of Borges's rejection of traditional realism is his preface to Bioy Casares's *La invención de Morel*, which I discuss extensively in the next chapter.

How could Argentina develop without abandoning the world market system? An European-style modernization did not seem to work, and going back to an exaggerated nationalism was not a viable solution either. It will then be necessary to find a "third way" to encourage progress and reach the level of development of the most advanced countries (which never ceases to be Borges's dream). Borges's literary alternative to Modernism and Realism, as I hope to show, was developed as an imaginary solution to the problem of (cultural) dependency, thus suggesting, indirectly, that some sort of "progress," cultural as well as economic and social, is possible in the periphery.

Before exploring any further Borges's attitude to the problem of dependency, however, it is necessary to return to the question of the meaning of realism in his work. So far I have presented a limited view of Borges's approach to realism in literature. I have mainly concerned myself with Borges's evaluation of traditional realist writing. But his understanding of this literary form is, in fact, a richer and more complex one. The problem of realism in literature was, so to speak, one of Borges's lifelong obsessions. Exploring his ideas on the topic will eventually take us back to the problem of internationalism and nationalism, to the question of whether modernization and tradition (or local culture) can coexist.

It is interesting to notice that after rejecting the style of "Street Corner Man," realism makes a return in Borges's fantastic fiction by way of some literary devices to which he attributes the power to create a "more realistic" impression than the one created by traditional realistic writing. In an essay included in *Discusión* ("The Postulation of Reality" [*Obras* 1.217-21; *Reader* 30-34]), Borges talks about three realistic techniques or "modes of postulating reality." Although the essay was probably written around 1932, he rarely used any of these realistic devices until much later, when he began to write fantastic literature. One of the devices, the one that Borges most frequently uses, consists in "imaginar una realidad más compleja que la declarada al lector y referir sus derivaciones y efectos" (*Obras* 1.219).[17] This effect is achieved by inserting in the narration phrases or fragments that are left unexplained, thereby producing the sensation that reality is so rich and complex that a narrative text can only cover some aspects of it (Molloy makes an important analysis of these ideas in *Signs of Borges* 105-33; see also Borges's "La poesía gauchesca," *Obras* 1.179-87). Silvia Molloy has found several examples of this technique in Borges's best-known tales:

> [In] Borges, certain syntactical surprises, insertions appearing to be trivial, obliquely open up the story. Think, for example, of the narrator's surprisingly personal intervention in "The Lottery in Babylon": "I don't have much time left; they tell us that the ship is about to weigh anchor"; or the provocative parenthesis interrupting Yu Tsun's list as he goes through his pockets in "The Garden of Forking Paths" and finds a letter "which I resolved to destroy immediately (and which I did not destroy)"; or the use of a demonstrative in "The Waiting": an "Uruguayan twenty-centavo piece which had been in his pocket since *that* night in the hotel at Melo." (64-65; Molloy's italics)

The meaning of these objects and statements is never explained to the reader because they are not directly related to the story being told. Their function in the text is to suggest the existence of "other stories" which are not revealed to the reader. Through them the reader realizes that reality is more complex than the way it appears in a written text.

Of the other two techniques proposed by Borges in his essay, one is merely a second version of the one described above and the other is simply explained as a "una notificación de los hechos que importan" ("narration of the important facts"). As Molloy points out, all three

---

[17]"imagining a more complex reality than the one stated to the reader and recounting its derivations and effects." (*Reader* 32)

devices could be summarized by the latter description.[18] What Borges means by it is that in our everyday life we do not pay attention to all those details that nineteenth-century realist writers were so fond of describing. Our minds only register the important or immediate aspects of a place or event. For example, one does not notice all the details of a building, only its general shape or its most interesting features. Similarly, in a literary text the author can only include a limited amount of information and, obviously, most of this has to be related to the story being told, that is, the *interesting* part of the story.

In a 1951 text (*Antiguas literaturas germánicas*) Borges comments again on the question of producing realism in literature. Here Borges is praising the paratactic style of Icelandic sagas, but at the same time seems to be talking about (or justifying) his own style:

> El estilo [de las sagas] es breve, claro, conversacional... El orden es estrictamente cronológico; no hay análisis de los caracteres; los personajes se muestran en los actos y en las palabras. Este procedimiento da a las sagas un carácter dramatico que prefigura la técnica del cinematógrafo. El autor no comenta lo que refiere. En las sagas, como en la realidad, hay hechos que al principio son oscuros y que luego se explican y hechos que parecen insignificantes y luego cobran importancia. (Borges and Ingenieros 70)[19]

---

[18]"Borges calls the third device "circumstantial invention." "The three modes of postulating reality," explains Molloy, "are different ways of achieving the same purpose: to narrate only the important facts" (114).

[19]"The style in which sagas are written is concise, conversational. ... It employs a strictly chronological order; there is no psychological analysis of the characters; characters show their personality through their acts and words. This writing technique foreshadows the cinematographic technique. The author does not comment on his narration. In Icelandic sagas, as in real life, there are events that are unclear at first and are only explained later, and events that seem insignificant and later they acquire importance."

Borges gives an example from *Njal Saga* in which a woman lets her husband die in the hands of his enemies because he once slapped her in the face and she was still angry about the incident. Borges then adds: "El narrador no nos había dicho que Hallgerd [the wife] guardase rencor a su marido; ahora lo sabemos bruscamente, como suelen revelarse las cosas en la realidad" (71).[20] This realistic method differs from the ones presented in *Discusión* in that events are not left entirely unexplained. The explanation, however, is not given directly and the readers have to find it by themselves, so to speak. Examples of this technique are also frequent in Borges's fantastic stories. The dramatic endings of "Emma Zunz," "The Shape of the Sword" and "The Garden of Forking Paths," just to mention a few stories, depend on this "realistic" technique that Borges found in Icelandic sagas. It is obvious that this method, like the ones proposed in *Discusión*, is ruled by the idea of creating the effect of realism by omitting information. In fact, Borges's "Theory of Realism" could be explained as the art of omitting facts in order to produce the sensation of reality.

I have mentioned the paradoxical fact that Borges puts in practice his theory of realism in his fantastic fiction. One could say that it is Borges's conception of realism as being the result of *literary devices that give the impression of reality* that allowed him to include "realism" within his fantastic short stories. He was arguing that there was no need to reproduce reality faithfully (as nineteenth-century realist writers tried to do) in order to be realistic. But even if Borges's strategy was successful, one has to wonder about its meaning—i.e., what is the meaning of the persistence of realism (in any of its forms) in Borges's work? If he had already rejected the realistic style of "Street Corner Man," why, then, did he incorporate it into a non-realistic genre? But a full interpretation of the residual presence of realism in Borges can only be given later, when I analyze why Borges sees his fantastic fiction as an imaginary solution to the problem of modernity in Latin America.

---

[20]"The narrator had not told us that Hallgerd [the wife] hated her husband; now we learn about it unexpectedly, as things are usually discovered in real life."

We have already seen that Borges associated Modernism with internationalism (openness to foreign influences in all social and economic aspects) and Realism with nationalism. This diagram is complicated by the additional meanings that Borges attached to these literary forms. The confrontation between Realism and Modernism appears not only at the level of form but also at the level of content. The conflict is symbolized by the civilization/barbarism opposition that, in so many different ways, so frequently appears in Borges's fiction. To understand these correlations and, especially, the less evident one (Realism = barbarism), one has to know the background against which Borges was writing. I am referring to the popularity and predominance of realistic novels whose main theme was the civilization/barbarism conflict, during the years preceding the composition of Borges's first stories. The most popular type of realistic fiction at the time in Spanish America was the so-called *novela de la tierra* genre, which flourished during the 1920s and was "read by its critics and even promoted by its authors as the realistic novel that Latin America had lacked" (González Echevarría, *Voice* 45). The *novelas de la tierra* were, in fact, allegories about the modernization of Latin American societies. These narrations often told the story of the struggle to liquidate a premodern social structure and replace it with new patterns of behavior and a modern economic system. Regardless of whether the authors of these novels were in favor of (Gallegos) or against modernization (Güiraldes), the fact is that they were using their realistic prose to write *about* "barbarism" and about the latter's futile resistance to the modernizing forces. In these novels "barbarism" was invariably represented by Nature, by typical characters (e.g., the gaucho) or by traditional ways of doing things that could be considered opposed to modern life (that is, European culture). Barbarism always appears linked to a premodern economy and/or a precapitalist style of life. What takes place then in Borges's writings is a rejection of the realism promoted by his contemporaries and a complex rewriting of the civilization/barbarism problem. Borges is writing *about* civilization and about how barbarism continuously stops the "civilizing" (modernizing) process. And the account is, of course, written in a non-realistic prose.

With the 1929 crisis the economic dependency of Argentina became evident, but for Borges, it seems, that which was stopping development was the existence of "barbarism." Barbarism must be understood as a whole set of social, political and even "psychological" conditions that prevented the development of Argentina.[21] This is not to say that Borges was not aware of the problem of economic and cultural dependency of his country—after 1929 hardly anyone could ignore it—and its effects on the Argentine society. But, as I said before, he initially thought that the problem could be easily overcome and that it was not a real impediment for Argentina's development. It is precisely because he was aware of the problem that Borges tried to rationalize the condition of dependency in such a way that it could become an advantage instead of a disadvantage for the Latin American writer.

There is a passage at the beginning of "The Zahir" that shows perfectly well Borges's awareness of the problem of cultural dependency in Latin America. In this story, the modernist obsession with the New is represented by the figure of a high-society lady who closely and minutely follows the new trends of fashion in Europe and the United States:

> Teodelina Villar se preocupaba menos de la belleza que de la perfección [...]. Buscaba, como el adepto de Confucio o el talmudista, la irreprochable corrección de cada acto, pero su empeño era más admirable y más duro, porque las normas de su credo no eran eternas, sino que se plegaban a los azares de París o de Hollywood. Teodelina Villar se mostraba en lugares ortodoxos, a la hora ortodoxa, con atributos ortodoxos, con desgano ortodoxo, pero el desgano, los atributos, la hora y los lugares caducaban casi inmediatamente y servirían (en boca de Teodelina Villar) para la definición de lo cursi. Buscaba lo

---

[21]On the character traits of the Argentines that Borges criticized, see "Our Inadequacies" (*Ficcionario* 41-44; *Reader* 28-30).

absoluto, como Flaubert, pero lo absoluto en lo momentáneo. (*Obras* 1.589)[22]

As Modernity shattered the traditional social structure, modern subjects found themselves with an "overwhelming sense of fragmentation, ephemerality and change" (Harvey 11). Under these conditions, any sense of historical sequence is lost. This disbelief in history became then another essential characteristic of Modernism. Modern movements and writers often wished to start from scratch, to discard all the traditional rules of art. But in order to avoid becoming part of history, modernist art movements had to continue renovating themselves constantly. Borges shows perfectly well in the paragraph just quoted the contradiction of modernity: in order to keep innovating, rejecting all tradition, modernity also has to reject its own innovations. The process is of course endless and futile since modernity cannot avoid becoming part of history, it can never be purely "ahistorical."[23] One of the early concerns of the critics and commentators of modernity was its connec-

---

[22]"Teodelina Villar was interested less in beauty than in perfection. . . . Like any Confucian adept or Talmudist, she strove for irreprochable correctness in every action; but her zeal was more admirable and more exigent than theirs because the tenets of her creed were not eternal, but submitted to the shifting caprices of Paris or Hollywood. Teodelina Villar appeared at the correct places, at the correct hour, with the correct appurtenances and the correct boredom; but the boredom, the appurtenances, the hour and the places would almost immediately become passé and would provide Teodelina Villar with the material for a definition of cheap taste. She was in search of the Absolute, like Flaubert; only hers was an Absolute of a moment's duration." (*Labyrinths* 156-77)

[23]"Modernity and history," writes Paul de Man, "relate to each other in a curious way that goes beyond antithesis or opposition. If history is not to become sheer regression or paralysis, it depends on modernity for its duration and renewal; but modernity cannot assert itself without being at once swallowed up and reintegrated into a regressive historical process" (*Blindness* 151).

tion to fashion (Frisby 18-19 and 95-102). Perhaps nothing represents the constant flux of changes in modern life better than fashion. But, for Borges, fashion also represents the way in which modernization affected countries on the periphery of Europe. The passage from "The Zahir" must be taken as a critique of the dependency of the Latin American culture on the latest fashions coming from European centers. Calling Teodelina Villar an "artist" is a way of making fun of the many Latin American artists who during the first decades of the century were more concerned with imitating the latest artistic trends in Europe than with developing their own original work. The nature of Teodelina's pseudo-Modernism also reminds us of the fact that since the nineteenth century the Latin American elites were obsessed with possessing European commodities. The "modernization" that took place in most Latin American countries was only a cosmetic one that simply gave to the cities the appearance of progress, without any substantial progress taking place in them. Borges shows, if we follow the story of Teodelina Villar, how fragile and dependent on the European markets is this type of Modernism:

> La guerra le dio mucho que pensar. Ocupado París por los alemanes ¿cómo seguir la moda? Un extranjero de quien ella siempre había desconfiado se permitió abusar de su buena fe para venderle una porción de sombreros cilíndricos; al año se propaló que esos adefesios *nunca se habían llevado en París* y por consiguiente no eran sombreros, sino arbitrarios y desautorizados caprichos. Las desgracias no vienen solas; el doctor Villar tuvo que mudarse a la calle Aráoz y el retrato de su hija decoró anuncios de cremas y de automóviles. (¡Las cremas que harto se aplicaba, los automóviles que ya *no* poseía!) Esta sabía que el buen ejercicio de su arte exigía una gran fortuna; prefirió retirarse a claudicar. (*Obras* 1.590)[24]

---

[24]"The war [World War II] gave her much to think about: with Paris occupied by the Germans, how could one follow the fashions? A foreigner whom she had always distrusted presumed so far upon her

On one level, it is possible to see in this paragraph a comment on the necessity of those Latin American "modern" artists (for Teodelina Villar believes herself to be an artist) to maintain a direct contact with the European metropolises. Any disturbance of such a connection could have disastrous consequences for the project of replicating European Modernism in Latin America. The result of an improper translation of modernization could be (and, in fact, it has been on many occasions) a complete transformation of the original project. On another level, there is a close relationship suggested between the war that has stopped the flow of luxury consumer goods from Europe and the economic crisis that in the end forces Teodelina Villar to quit the practice of her "art." Borges connects both events in a casual manner: "And troubles never come singly" is the linking phrase. However, their juxtaposition suggests that the great fortune of doctor Villar, which allowed him to acquire all those expensive European imports for his daughter, was also dependent on the accessibility of the European markets.

Dependency always affects directly or indirectly the composition of literary texts in countries that are part of the periphery. It does not matter whether the author of such a text recognizes the problem of dependency or not, although being aware of that condition increases the chances of overcoming cultural dependency. In Borges's case, it seems that he decided to rationalize the problem of dependency and, through the justification of that cultural condition, find a (literary) solution to the problem.

Borges's understanding of the situation of the Latin American writer is contained in the essay "The Argentine Writer and Tradition"

---

good faith as to sell her a number of cylindrical hats; a year later it was divulged that those absurd creations *had never been worn in Paris at all!* Consequently they were not hats, but arbitrary, unauthorized eccentricities. And troubles never come singly: Dr. Villar had to move to Aráoz Street, and his daughter's portrait was now adorning advertisements for cold creams and automobiles. (The cold cream that she abundantly applied, the automobiles she *no longer* possessed.) She knew that the successful exercise of her art demanded a large fortune, and she preferred retirement from the scene to halfway effects." (*Labyrinths* 157)

(1954). Although some of the ideas in it are already present in earlier texts, it is here that he presents them most coherently. In this essay Borges discusses the problem of which literary or cultural tradition Argentine writers should follow. The three possible traditions available to an Argentine writer, according to Borges, are the local (Argentine one), the Spanish one, and a universal tradition. Borges is interested in attacking what he considers to be a nationalistic view of literature. This view promotes the idea that Argentine writers should write about local topics and not about places or cultures from other countries. The rationale behind the idea seems to be that if local artistic production is not based on local traditions, it will never be more than an imitation of foreign artistic expressions. Whatever the reasons are for adopting what Borges calls a nationalistic perception of literature, it is clear that he rejects it. Borges concludes that to be "Argentine" does not have to mean that writers must limit themselves to deal with local topics.

Borges compares the situation of the Latin American writer in relation to Western literature with that of Irish writers and philosophers to the English culture or of Jewish people in general to the Western world. Because Irish and Jewish people belong to "marginal" or peripheral cultures, Borges argues, they can treat the primary or hegemonic culture with irreverence. It is thanks to this attitude of irreverence that they are able to innovate, to be original. Argentine writers, Borges says, must feel that their "patrimony is the universe" and that they do not have to limit themselves to treating local topics in order to create an authentic Argentine literature: "[debemos] ensayar todos los temas, y no podemos concretarnos a lo argentino para ser argentinos: porque o ser argentino es una fatalidad y en ese caso lo seremos de cualquier modo, o ser argentino es una mera afectación, una máscara" (*Obras* 1.273-24).[25]

---

[25]"we should essay all themes, and cannot limit ourselves to purely Argentine subjects in order to be Argentine; for either being Argentine is an inescapable act of fate—and in that case we shall be so in all events—or being Argentine is a mere affectation, a mask." (*Labyrinths* 185)

One of Borges's strategies to overcome the condition of dependency, then, is the elimination of any trace of local color from his writings. By "local color" he means the overuse or exaggerated emphasis on local topics but also the use of local expressions, places, behavior. Thus, he criticizes Argentine writers who try to imitate popular poetry because they employ a high degree of regionalisms, something that not even the real popular poets do: "[U]n colombiano, un mejicano o un español pueden comprender inmediatamente las poesías de los payadores, de los gauchos, y en cambio necesitan un glosario para comprender, siquiera aproximadamente, a Estanislao del Campo o Ascasubi" (*Obras* 1.268).[26] Borges condemns this practice because, he says, it gives an appearance of unauthenticity to literature:

> Gibbon observa que en el libro árabe por excelencia, en el *Alcorán*, no hay camellos; yo creo que si hubiera alguna duda sobre la autenticidad del *Alcorán*, bastaría esta ausencia de camellos para probar que es árabe. Fue escrito por Mahoma, y Mahoma, como árabe, no tenía por qué saber que los camellos eran especialmente árabes; eran para él parte de la realidad, no tenía por qué distinguirlos; en cambio, un falsario, un turista, un nacionalista árabe, lo primero que hubiera hecho es prodigar camellos, caravanas de camellos en cada página. (*Obras* 1.270)[27]

---

[26]"[A] Colombian, Mexican or Spaniard can immediately understand the poetry of the payadores, of the gauchos, and yet they need a dictionary in order to understand, even approximately, Estanislao del Campo or Ascasubi." [*Labyrinths* 179]

[27]"Gibbon observes that in the Arabian book *par excellence*, in the Koran, there are no camels; I believe if there were any doubt as to the authenticity of the Koran, this absence of camels would be sufficient to prove it is an Arabian work. It was written by Mohammed, and Mohammed, as an Arab, had no reason to know that camels were especially Arabian; for him they were a part of reality, he had no reason to emphasize them; on the other hand, the first thing a falsifier, a tourist, an

A writer uses local color because s/he is either seeing a culture from outside and can observe only its most superficial aspects, or because s/he is too conscious of the differences between his/her (marginal) culture and the hegemonic ones. Carlos J. Alonso has written a very interesting critique of the previous passage:

> The success of [Borges's] critique of the obsession with autochthony depends on the existence of an assumption shared by him and his reader that camels are indeed "especially Arabian," obviously the perspective of an outsider to that specific cultural reality. Paradoxically enough, then, there would appear to be a common rhetorical ground underlying both the discourse of the ardent cultural nationalist and that of the gawking, exoticizing foreigner. (4)

By assuming that camels represent the Arabian culture, Borges is also behaving like a "tourist."

Ironically, it is that consciousness of being different from the metropolis (from that center whose approval writers from the periphery are always looking for) that leads Latin American writers to add an explanation of those differences for the benefit of their potential European (First World) readers. As Angel Rama points out, from colonial times to the most recent, Latin American writers, in their desire to be read and understood by the inhabitants of the metropolis, have always felt the necessity to explain or define what they knew were typically Latin American words or objects, and therefore foreign to European readers. In the *novelas de la tierra*, for example, the authors usually included glossaries of local words at the end of the book. The same necessity to be understood by people from other cultures, explains Rama, leads a contemporary novelist like Alejo Carpentier to propose a style he calls "baroque" as the "literary language" most appropriate for Latin American literature:

Arab nationalist would do is have a surfeit of camels, caravans of camels, on every page." (*Labyrinths* 181)

> It is enough to say the word pine for us to see a pine; the word palm tree is enough to describe, to show a palm tree. But the word "ceiba"—the name of an American tree which blacks in Cuba call "the mother of all trees" is not enough to make people from other places see the shape of that gigantic tree, which looks like a column [*columna rostral*]. [This] is only achieved by means of an original combination of several adjectives, or, if we want to avoid the use of adjectives, by turning certain substantive into adjectives, which in that case will acquire a metaphorical function. If we are lucky—artistically speaking, of course—we achieve our purpose. The object becomes alive, one can see it, one can feel it. But the prose that gave it life and body, weight and shape, is a baroque prose, it has to be necessarily baroque. (Carpentier 24-25; qtd. in Rama, *La ciudad* 51)

In Rama's opinion, what has taken place in Carpentier's texts is a displacement of the earlier glossaries of the realist writers into the text itself. The glossary (i.e., explanations for the European or First World readers) has now become part of the style of the writer:

> It is obvious that it is not the words themselves that allow us to *see* a pine, a palm tree or a "ceiba" in a literary text but the various cultural contexts in which they occur. While European writers normally address their public without taking into consideration non-European readers, Latin American writers (like Carpentier) continue to yearn for the approval of European readers and critics. What [Alejo Carpentier] is proposing is the absorption of the extra-literary explanations—necessary for the cultural translation of a text—by the narrative style employed by the author. But this strategy is not enough to hide the presence of those explanations. [This literary practice] shows how, still in the twentieth century, the Latin American intellectual continues to feel that the real Civilization is located in Europe. Europe is the center that inspires Latin American writers and

the place where their reading public is located. (Rama, *La ciudad* 51-52)[28]

The same tactic or technique—to incorporate extraliterary explanations of the text as part of the very construction of the text—can still be observed in some recent writers whose "poetics," ironically, at first look so different from Carpentier's (see Barrada's comments about Luis Rafael Sánchez's style).

Borges is saying that by simply putting too much emphasis on a certain cultural context, be this Latin American or European, we are showing that we do not really belong to it. A writer who tries to "Europeanize" a text by adding emphasis on European elements betrays in this way his/her real origin as a writer from a peripheral culture. This is what Jean Franco points out, in relation to Rubén Darío, as a "mark" of the condition of dependency that the writers who try to Europeanize themselves sometimes cannot hide:

> [A] subtle gap is disclosed between the Spanish American writer who assiduously cultivated the manners and values of the metropolis and his European peers. This often took the form of explicit allusion to or exaggeration of that which could be left as understood (because obvious) in the primary culture. I am thinking here of the tendency of the Modernists [*Modernismo*, a sort of Spanish-American Symbolist movement from the turn of the century] and specially Rubén Darío to dwell on cultural references, classical allusions, and even luxury commodities for their own sake, implying a certain celebration of taste which in the metropolis could be taken for granted. (Franco, "Dependency Theory" 73)

---

[28]See also Rama, *La novela* 304-306. Both Borges and Rama present a very limited view of Latin American readers and writers. They assume that there is "one" type of European/Latin American reader. Their theories are too simple to account for more complex issues of reception and production in literature.

Darío, if we follow Borges's artistic judgment, would be classified as a "tourist" because, by adding too much European "local color" to his writings, is showing that he does not share the same cultural context with the Europeans.[29]

It must be clear from the analysis above that Borges identified a difference between European and Latin American writers that, at the bottom, seems to be a consequence of the latter's condition of being intellectuals living in peripheral or dependent countries. Latin American writers are too conscious of this cultural difference while the Europeans, as Rama rightly points out, simply do not think of the people living in

---

[29]In a 1937 article about Langston Hughes published in *El Hogar*, Borges employs similar ideas to analyze the African American literature of the time:

> Salvo en ciertos poemas de Counteé Cullen, la literatura negra, hoy por hoy, adolece de una contradicción que es inevitable. El propósito de esa literatura es demostrar la insensatez de todos los prejuicios raciales, y sin embargo no hace otra cosa que repetir que es negra: es decir, que acentuar la diferencia que está negando. (*Textos cautivos* 92)

> (With the exception of a few poems by Counteé Cullon, Black literature today contains within itself an unavoidable contradiction. The goal of that literature is to show the stupidity of racial prejudice; however, it never ceases to mention the fact that it is black: that is to say, it emphasizes the difference that it wants to disprove.)

No other passage does more to reveal the limitations of Borges's concept of a "universal" tradition than this one. According to Borges, an African-American writer can only write "authentic" AfricanAmerican literature if s/he suppresses that "emphasis" on specific AfricanAmerican cultural topics. The problem with Borges's view is that it equates the hegemonic cultural discourse with a "universal culture." Needless to say, an African American literature that does not deal with African American topics loses its power to challenge this discourse.

the periphery of their countries when they write. Borges's attacks on the exaggerated emphasis on local color by Latin American writers are then part of a very smart strategy to "overcome" or at least to hide the effects of cultural dependency. If omitting local color makes it easier for the Latin American writer to "elevate" his writings to the level of the European ones, then, by the same token, it is possible for the same Latin American writer to employ European topics. In other words, a Latin American can write like an European by employing the same approach: to omit all the cultural allusions that European readers do not need because they already know the cultural context from which these topics come. Borges's project (his suggestion to the Latin American writer) is to write like an European by assuming that all his/her readers share the same cultural context. Therefore, writers from the periphery do not need to add "unnecessary" explanations, neither for local nor for European readers.[30] One might rightly argue that it is impossible to reduce something so complex as cultural dependency to the presence or absence of a literary element. But for Borges the elimination of local color became a valid strategy to deal with the problem of dependency in literature.

It is only in relation to Borges's attempt to overcome cultural dependency that we can now begin to understand his lifelong search for a unique *form*. Borges is trying to find an alternative to both a modernity that has never fully taken place in Argentina (symbolized by avant-garde literary forms) and to archaic social elements that he hopes some day will disappear (realism). As we have seen, it was Borges's pessimism that led him to abandon his modernist aesthetics. This was

---

[30]It is difficult to understand why Borges followed the same practice that he was criticizing when translating his works into English: "Working closely together in daily sessions, we [i.e., Borges and Thomas Di Giovanni, his translator] have tried to make these stories read as though they had been written in English. . . . This venture does not necessarily mean that we have willfully tampered with the original, though in certain cases we have supplied the American reader with those things—geographical, topographical and historical—taken for granted by an Argentine" (*The Aleph* 9-10).

a pessimism grounded on the impossibility for his native country to reach the level of modernization apparently being achieved in some European societies. Borges's intention is to adopt a literary model that neither copies European Modernism nor goes back to the archaic type of Realism practiced by many of his contemporaries. This new model has to go beyond the discarded ones while, at the same time, asserting the right of Latin American culture to be part of Western culture. Borges recognizes that as Argentina is part of a world economic system, it is also part of a world "cultural" system. Whether a modern (Western) culture will in the end impose itself over the world or not, the solution to this is not isolating oneself economically and culturally. This is one of the reasons why Borges rejects political nationalism as well as nationalistic views of literature. He believes in the possibility of progressing (culturally and economically) *without* fighting the world system. But this remains a fantasy that can only be realized in his literary work.

The form of the Borgesian texts about which we have been talking for so long now, that narrative model that pretends to transcend Modernism and Realism, is the fantastic tale. I have already mentioned that Borges's problem, as a writer from the periphery, was to use "First World" culture in an innovative way. Borges's solution is to use a literary form that is considered to be secondary or marginal in the history of Western literature. Although the fantastic tale is a form long practiced in Western literature, it has never been a major genre (for a definition of the fantastic tale as a genre, see Todorov). It remains a type of literature that is not widely practiced, and it is not considered as important as other genres are. And yet it is part of the Western cultural tradition; it has its own history and rules.

Borges's idea was to write stories about "universal" themes (such as time, memory, history) but giving them a fantastic interpretation. And this he achieves by treating those topics with "irreverence." He writes from a peripheral or marginal country and culture using a literary form considered marginal in the history of Western literature. But this is not all. Borges also tries to include or rewrite within this marginal form the other two that he has abandoned (Modernism, Realism), in such a way that they can be both "neutralized" and replaced by the new one. This is perhaps one of the reasons why he tried to make realism part of his fantastic writings. We saw earlier that his "theory of realism" aimed at freeing that notion from the nineteenth-century idea of reproducing reality faithfully. By arguing that realism, or the realistic effect in literature, is only the result of literary devices, Borges prepares the way to incorporate "realism" into his nonrealistic fiction. The same can be argued about Borges's treatment of Modernism. Although he seems to have rejected avant-garde forms of writing and the modern search for the New, Borges employs in his stories the most typical modernist topics: I am referring, of course, to the issues of self, time, memory, relativity of point of view, loss of individuality, with which Borges constantly plays in his fiction. However, Borges's relation to modernist poetics goes beyond the simple use of classical modernist topics in his writings. In fact, one could say that he took many aspects of modernist literature and modified them within his short stories. This rewriting of modernist poetics that takes place in his stories is so complex that I have dedicated a great part of my study to discussing it.

It is not by completely rejecting Modernism and Realism that Borges is going to find an alternative to them, but by rewriting, "renovating" these modes of writing. He wants his fantastic fiction to incorporate realist and modernist elements in order to go "beyond" those artistic forms. This is a reaction to Modernism that does not go back to outmoded artistic expressions. Borges's solution to the problem of form, that is, his writing fantastic fiction in a style that is different from the styles of the other two—the avant-garde, the realist—can be considered as a personal way of overcoming literary dependency. He turns his situation as a subject from a peripheral society and a peripheral culture into an advantage. The political meaning of his aesthetics is also obvious. It clearly suggests that being in the margins (subjected culturally and economically to the "First World") is not an impediment to progress.

However, there are reasons to believe that Borges's confidence in this new literary project did not last long. After the 1960s Borges became more pessimistic about the possibility of progress in his country (progress, of course as he defined it: achieving the level of development of the industrialized countries). This perhaps explains why, after *Ficciones* (1944) and *El Aleph* (1949), Borges stopped writing fantastic literature. In 1970, after several years of silence, Borges published *Doctor Brodie's Report*, in which he returns to realistic writing. His realistic style in this short story collection is, however, radically different from the one employed in "Street Corner Man," and Borges is quick to point out these differences in his prologue to the book. Although Borges never mentions "Street Corner Man," in the prologue he seems to be alluding to the story. He states, for example, that he does not use slang in *Doctor Brodie's Report*. And after explaining that he has tried "to write straightforward stories," Borges adds, quite unexpectedly, that he wants to make clear that he is not, nor has he ever been what "ahora [se llama] un escritor comprometido" (*Obras* 2.399)[31] nor a nationalist. Let us not forget also that it is in this collection of short stories that "Rosendo's Tale" (his rewriting of "Street Corner Man") is included. It is obvious that he is trying to distance these new realistic stories of *Doctor Brodie's Report* from the realism of "Street Corner Man." This time his return to traditional realism does not respond to a nationalistic reaction in face of social problems, as was the case earlier.

However, this new change in the form of his fiction is not completely void of political meaning. I have established that the unique form of Borges's 1940s and 1950s writings (fantastic tales) sprang partly from his belief that innovation (progress) was still possible in Latin America, even if the continent was dependent on the industrialized nations. By practicing a Henry Jamesian type of realistic writing in *Doctor Brodie's Report*, Borges is giving up his last utopian dreams. Borges's loss of faith in his literary (and cultural) project of the 1940s and 1950s appears to have been a consequence of his pessimism toward the future of Latin America. It would be a mistake, however, to see his pessimism as simply the result of what he experienced during the 1930s and as a feeling that kept growing as the years went by, totally unaffected by what happened in his life afterwards. If, as we have seen, the period of the early 1930s is a decisive one in Borges's development of a style of writing, no less important is the period that goes from the mid 1940s to 1955, that is, the years that Perón was in power. An analysis

---

[31]"is now known as a committed writer." (*Reader* 296)

of this period of Borges's life is especially important for an understanding of the political position that he took during those last couple of decades of his life, especially his well-known attacks on democratic institutions. I have chosen to leave the study of the events that shaped Borges's ideology during the Perón years for my last chapter.

But the turn in Borges's writings described above does not really question the theory that he was proposing with his fantastic writings. That is, Borges still believed that he had found a way to overcome the problem of "dependency" as he understood it. He thought that he could write a text that was "universal" and did not bear any traces of the culture in which it was produced. The question that should be raised now is whether he was really able to do that. I will outline in the paragraphs that follow the possibility of a different reading of Borges's stories, one in which the return of elements from premodern cultural periods is seen as the symbolic representation of a condition of dependency from which he cannot fully escape. I wish to interpret Realism and barbarism as standing for residual and even archaic elements that Borges simply cannot erase from his creative work. Both elements, as we know, are interrelated in his writings. At various moments Borges associated Realism with barbarism and nationalism. Barbarism in his work is almost always a keyword for nationalism while the opposition civilization/barbarism equates that of internationalism (Europeism)/nationalism. The mature Borges always sided with internationalism and civilization, even in spite of his pessimism about the possibility of "civilizing" Latin America.

Borges came to see the civilization/barbarism conflict as eternal. This is evident from his interpretation of Argentina's history: he saw it as composed of a series of efforts to civilize (modernize) the country that were constantly frustrated by a prevalent barbarism. This cyclical confrontation is perhaps best represented in his "Story of the Warrior and the Captive." This tale is in reality two different stories loosely linked together. The first one is about a Lombard warrior during the fall of the Roman Empire. The Lombard, after seeing a city for the first time, decides to abandon his tribe and fight for the Roman Empire, against his people. The second story takes place in nineteenth-century Argentina. It is a story supposedly told to Borges by his grandmother about an English girl who was living among Indians. Her parents emigrated to Argentina but were killed by Indians who then kidnapped the girl. Now she had become one of them. In a typical Borgesian ending, the two main characters—symbolizing civilization and barbarism—are said to be the two sides of the same coin. It could be argued, based on the ending, that Borges is erasing all distinctions between the two concepts, thus suggesting that they are one and the same. However, we should not overlook that the main theme is about how a barbarian becomes civilized when he enters in contact with the Roman (read European) culture, and how an English woman becomes barbaric in South America. At least one critic recognizes that the central topic of the story no longer seems to be of any importance in a contemporary world: "Perhaps the only problem with the story is its unstated central dichotomy (civilized versus barbarian), today a somewhat dated view" (Bell-Villada 157), and he goes on to suggest that a contemporary reader may even "resist" that central presupposition. What is most interesting about this statement is that it suggests the need to find an explanation for the constant presence of that topic not only in Borges, but also in other contemporary Latin American writers who have felt the necessity to treat it.

Rosalba Campra, in her book *América Latina: la identidad y la máscara*, briefly traces the trajectory and the multiple transformations of this topic throughout the history of Latin American literature. Beginning with Sarmiento's archetypical text (*Facundo: civilización y barbarie*), she shows how the long standing idea of nature as an enemy and as the origin of a barbarism that opposes civilization and therefore has to be conquered, slowly changed into a positive one. In the hands of Horacio Quiroga and others the barbarism/nature equation is revalued and given a new meaning. Finally, in Carpentier's *Los pasos perdidos* (1953) the opposition is completely reversed, and civilization acquires negative connotations: going back to nature, to a primitive way of life, is seen as a way out of the alienation of the urban world. A different, more contemporary, treatment of the same conflict is presented in Vargas Llosa's *Pantaleón y las visitadoras* (1973), where the stereotypical views of both concepts are parodied (Campra 49-53). However, I think that the point to be emphasized is not how the idea is reinterpreted in different works or in different historical situations but that its continuous presence tells us that it still responds to some psychological necessity on the part of Latin American writers.

The conflict between civilization and barbarism undeniably represents a stage that has not passed or that has not yet been overcome. That is to say, the presence of a precapitalist, or more exactly a premodern world in Latin America. What the persistence of this topic represents in Borges's fiction is the return of "barbarism" or a premodern epoch, no longer as some natural force that impedes modernization, but as a non-modern world that coexists—if that is the right word—with the modern one. Barbarism symbolizes in these texts the uneven development of Latin America. Like Realism (an "outmoded" literary form that fascinates Borges nonetheless), barbarism's presence in these modernist or postmodernist texts of Borges stays as a visible "mark" of his origin. Borges managed to hide the effects of dependency by erasing local color from his writings. The fact that he belongs to a peripheral country where life is not as modern as in the metropolis could not, however, be totally or effectively erased.

THINKING AS PLEASURE: BORGES AND THE CULTURE INDUSTRY

> Que nadie quiera rebajarnos a ascetas. No hay placer más complejo que el pensamiento y a él nos entregábamos–Borges, "El inmortal"
>
> Pleasure always means not to think anything–Adorno, *Dialectic of Enlightenment*

When Adorno first proposed his Culture Industry theory, he saw popular or mass culture as completely opposed to high culture. Art could only be high art; all the rest was debased art. Popular art only provides entertainment as relief from labor (Adorno and Horkeimer 120-67). In Adorno's view, modern art is partly the result of this division between high and popular culture. Modernism was against the commercialization of life, against mass consumption and reification. Unlike popular art, modernist or high art was not easy to understand, it was sometimes incomprehensible, and "unsealable." Modernist works of art were not oriented towards the masses. Adorno's classical argument for favoring high art over popular art is that popular art is a mere distraction or entertainment which is passively internalized by the public. Contemporary revaluations of popular culture, however, claim that it is possible to detect the presence of moments or elements of resistance to commercialization *within* popular art (Kellner 121-67). This revaluation of popular art is accompanied by a literary tendency, Postmodernism, that seeks to erase the old division between high and popular art that informed the modernist aesthetics. Postmodern literature is said to purposely appropriate the forms of popular art with the intention of blurring the distinction between these two realms of culture. This postmodern ability to move freely from one discourse to another, from high art to popular art, is often seen as part of a general attempt by postmodern artists to break down the barriers between different fields of knowledge. Postmodern texts try to overcome the modern fragmentation of knowledge by creating a postmodern "discourse" that includes other kinds of "discourses." The divisions among specialist disciplines are erased (Hutcheon 20-21). Since the division between high and popular culture is a reflection of the same atomizing process, it also has to be erased.

In the following pages I wish to study further the relationship between the use of popular forms of art in postmodern literature and the desire to overcome specialization. I will do this by studying the presence of popular forms of art in Borges's short stories. The choice of Borges is a particularly appropriate one since, first of all, he is often considered to be one of the first postmodern writers and, second, the problem of human knowledge is said to be one of the central themes of his fictional work (see Alazraki, *La prosa* 7-9).

The best known relation between Borges and the Culture Industry is almost a commonplace in Borges criticism. I am referring to the idea that Borges's fantastic writings were influenced by his childhood readings and that, to a certain extent, he modeled his own fictions on these texts, perhaps trying to reproduce in his work the same pleasure that he received from his early readings (Balderston, *El precursor*; Bell-Villada 20-28). Borges himself has contributed to this mystification of his childhood years:

> [M]e crié en un jardín, detrás de una verja con lanzas, y en una biblioteca de ilimitados libros ingleses. Palermo del cuchillo y de la guitarra andaba (me aseguran) por las esquinas, pero quienes poblaron mis mañanas y dieron agradable horror a mis noches fueron el bucanero ciego de Stevenson, agonizando bajo las patas de los caballos, y el traidor que abandonó a su amigo en la luna, y el viajero del tiempo, que trajo del porvenir una flor marchita, y el genio encarcelado durante siglos en el cánta-

ro salomónico, y el profeta velado del Jorasán, que detrás de las piedras y de la seda ocultaba la lepra. (*Obras* 1.101)[1]

Borges's preference for what we would now consider light or even children's literature is generally regarded as one of the evidences that supports the common psychological reading of Borges. I will analyze closely later the most widely accepted of these theories, which tries to explain Borges's beginnings as a short story writer in relation to a problematic son/father relationship. Suffice it to say, for the moment, that Borges is often seen as a "child that never grew up" (Bell-Villada 24) or, in the most sophisticated readings, as being unable to fill the void left by the death of his father.

Critics seem to agree that there is an obvious relation between Borges's preference for the precursors of present-day popular literature and his own fantastic writings, but it is very difficult to explain with precision the nature of that relation or how it is reflected in Borges's texts. One way in which Borges criticism has always gone around this problem is by asserting that Borges has borrowed techniques from the "old adventure tales" and employed them in the construction of his fictions (see Balderston). In fact, given the eclectic nature of Borges's

---

[1]"I grew up in a garden, behind a fence of iron palings, and in a library of endless books. The Palermo of the knife and guitar throve (I am told) just around the corner, but those who populated my days and gave a pleasant shiver to my nights were Stevenson's blind buccaneer, dying under the horse's hooves, and the traitor who left his friend behind on the moon, and the time traveler who brought back from the future a withered flower, and the genie imprisoned for centuries in a Salomonic jar, and the Veiled Prophet of Khurasan, who hid his leprosy behind silk and precious stones." (*Evaristo Carriego* 33)

The text was published in *Sur* in 1945 and reprinted later as the preface to the second edition of *Evaristo Carriego* (1930; 2nd ed., 1955). In other texts, and in interviews, Borges gives different lists (see, for instance, his "Autobiographical Essay" 25). According to Balderston (*El precursor* 14-17) the only texts that all the lists have in common are the *Arabian Nights* and Stevenson's writings.

childhood readings, the label "literature of adventure" seems to be the only one capable of encompassing texts as different as *Treasure Island*, *Arabian Nights* and the now-forgotten Thomas Moore's *Lalla Rookh* (which are some of the texts alluded to in the preface to *Evaristo Carriego* quoted above). One can tentatively define all of these texts as being different types of "adventure" tales. Once one has classified them as adventure books it is easy, as we will see, to associate them with Borges's views on literature and literary composition.

In his most theoretical essays, Borges has defended what he called the "novel of adventure" while at the same time attacking the realist novel. His views on the subject are succinctly summarized in a preface that Borges wrote for his close friend Adolfo Bioy Casares's novel, *La invención de Morel* (1940). Borges begins the "Preface" by attacking the intellectuals' disdain for the novel of action and the contemporary preference (at that time, 1940) for the psychological and/or realistic novel. He argues for the superiority of the adventure tale on the grounds that psychological fiction is amorphous:

> La novela característica, "psicológica", propende a ser informe. Los rusos y los discípulos de los rusos han demostrado hasta el hastío que nadie es imposible: suicidas por felicidad, asesinos por benevolencia; personas que se adoran hasta el punto de separarse para siempre, delatores por fervor o por humildad... Esa libertad plena acaba por equivaler al pleno desorden. Por otra parte, la novela "psicológica" quiere ser también novela "realista": prefiere que olvidemos su carácter de artificio verbal y hace de toda vana precisión (o de toda lánguida vaguedad) un rasgo verosímil. (*Ficcionario* 160)[2]

---

[2]"The typical psychological novel is formless. The Russians and their disciples have demonstrated, tediously, that no one is impossible. A person may kill himself because he is so happy, for example, or commit murder as an act of benevolence. Lovers may separate forever as a consequence of their love. And a man can inform on another out of fervor or humility. In the end such complete freedom is tantamount to chaos. But the psychological novel would also be a "realistic" novel,

These two objections, the lack of form and the exaggerated realism of the psychological novel, are in reality one. It is because it tries to copy reality faithfully that the realist novel is amorphous. Realism does not attempt to impose an order on the elements of the outside world; it limits itself to a mere representation of them. This is not the case with the adventure tale:

> La novela de aventuras, en cambio, no se propone como una transcripción de la realidad: es un objeto artificial que no sufre ninguna parte injustificada. El temor de incurrir en la mera variedad sucesiva del *Asno de oro*, del *Quijote* o de los siete viajes de Simbad, le impone un riguroso argumento. (*Ficcionario* 160)[3]

Since writers of adventure stories are not trying to imitate reality, Borges explains, they can limit themselves to include in their texts only those elements that are directly related to the plot. This allows adventure novels to be more coherent, less "amorphous," than their realist counterparts. For Borges the more coherent, the more artistic a literary work is. Hence the novel of adventures is the superior one (on the influence of Stevenson on this preface, see Balderston, *El precursor* 17-26). One of Borges's purposes in this preface is to correct the misconception that contemporary writers are not capable of creating interesting plots. He wants to prove that adventure novels can still please a contemporary, and apparently more demanding, public. To do so, he proceeds to argue that twentieth-century fiction has invented plots that are superior, more "admirable," than those created in any previous cen-

---

and have us forget that it is verbal artifice, for it uses each vain precision (or each languid obscurity) as a new proof of verisimilitude." (*Reader* 122-23)

[3]"The adventure story, on the other hand, does not propose to be a transcription of reality: it is an artificial object, no part of which lacks justification. It must have a rigid plot if it is not to succumb to the mere sequential variety of *The Golden Ass*, the *Seven Voyages of Sindbad*, or the *Quixote*." (*Reader* 123)

tury. Thus, Kafka's arguments are better than De Quincey's, even though, according to Borges, both writers were interested in similar topics (*Ficcionario* 161; *Reader* 123).

It is interesting that one of Borges's explanations for the need of a careful construction of the plot in the adventure tale is that it tries "not to succumb to the mere sequential variety of *The Golden Ass*, the *Seven Voyages of Sindbad*, or the *Quixote*." Borges is unconsciously alluding here to the historical development of the novel of adventure as a genre. The *Golden Ass* and Cervantes's *Quixote* are, to be sure, adventure stories of an "older" kind. The structure of the adventure tale, since its origins in the early Greek and Roman "novels" (e.g., *Satyricon*) up to the eighteenth century did not change much. The old adventure story was a narration of a series of loosely connected episodes, sometimes not directly related to the plot. Because the early action tale was not yet an independent genre, the nature of the events in the story was determined by other forms of writings to which the "adventure tale" was subordinated. As Jean-Yves Tadié explains, it is only in the nineteenth century that the novel of adventure becomes an autonomous genre and adopts the carefully structured plot that Borges so much admires:

> The structure of the adventure novel has always imitated the one of the novels of its time. In the Middle Ages, it followed the structure of the chronicle, which consisted in a series of events loosely linked to one another, even if there was not necessarily a connection among them. The Spanish picaresque novel, and later the English one, kept that freedom that makes one await the happy outcome with a light heart. It is in the nineteenth century when the novel of adventures devotes itself to a great adventure. In *Treasure Island*, Jim Hawkins makes only one trip. Captain Mac Whirr [in Conrad's *Typhoon*] encountered a terrible storm, and that is what he narrates to us. An injustice and a vengeance are the main topics of *The Count of Monte-Cristo* and *Mathias Sandorf* respectively. This unique adventure organizes the novel of adventures in the nineteenth century with a rigor unknown until then. Thus, after Walter

Scott, an order is slowly imposed on the most fantastic of genres. (6; see also Tadié 19-23)

It is not really that the contemporary adventure story only narrates *one* adventure, but that all the "small" or secondary adventures are subordinated to the "great" or central one. Despite Borges's claim in the preface to *La invención de Morel* of being "free from every superstition of modernity, of any illusion that yesterday differs intimately from today or will differ from tomorrow" (123; 161), his preference for this version of the adventure tale and for the well-ordered plot is in fact a very modern one. As I said above, many critics see Borges's interest in the adventure novel and popular literature in general as springing from his childhood reading experience. However, with a few exceptions most of the books that Borges lists in the opening pages to Carriego's biography can only be collectively described as "adventure" books if we apply to them the older definition of the adventure story that he openly rejects in the preface to *La invención de Morel*. They are "amorphous" collections of adventures. This means that the influence of mass cultural products on Borges's writings cannot be simply explained as a regression into childhood. And one of the purposes of this chapter is to provide a sophisticated reading of the popular elements in Borges's work.

Another type of fiction that Borges praises in the preface for its plot construction is the detective or crime fiction. This is certainly a genre that immediately comes to one's mind whenever one thinks about Borges's use of popular culture in his writings. And for an obvious reason: Borges has created some extraordinarily innovative detective stories. No doubt he was one of the writers that helped to renew this genre. Borges considers detective fiction another example of the novel of adventure, in spite of its analytical character, which is supposed to emphasize reflection and abstract analysis over action. For Tadié also the detective fiction is a subgenre of the adventure tale (from which it detached itself in the nineteenth century), but one in which adventures are reduced [*ramenée*] to a particular type of adventure: the crime and the intrigue involved in the solution of the mystery. The most important part of the story is the understanding of the conditions of possibility (how, why and who did it?) of the crime: "Hence the intellectual look of this type of stories, a characteristic completely foreign to the novel of adventures" (Tadié 13). Of course, one must also remember that there are a series of adventures, in a more traditional sense, that the detectives (or their allies) experience in the process of solving the central mystery of the story. Not everything in the detective story is analysis and deduction. At least part of it is also composed of action and adventure.

In the case of the detective story, the major influence on Borges was exerted by the writings of G.K. Chesterton, whose name appears time and again in Borges's texts. Chesterton is mentioned, most famously, in another of Borges's theoretical essays on fiction, "Narrative Art and Magic" (1932). In this essay, Borges explains that there are two ways in which one can establish connections among events in a fictional text: the realist and the "magical." The realist way consists in reproducing or mimicking the causality that one normally experiences in the world. The magical, on the other hand, is the one that rules the novel of adventures ("la novela de continuas vicisitudes" [*Obras* 1.230; *Reader* 37]): events are not connected because of any causative relation among them, but by means of the principle of "sympathy." By sympathy Borges means that events that occurred in different places and under different circumstances can be linked to one another through an indirect association, like a resemblance in the way they took place (he calls this, their "figure" or shape) or a previous and unimportant contact between two events. Borges gives the following example from Chesterton to illustrate his point:

> Todo episodio, en un cuidadoso relato, es de proyección ulterior. Así, en una de las fantasmagorías de Chesterton, un desconocido acomete a un desconocido para que no lo embista un camión, y esa violencia necesaria, pero alarmante, prefigura su

acto final de declararlo insano para que no lo puedan ejecutar por un crimen. (*Obras* 1.231)[4]

Borges employs the same technique to write his short stories. Future events in Borges's stories are always foreshadowed by other, apparently insignificant, actions or elements within the text. The literary text, for Borges, becomes an organically structured object in which textual elements echo one another in an apparently endless game of internal allusions: "[una novela] debe ser un juego preciso de vigilancias, ecos y afinidades" (*Obras* 1.231; "[A narration] should be a rigorous scheme of attentions, echoes and affinities" [*Reader* 38]). I shall refer to this way of structuring fiction as the "geometrization" of narrative, a name given to Borges's writing practice by one of his contemporaries, and ideological adversary, the Argentine writer Ernesto Sabato (the author of one of the first critiques of Borges's writing practice [73-78]).

In his writings on the detective novel[5] Borges always emphasized both the importance of plot construction (see *Ficcionario* 192; *Reader* 148) and the analytical character of this genre. The adventures of the characters are not very important for Borges. In fact, the perfect detective story, he thinks, would avoid "physical" action and confine itself to the abstract solution of a problem, which suggests that the

---

[4]"Every episode in a painstaking piece of fiction prefigures something still to come. Thus, in one of Chesterton's phantasmagorias, a man suddenly shoves a stranger out of the road to save him from an oncoming motorcar, and this necessary but alarming violence foreshadows the first man's later act of declaring the other man insane so that he may not be hanged for murder." (*Reader* 38)

[5]Borges's major essays on detective fiction are "Los laberintos policiales y Chesterton" ("Chesteron and the Labyrinths of the Detective Short Story"; 1935) (*Ficcionario* 96-99; *Reader* 71-73), "Modos de G. K. Chesterton" ("Modes of G. K. Chesteron"; 1936) (*Ficcionario* 117-22; *Reader* 87-91), and "Roger Caillois: 'Le roman policier'" (1942) (*Ficcionario* 191-92) [translated as "On the Origins of the Detective Story" (*Reader* 147-48)].

adventures of the characters could easily be eliminated without affecting the essence of the detective story:

> El genuino relato policial...rehúsa con parejo desdén los riesgos físicos y la justicia distributiva. Prescinde con serenidad de los calabozos, de las escaleras secretas, de los remordimientos, de la gimnasia, de las barbas postizas, de la esgrima, de los murciélagos de Charles Baudelaire y hasta del azar. En los primeros ejemplares del género (El misterio de Marie Roget, 1842, de Edgar Allan Poe) y en los últimos (*Unravelled Knots*—Nudos desatados—, de la baronesa de Orczy) la historia se limita a la discusión y a la resolución abstracta de un crimen, tal vez a muchas leguas del suceso o a muchos años. Las cotidianas vías de la investigación policial—los rastros digitales, la tortura y la delación—parecerían solecismos ahí. (*Ficciones* 96)[6]

All of this suggests that Borges considers the detective novel to be a novel of adventures simply because of its attention to plot. He is no doubt right in noticing the "primacy of the plot" in this genre, but, again, this seems to be merely the result of a historical process. Leroy Panek explains how the development of narrative writing in the late nineteenth century and early twentieth century affected the form of the detective short story:

---

[6]"The genuine detective story . . . rejects with equal contempt physical risks and distributive justice. It serenely does without jails, secret stairways, remorse, gymnastics, fake beards, fencing, the bats of Charles Baudelaire, and even the element of chance. In the earliest examples of the genre ("The Mystery of Marie Roget," by Edgar Allan Poe, 1842) and in one of the most recent (*Unravelled Knots* by the Baronesse Orczy), the story is limited to the discussion and abstract resolution of a crime, perhaps quite distant from the event or after many years. The everyday methods of police investigation—fingertips, interrogation, and confession—would seem like solecisms therein." (*Reader* 71-72).

> At its inception, the novel was a slow-paced and rambling form written for people of leisure. We amble along with Joseph and Parson Adams on their picaresque adventures, we jog down an odd series of crooked paths and cul-de-sacs with Tristram Shandy, and we drag along Pamela's rocky road to the altar. A few more episodes, letters, or digressions make little difference. From the prose romance, eighteenth-century writers like Fielding took the unexpected ending, like the astonishing revelation of someone's ancestry, as a tongue-in-cheek method of concluding their fictions. The use of this sort of structural mystery descended to Mrs. Radcliffe, then to Lytton and Dickens. . . . The demands of serial publishing and three volume format for novels almost insured that this was as far as mystery and suspense would go in the novel. The invention of the short story and the slimming down of novels changed all of this. Joined with this, we find a reaction against the loose structure patterned on the romance and a movement toward the well-ordered novel. Here we need to note that early in its development, with Poe and Doyle, the successful detective story is the short story. Because of its need for economy, compression and consistency, the short story cannot afford the casualness of romance. (Panek 10)

In his "theory," Borges equates the well-ordered novel with the adventure novel and the realist novel with what Panek calls "casualness." Panek's observations serve here as a complement to Tadié's analysis of the emergence of a more coherent order in the narrative of adventure in the nineteenth century. It is obvious that this type of organization of the textual material cannot be ascribed exclusively to the adventure tale or novel but that it is, more exactly, the result of the modern development of narrative. In fact, a detective (or adventure) novel can also be a "novel of characters" as Borges himself points out in one of his essays in reference to Wilkie Collins' classic detective novel *The Moonstone* (1868) (*Ficcionario* 97). One of the problems of classifying Borges's stories as adventure tales is that the "structure" of the adventure tale that Borges is suggesting as the basic one (i.e., the geometrization of narrative) is not necessarily related to this genre. Borges himself recognizes the same kind of textual organization in Joyce's *Ulysses* and in Hollywood's films (*Obras* 1: 232). The technique of "geometrization" does not belong exclusively to popular literature.

It is not difficult to see how different today's popular literature is from those old forms of popular literature that Borges held as a model. In the nineteenth-century adventure novel, for example, one still finds a complexity and depth of plot and characters that is completely absent from the most streamlined cultural products of today:

> When the journalist Defoe and the printer Richardson calculated the effect of their wares upon the audience, they had to speculate, to follow hunches; and therewith, a certain latitude to develop deviations remained. Such deviations have nowadays been reduced to a kind of multiple choice between very few alternatives. The following may serve as an illustration. The popular or semi-popular novels of the first half of the nineteenth century, published in large quantities and serving mass consumption, were supposed to arouse tension in the reader. Although the victory of the good over the bad was generally provided for, the meandering and endless plots and subplots hardly allowed the readers of Sue and Dumas to be continuously aware of the moral. Readers may expect anything to happen. This no longer holds true. Every spectator of a television mystery knows with absolute certainty how it is going to end. (Adorno, *Culture Industry* 138)

To this one must add the profound changes that the process of characterization has undergone in contemporary forms of popular writing: "The accents on inwardness, inner conflicts, and psychological ambivalence (which plays so large a role in the earlier popular novels and on which their originality rests) have given way to unproblematic, cliché-like characterization" (Adorno, *Culture Industry* 139). It would seem that Borges's work, with his economy of words and deliberate exclusion of psychological traits from his characters, is closer to contemporary forms of mass culture than to the old adventure tale. But here

José Eduardo González   69

I would like to mention another aspect of Borges's writings that not only distances them from the adventure genre but also from contemporary popular literature. I am referring to the absence of action, of "adventures" in the popular sense of the term, from his fantastic fictions, to the fact that very often little, almost nothing, happens in these stories.

It is often said that Borges's fictions are "cerebral," in the sense that they supposedly deal less with "real" events than with the process of thinking, with the way the mind creates totalizing systems to explain the reality. The persuasiveness of this reading depends partly on the astounding absence of physical action, of adventures, in a group of writings that are said to seek to imitate traditional adventure writings. Today one may be skeptical of Carter Wheelock's old (but often quoted) assertion that Borges's work does not deal with "external" events but that in his writings the mind turns inward to contemplate its own activity. But the fact is that such theories and studies (including recent ones [see Lapidot; Merrell]) on the relation of Borges's narrative with abstract thinking, can gain credibility from the overwhelming amount of comments and allusions to mental constructs present in these stories: cosmologies, theological problems, philosophical concepts. This characteristic of Borges's prose, which constitutes the most obvious high-brow aspect of his work, frequently overburdens his stories to the point of almost obliterating the actions of the characters. There are stories in the Borges canon where no adventure ever takes place ("The Sect of the Phoenix," "The Library of Babel") and others that can be best described as a meditation on a single central idea ("Funes the Memorious"). Like the narrator of "The Lottery in Babylon" who mentions in passing many of the adventures that the lottery system has allowed him to experience but which the reader never "sees" him actually experiencing, Borges often talks about the diversity of his main characters' adventures but does not describe the events themselves as they happen. Thus, one often comes across those succinct catalogues of the different events experienced by a person/character in his/her life. In "Story of the Warrior and the Captive," for example, the adventures of an Englishwoman living among the Indians are summarized in a few lines:

[D]etrás del relato se vislumbraba una vida feral: los toldos de cuero de caballo, las hogueras de estiércol, los festines de carne chamuscada o de vísceras crudas, las sigilosas marchas al alba; el asalto de los corrales, el alarido y el saqueo, la guerra, el caudaloso arreo de las haciendas por jinetes desnudos, la poligamia, la hediondez y la magia. (*Obras* 1.559)[7]

The presence of these catalogues in Borges's fiction used to be explained in traditional Borges criticism as the result of his "poetics of briefness" (i.e., his preference for allusions rather than description [see Christ]). Later I will propose a reinterpretation of Borges's preference for briefness and minimalism. For the moment, this observation allows us to notice the difference between Borges's narrative and the traditional adventure fictions. I must point out that, on the one hand, in popular adventure stories the adventures of the main characters occupy a central position in the narration. On the other hand, the bulk of the body of a typical Borges text is devoted to the setting or background, to the conditions of possibility and to the fantastic consequences of the main event around which the narrative is constructed. Only a minimal part deals with the actual adventures of the characters. If "adventure," as it is defined by the theorists of this genre, consists of mainly physical action, as opposed to thought and analysis, then Borges's fictions are far from being adventure tales.[8]

---

[7]"[B]ehind her story one could glimpse a savage life: the horsehide shelters, the fires made of dry manure, the feasts of scorched meat or raw entrails, the stealthy departures at dawn, the attacks on corrals, the yelling and the pillaging, the wars, the sweeping charges on the haciendas by naked horsemen, the polygamy, the stench and the superstition." (*Labyrinths* 130)

[8]Green, like most critics of the adventure tale, defines it as a type of narration in which action takes precedence over thinking. "Adventure" is opposed to abstract thinking, to analysis. Green notices the importance that the body acquires in these narratives: "The adventure tale pays quite as much attention to the body and finds as much dignity in it (when that value comes in conflict with other values) as the love sto-

It should be clear that when I argue that there is no direct imitation of the detective novel or of the adventure tale in Borges, I am not saying that these forms of popular writing are not present in his fiction. They *are* present but not as some master form or paradigm underlying all of Borges's stories. Instead of trying to analyze Borges's stories as if they were detective or adventure stories, it would be more productive to consider them as possessing a unique form, which is different from that of popular modes of writing. However, it is a *form*, as it will be shown later, that has the capacity to absorb these two popular genres.

But when the absorption of popular forms of writing by Borges's fiction is so successful that they are taken to be the central textual structure, the appropriate questions to ask would be: How can these high-brow/modernist writings incorporate popular elements? Or how can the omnipresent high-brow cultural elements in Borges be rewritten in such a way that these "cerebral" fictions can be considered to be close to popular modes of writing? In other words, how is it possible that a group of stories dealing with such metaphysical topics and containing so many learned quotations and literary and historical allusions are so entertaining that the pleasure of reading them can be compared to the pleasure of reading popular literature (Savater 171-8)? Answering these questions requires that we reconstruct the conditions under which Borges carefully transformed himself from a poet into a short story writer and that we examine as well how the emerging Culture Industry in Argentina at that time affected that process. In those historical conditions we will find the origin of what I will call Borges's *post*-modern

---

ry. . . . Even in *Robinson Crusoe*, a Puritan and nonsensual novel, Robinson's experience of sickness dramatizes the vulnerability of the subject's body, while the description of Friday, which is reminiscent of slave-market descriptions, translates the excitement of property into somatic terms. *The Three Musketeers*' focus is characteristically on the body's forms of movement, running, leaping, riding, dueling; even in a seated and sculptural form (as in Doré's statue of d'Artagnan) the hero seems to move" (19).

literary project: to popularize, that is, to make accessible and enjoyable, the modernist literary enterprise.

Borges employs the traditional modernist topics as the central themes around which his fictions are constructed. Borges's topics such as the uncertainty about the individuality and coherence of the Self; the distrust of the linear conception of time; the relativity of point of view; and memory and how it relates to knowledge are also some of the most typical themes of High Modernism. Unlike popular literature, the modernist literature was concerned with complex topics and explored them using very complex forms of writing. Modernist literature was "difficult" reading as opposed to the light reading provided by mass literature. We will see shortly the origin of this "difficulty" and why Borges rejects it. It must be stated in advance that Borges's strategy was to rewrite modernist fiction in such a way that, without excluding the "difficult" modernist topics or parodying them, these ideas became not only more accessible but also much more entertaining to read.

Borges's strategy to turn what otherwise would be difficult reading—a reading that includes dealing with philosophical or theological themes—into a very pleasant activity, requires that he make the reader enjoy "thinking" about these topics. Readers must feel attracted to these "theories" about Time, Self, History, Order, and Chaos, etc. in the same way that they feel attracted to a sequence of events in an adventure tale or to any type of popular literature in general. In other words, these "great" topics are transformed into the opposite of that which they are supposed to be: they are not used to make readers think, but to entertain them. Knowledge in these stories has been reified to the point that it becomes a series of "theories" or "ideas" which have value only if there are readers interested in consuming them. Borges's purpose can be best described as a desire to turn the act of thinking, a mental process, and knowledge itself, into what I would call a "commodity," for the lack of a better term. The term itself ("commodification of knowledge") comes from Jean-Francois Lyotard's famous book on postmodernism, which is, even though critics often seem to forget about this, a study on the condition of knowledge in contemporary societies (xxiii). "Commodification of knowledge" describes for Lyotard the postmodern perception of knowledge:

> The old principle that the acquisition of knowledge is indissociable from the training (*Bildung*) of minds, or even of individuals, is becoming obsolete and it will become even more so. The relationship of the suppliers and users of knowledge to the knowledge they supply and use is now tending, and will increasingly tend, to assume the form already taken by the relationship of commodity producers and consumers to the commodities they produce and consume—that is, the form of value. Knowledge is and will be produced in order to be sold, it will be consumed in order to be valorized in a new production: in both cases, the goal is exchange. Knowledge ceases to be an end in itself, it loses its "use-value." (4-5)

It will become clear as my interpretation moves along that there are many similarities between Borges's use of "knowledge" and the phenomenon described by Lyotard in his book. The commodification of knowledge in Borges can be defined as the project of making accessible to the non-specialized reader the products of highly specialized fields of knowledge in a form designed to make it easier for the reader to "consume" them—and enjoy consuming them. My purpose at this moment is to understand how Borges achieves this popularization of knowledge. In other words, which are the strategies in his writings that are directly intended to turn knowledge into an object of nonspecialized consumption? In order to do this, however, one must analyze first the difference between Borges's view of literature and that of modernist artists: why and how Borges distances himself from modernist poetics. Borges's ambiguous reaction towards Modernism (he appropriates modernist topics and concerns but rejects, as we will see, the traditional modernist view of literature) can be explained in reference to a concept that was decisive for the creation of a new modernist perception of the artist and the work of art: the idea of *literature as work*.

During the high modernist years (1880-1930), and apparently as a reaction to the increasing influence of mass-produced art and to the specialization of work in Western societies, writers began to take refuge in their creative activity, turning the latter into a complex and difficult process. We witness as a consequence the birth of the "poet as a craftsman," a new type of writer who is going to put as much emphasis on the construction of the text (on style and form) as on the content. Writing becomes a difficult and sometimes painful action to which the author must devote most of his time and energy (his entire life in extreme cases). In clear opposition to the mechanization of work taking place in their societies, these writers chose to turn back to a medieval notion of work, in which the worker takes part in every aspect of the production of the final object. Writing was their "craft" and the literary work was a "product" that could not be created in factories (in an assembly line) and was not subjected to the capitalist division of labor. This modernist attitude was evident, for example, in Ezra Pound's complaints about the editors of the literary magazines: "The whole matter is that the editor wants one man to make screws and one man to make wheels and each man in his employ to do some one mechanical thing that he can do almost *without the expenditure of thought*, so the magazine producer wants one man to provide one element, let us say one sort of story and another articles on Italian cities and above all, nothing personal" (qtd. in Knapp 31; my emphasis).

Roland Barthes, in his now classical book *Writing Degree Zero*, traces this tendency to make literary writing a "job" back to mid-nineteenth century. Barthes's explanation of how this notion of writing as craftsmanship originated differs from the most traditional accounts. Unlike standard interpretations, accepted by both critics of the right and left alike, Barthes does not see this concept of art only as a simple reaction towards mechanization and commodification in society. For him it is mainly the result of a need for self-justification felt by the modern European writer (Barthes's point of reference is, as always, France and French literature):

> [The] 1850s bring the concurrence of three new and important facts in History: the demographic expansion in Europe, the replacement of textile by heavy industry, that is, the birth of modern capitalism, the scission (completed by the revolution of June 1848) of French society in three mutually hostile classes, bringing the definitive ruin of liberal illusions. These circumstances put the bourgeoisie into a new historical situation.

> Until then, it was bourgeois ideology itself which gave the measure of the universal by fulfilling it unchallenged. The bourgeois writer, sole judge of other people's woes and without anyone else to gaze on him, was not torn between his social condition and his intellectual vocation. Henceforth, this very ideology appears merely as one among many possible others; the universal escapes it, since transcending itself would mean condemning itself; the writer falls a prey to ambiguity, since his consciousness no longer accounts for the whole of his condition. . . . Whenever the writer assembles a network of words it is the existence of Literature itself which is called into question. (60-61)

Since the usage of literature has been called into question, he argues, writers begin to put the value of writing in the work that creating art has cost them. (In relation to the idea of the author as worker, see also Walter Benjamin, 220-38.)

The consequence of this new perception of literature was that work was placed inside the very process of writing. Writers, Barthes explains, began to put the "work-value" of writing in place of its "use-value":

> Writing is now to be saved not by virtue of what it exists for, but thanks to the work it has cost. Here begins now to grow up an image of the writer as a craftsman who shut himself away in some legendary place, like a workman operating at home, and who roughs out, cuts, polishes and sets his form, exactly as a jeweller extracts art from his material, devoting to his work regular hours of solitary effort. . . . Labour replaces genius as a value, so to speak; there is a kind of ostentation in claiming to labour long and lovingly over the form of one's work. (62-63)

It is impossible not to recall at this moment the image of a Proust withdrawing himself from the "world" into his cork-lined room in order to write his masterpiece or that of Joyce always working on his never-ending work in progress. For Barthes, it was Flaubert "who most methodically laid the foundations for this conception of work as craft" (64). This statement may very well have come from Borges himself, who also recognized the writings of Flaubert as the first expression of this new view of the writer and the writing process: "Flaubert, que fue el primer Adán de una especie nueva: la del hombre de letras como sacerdote, como asceta y casi como mártir" (*Obras* 1.263);[9] "[P]ensar en la obra de Flaubert es pensar en Flaubert, en el ansioso y laborioso trabajador de las muchas consultas y de los borradores inextricables" (*Obras* 1.265).[10] Borges wrote two essays on Flaubert, both of which were published in the second edition of *Discusión* in 1957. The one I have quoted from is "Flaubert y su destino ejemplar" (*Obras* 1.263-66); the other one is entitled "Vindicación de 'Bouvard y Pécuchet'" (*Obras* 1.259-62). Curiously, according to Rodríguez Monegal (*Literary Biography* 118), these essays were originally written and published in 1954, which is around the time that Barthes published his book (1953), which Borges probably never read.

If turning writing into a craft was a reaction against the modern division of labor, it was also part of a tendency at the time to separate high art from popular art. Modernist art's opposition to popular forms of art is, then, part of a more general rejection of cultural commoditification in modern societies. This rejection of the commercialization of life was expressed by the modernist authors through the elimination of the notion of pleasure from the work of art. Modernist art was not only difficult to produce, but it also became difficult to consume. What was being attacked, however, was not pleasure itself, but the idea of pleasure as amusement or entertainment, such as the one that mass art offers:

---

[9]"Flaubert was the first Adam of a new species: that of the man of letters as a priest, as an ascetic and almost a martyr."

[10]"To think about Flaubert's work is to think about Flaubert himself, about that anxious and laborious worker of many revisions and inextricable drafts."

> Amusement under late capitalism is the prolongation of work. It is sought after as an escape from mechanized work, and to recruit strength in order to be able to cope with it again. Meanwhile, however, mechanization so dominates the resting worker's leisure and happiness, and so profoundly determines the manufacture of amusement goods, that his experiences are inevitably mere after-images of the work process itself. . . . What happens at work, in the factory or in the office, can be evaded only by approximation to it in one's leisure time. Pleasure hardens into boredom because, in order to remain pleasure, it must demand no effort and thereby moves rigorously in the worn grooves of association. (Adorno and Horkeimer 137)

Modern writers thought that if they did not want their art to become another commodity, they had to make the consumption of art a difficult task for the reader. Readers had to "work hard," as it were, to understand modernist literature, almost as hard as the writers themselves labor to create that literature. As a result, modernist literature is not only unpleasurable but also "unintelligible," that is, very *difficult* to read. Its aim is not to entertain or amuse the readers, but to shock/annoy them, to make them think—which is not, by definition, pleasure.

Borges's attitude towards this aspect of modernist poetics is one of complete rejection. Thus, in his story about the imaginary writer Herbert Quain, Borges writes:

> Flaubert y Henry James nos han acostumbrado a suponer que las obras de arte son infrecuentes y de ejecución laboriosa; el siglo dieciséis (recordemos el *Viaje del Parnaso*, recordemos el destino de Shakespeare) no compartía esa desconsolada opinión. Herbert Quain, tampoco. Le parecía que la buena literatu-

ra es harto común y que apenas hay un diálogo callejero que no la logre. (*Obras* 1: 461)[11]

But if this is obviously a critique of the idea of the writing process as work, he also criticized the notion of reading as work. The modern tendency to make literature inaccessible to the common reader, to make the reader work hard to discover the hidden "meaning" of a literary text is, for instance, the target of his well-known attack on the novel genre in the "Preface" to *Ficciones*:

> Desvarío laborioso y empobrecedor el de componer vastos libros; el de explayar en quinientas páginas una idea cuya perfecta exposición oral cabe en pocos minutos. Mejor procedimiento es simular que esos libros ya existen y ofrecer un resumen, un comentario. (*Obras* 1.429)[12]

Borges's self-acknowledged incapacity to finish the reading of classical modernist texts like *Ulysses* must be understood as an open critique of the modernist transformation of writing into "work." In "Fragmento sobre Joyce" (["Fragment on Joyce"] *Ficcionario* 175-77; *Reader* 134-36), Borges writes: "Nadie ignora que para los lectores desprevenidos, la vasta novela de Joyce es indescifrablemente caótica... Yo (como el resto del universo) no he leído el *Ulises*, pero leo y releo con

---

[11]"Flaubert and Henry James have accustomed us to suppose that works of art are infrequent and laboriously composed [*de ejecución laboriosa*]. The sixteenth century (we need only to recall Cervantes' *Viaje al Parnaso*, or Shakespeare's destiny) did not share this disconsolate opinion. Neither did Herbert Quain. He thought that good literature was common enough, that there is scarce a dialogue in the street that does not achieve it." (*Ficciones* 73-74)

[12]"The composition of vast books is a laborious and impoverishing extravagance. To go on for five hundred pages developing an idea whose perfect oral exposition is possible in a few minutes! A better course of procedure is to pretend that these books already exist, and then to offer a résumé, a commentary." (*Ficciones* 15)

felicidad algunas escenas" (*Ficcionario* 176).[13] In "El arte narrativo y la magia" ("Narrative Art and Magic"), he suggests to his readers to take a look at Stuart Gilbert's book on *Ulysses* instead of reading the novel: "Basta el examen del libro expositivo de Gilbert o, en su defecto, de la vertiginosa novela" (*Obras* 1.232).[14] (See also "Joyce y los neologismos" ["Joyce and Neologisms"], *Ficcionario* 136-38; *Reader* 103-105). Ideas that foreshadow these positions can also be found in some of his early writings (Rodríguez Monegal, *Literary Biography* 169). Another example of Borges's rejection of modernist aesthetics is his special use of "spatial form." Spatial form was the name given to the modernist experimentation with literary structure, especially when it was used with the intention of expressing an author's disagreement with a linear concept of time. This formal experimentation, however, is one of the characteristics that make modernist literature so difficult to read. So when Borges plays with the idea of spatial form to represent a different conception of time, he prefers to describe or summarize what this form will look like rather than use formal experimentation in his stories. A good example is Herbert Quain's novel, *April March*, whose structure is carefully described for us (Borges even draws a diagram to *help* the reader understand the form of this imaginary novel). Another example is Ts'ui Pên's novel in "El jardín de senderos que se bifurcan." Borges is fascinated by the structure of these novels, but he always spares his readers the trouble of reading them. In the latter story, Yu Tsun represents the common reader, and his reaction to the novel recreates the reaction that the readers of the first modernist works probably had: "El libro [*El jardín de senderos que se bifurcan*, Ts'ui Pên's novel] es un acervo indeciso de borradores contradictorios. Lo he examinado alguna vez: en el tercer capítulo muere el héroe, en el cuarto

---

[13]"Everyone knows that for the unprepared reader, Joyce's vast novel is undecipherably chaotic. . . . Like the rest of the world I have never read all of *Ulysses*, but I happily read and reread some scenes." (*Reader* 135)

[14]"One need only to look into Stuart Gilbert's study or, in its absence, into the dizzying novel itself." (*Reader* 38)

está vivo" (*Obras* 1.476).[15] It is significant that only an "expert reader," a scholar, like Stephen Albert, may enjoy reading this modernist novel *avant-la-lettre*.[16]

Other examples of this critique of Modernism in his writings could be added, but what interests us now is to explain how the elimination of the notion of "work" from literature plays a central role in Borges's rewriting of modernist aesthetics. It will be convenient to try to localize the origin of his position.

Borges's rejection of writing as work may be inextricably related to his beginnings as a fiction writer. Familiar to all of us is the story of how after his father died, Borges had a near-fatal accident when he hit an ajar window frame with his head (he retells the story with some variations in "The South" [*Ficciones* 167-74; *Obras* 1.525-30]). The wound became poisonous and he had to be operated on (Rodríguez Monegal, *Literary Biography* 320-21). Borges was afraid that he had lost his capacity to read and write because of the operation. So he explains that after recovering from the accident, he began, "for the first time in his life," to write short stories. His rationale was that if he failed, he could always argue that it was because he had never written stories before and that it was not a consequence of the accident (Borges, "Essay" 45). But the stories, the first one of which was supposedly "Pierre Menard," were highly successful. It is known that the account is partly false and that Borges is probably mystifying his readers: he had written, besides the tales in *A Universal History of Infamy*, at least two original short stories before the accident took place ("Street Corner

---

[15]"The book is a shapeless mass of contradictory rough drafts. I examined it once upon a time: the hero dies in the third chapter, while in the fourth he is alive." [*Ficciones* 96])

[16]Borges's rejection of spatial form is also evident in his evaluation of Eisenstein's movies. Although he recognizes Eisenstein's genius, he absolutely dislikes Eisenstein's concept of "intellectual montage" (Cozarinsky, *Cine* 27). Intellectual montage was the cinematic version of spatial form in literature. Borges preferred Hollywood's movies, whose structure, based on the use of parallelisms, is closer to his theory of narrative (*Obras* 1.232).

Man"; "The Approach to Al-Mu'tasim"). Psychological interpretations of these events—and of Borges's retelling of them—go from the ones that see the accident as self-punishment (a Borges suffering some kind of Oedipal complex was feeling guilty about the death of his father [Matamoro 51-57]) to the ones that consider it an act of psychological liberation from the father's tutelage, which had as a consequence the release of Borges's artistic powers (Rodríguez Monegal, *Literary Biography* 323-31). Similar explanations are found in pseudo-psychological readings of Borges as well as the most sophisticated ones, such as Didier Anzieu's and Woscoboinik's. Anzieu argues, like Rodríguez Monegal, that the accident freed Borges from his father's influence and that having overcome this problem, he could begin to develop as a writer at a different level (Anzieu 190). Julio Woscoboinik in *El secreto de Borges* (51-54) agrees with Rodríguez Monegal's and Anzieu's analyses.

These interpretations, however, generally obscure the undeniable relationship that exists between Borges's creative work and his financially remunerative work, which, after he became the head of the household, was going to be the only means of support for his family. To fully understand the origin of the separation of labor and writing in Borges, one has to go back to the moment when he *really* began to write fiction, namely that period of his life (late 1920s/early 1930s) which I have already pointed out as the central key to understanding his artistic and political positions.

A certain "division of labor" was present in Borges's life from the very beginning, since his father (who always wanted to be a writer) never allowed Borges to work so that he (Borges) could dedicate all his time to reading and writing. In other words, Guillermo Borges always worked so that Jorge Luis Borges could create art. It is important to notice that the separation between the two kinds of activities (one more corporeal, the other more cerebral), was present in his early relationship with his father because it is the very real dissolution of the separation between work and writing (and not some psychological problem that Borges might have had) that should be the focus of our attention.

It is difficult to establish with precision the financial situation of the Borgeses during the late 1920s and early 1930s (which is when the financial problems of the family began), especially because the main

82   Thinking as Pleasure: Borges and the Culture Industry

biographical sources available pay little or no attention to these matters. With the exception of Rodríguez Monegal's *Literary Biography* and Borges's own "Autobiographical Essay" there are very few historical sources that one could use to document this period of Borges's life. Rodríguez Monegal's biography of Borges is very confusing in its description of this transitional period. However, we know that by 1927 Borges's father was almost blind and that he had stopped working ten years before (in 1917). Since then he had been receiving a pension with which he supported the entire family. That year (1927) the Borgeses had to move from their old house to an apartment in downtown Buenos Aires, and even though nowhere in the biographical sources are we told the reasons for the change, this is obviously a sign of the financial problems yet to come (Rodríguez Monegal, *Literary Biography* 214).[17]

---

[17]The Borgeses lived in this apartment until 1938, when Borges's father died. Borges's sister, Norah, and her husband were living with Borges and his mother during this time. They had been forced to leave Spain (because of the Civil War there) and returned to Argentina that year. In 1939 (after Borges's accident) they all moved to a house on Anchorena Street ("It was a two-story building in the Andalusian style, with a garden" [Rodríguez Monegal, *Literary Biography* 341]). It is obvious that it was thanks to the help of his sister and her husband (Guillermo de Torre) that Borges was able to live comfortably until 1943, when (for unknown reasons) he and his mother moved to an apartment on Quintana Avenue. "For the last three decades of their lives together, Borges and his mother lived in the same two-bedroom apartment on the sixth floor of a house on Maipú Street, in downtown Buenos Aires. . . . The Borgeses moved to that apartment in 1944, after a rather unsuccessful attempt at sharing lodgings with Norah and her family and a transitional stay at an apartment on Quintana Avenue" (Rodríguez Monegal, *Literary Biography* 467). A very romanticized description of the apartment is given by Rodríguez Monegal in the last pages of Borges's biography. A most accurate description of Borges's daily life in 1945 is the one offered by Borges's nephew (son of Norah): "Seated on the bed, with his bare feet on the floor, [Borges] drank coffee slowly and gazed around his room. It was not actually a bedroom but the dining room of a small apartment, separated from the living

To this, one should add the fact that, also in 1927, Borges had to be operated for cataracts. This was going to be only the first of a series of operations that most probably worsened the family's economic burden (neither the number of operations nor the dates when they were performed are known). During the end of this decade and the beginning of the next one, with the economic crisis aggravated by the overthrowing of the local government (Irigoyen) by the army, the Borgeses probably experienced the most difficult moments of their lives. Borges was going to spend most of the thirties looking for a stable job that could allow him to contribute regularly to his family's income. In 1933, Borges took up a job as editor of the Saturday literary section of *Crítica*, an Argentine newspaper that followed the method of "United States' tabloids" (Rodríguez Monegal, *Literary Biography* 251). In his biography of Borges, Rodríguez Monegal presents the events as if they were completely unrelated to the economic situation of the writer: in fact, the critic seems to suggest that Borges took the job mostly because it presented a challenge to him. However, one cannot help thinking that working as an editor is not the most appropriate job for someone who had recently had a cataract operation. But it is even less understandable that Borges stayed for so long (supposing that he did it for "pleasure") in a job where, as Rodríguez Monegal himself says, "the pay was small, [his boss] very demanding, and the pace killing" (*Literary Biography* 251-52). Given that Borges did not have a university education nor possess any type of professional training, writing was for him the most immediate and accessible means of earning an income.

This was the first time in Borges's life that literature and (economically remunerative) work became intertwined. His "mental activity" was now directly affected by material concerns. The fictitious separation between mental and corporeal activities that his father wanted to preserve was being erased by the pressures of the real world. It was also

---

room by sliding doors that were always kept closed" (Torre Borges 90). With Borges's salary it was impossible for them to afford a better apartment. It is curious, however, that even after achieving international fame in the sixties, he decided to stay in the same apartment, until his mother's death.

during this time, while working for *Crítica*, that Borges began to write fiction: "Street Corner Man" was published in the newspaper in 1933, and his tales of infamy were soon to follow. Even the topics of these stories—hooligans, gangsters, pirates—were apparently determined by the popular character of the newspaper in which they appeared (Charbonier 62). Perhaps because Borges did not recognize these pieces of writing as his first fictional works, he never explained why he suddenly started to write fiction and practically abandoned poetry (his poetic work belonging to this period is almost nonexistent). Unlike the dramatic accident that years later he will claim was the reason why he started composing his famous *ficciones*, no reason whatsoever is given by him as the one that compelled him to start writing the narrations of *A Universal History of Infamy*.

In any case, it is interesting to notice that the creation of Borges's so-called "first" fantastic short stories ("Pierre Menard," "Tlön, Uqbar, Orbis Tertius" [1939-40]) is also preceded by a period of intense writing that was—like his work for *Crítica*—mostly aimed at consumption by the general public. Borges was writing "for money," so to speak; that is, in order to improve his family's economic situation he was selling his writings to magazines and newspapers. It is not difficult to understand why he suddenly needed to increase his income: by 1936 his father's pension, already eroded by inflation, was no longer enough to support the family. Also, his father's health had declined so much that everyone knew that he was not going to live much longer (Rodríguez Monegal, *Literary Biography* 306).[18]

As he did during most of this decade, Borges resorted to writing—his only marketable skill—to help his family. His literary output was never going to be greater than during this period (1936-38), when he seems to be preparing himself to take over his father's role in the family. Twice a month Borges would write book reviews and short articles for *El Hogar*. Occasionally, he would also prepare page-long articles on literary subjects for the same magazine. Although it is im-

---

[18]"By the beginning of 1937 Father was too ill to leave any doubts about the coming end." (Rodríguez Monegal, *Literary Biography* 317)

possible to say whether his book and movie reviews for *Sur* were paid (they probably were not), it is known that he was commissioned to translate several texts to be published in the magazine or in book form. The amount—and the quality—of Borges's translations during this period is impressive: André Gide's *Persephone* (1936); Virginia Woolf's *A Room of One's Own* (1936) and, issued as a book, *Orlando* (1937). His translation of Kafka's short stories dates from 1938 (Rodríguez Monegal, *Literary Biography* 291-92). He also translated Faulkner's *Wild Palms* in 1939. The increment in his literary production should give us an idea of the bad financial situation in which the Borgeses found themselves at that moment. In many cases Borges had to translate and review books that he did not like. And in some other cases, even though he was translating an author that he admired, he chose a text which he considered of inferior quality. This was the case with Faulkner's *Wild Palms*, which Borges did not consider one of Faulkner's best books (Rodríguez Monegal, *Literary Biography* 372-73). Perhaps Borges consciously chose texts that he did not like because he did not want to forget that translating and reviewing books at that moment was his *job*. But whatever the reasons were, it is clear that he was not doing this incredible amount of work for pleasure. Around this time (it is not known exactly when) Borges had another editorial job, which he describes in his "Autobiographical Essay": "[I]had been the editor of a pseudoscientific magazine called *Urbe*, which was really a promotional organ of a privately owned Buenos Aires subway system" (43). In a conversation with Sorrentino, Borges gives a fuller description of the nature of this job:

> Actually, I've had some rather strange jobs. For instance, I ran a magazine for a subway company, and there I wrote, under various pseudonyms, articles on the fourth dimension, on the possibility of reaching the moon, on extra-sensory perception, on group theory [in mathematics]; that is to say, the kind of articles an amateur might write on mystical or scientific subjects. I've also written the commentary for an Argentine news-

reel. In short, I've worked at some strange jobs, not very remunerative ones, either. (Sorrentino 133)[19]

In 1937, Borges was finally able to get a regular income as a librarian. In February 1938, his father died and for five months he stopped contributing to *Sur*: "[Borges] could not afford to stop writing for *El Hogar*, which at least paid him something, but he was in no mood to write the more demanding reviews and articles *Sur* needed" (Rodríguez Monegal, *Literary Biography* 318). After his father's death, Borges's fate had been sealed: work could no longer be avoided, since now both he and his mother depended on his salary. But things were still going to get worse. His meager salary as a librarian was initially intended to be a complement to the money that he was receiving for his writings and not a substitute for it. According to Borges, his salary as a librarian was not very high, but with the money that he was earning from his writings for *El Hogar*, it was "enough."

> **J.L.B.** . . . .I must have been there [working at the library in Almagro Sur] altogether some nine years, and I finally attained a salary of 240 pesos per month.
>
> **Fernando Sorrentino.** Was that a good salary in those days?
>
> **J.L.B.** No, but as I was also writing a couple of pages for *Hogar* and they paid me seventy-five pesos a page, it was a salary that was—I won't say magnificent—sufficient. (Sorrentino 133)

---

[19]Notice that his job was to present complex topics in a way that they could be understood easily by the general public. We will see later how he employed a similar technique in his short stories. Pseudoscientific articles like the ones that he mentions here (including one about the fourth dimension) also appeared in *Crítica*. See *Borges en Revista Multicolor*.

But by the middle of 1939, just as Borges had begun to have new responsibilities, the editors of *El Hogar* decided to cancel Borges's literary section.[20] For several years afterward, the library job was going to be his only source of steady income. During this troubled period of his life, in 1939, Borges began to write fiction again. But it is clear now that this was not the result of some magical release of creative powers after his accident or of a psychological conflict "solved" after his father's death. Fiction becomes at this point in Borges's life, as it did during the *Crítica* years, the only place where Borges can escape from real work.[21] Also, it was his father who originally taught Borges to see profit and literature as incompatible. With Guillermo Borges's death any possibility of going back to a time when work and literature were separated disappeared. Now that Borges needed to sell his writings to improve his financial situation, eliminating the notion of work from

---

[20]Rodríguez Monegal gives a detailed description of how Borges's section was slowly eliminated by the editors, until it ceased to appear after July 7, 1939 (Rodríguez Monegal, *Literary Biography* 341-42).

[21]In 1940, Borges wrote a story in which the main character ("Borges") commits suicide. "Since Father's death," writes Rodríguez Monegal, "and the accident of Christmas Eve, suicide had become an obsession" (348). But, it is also very probable that the fact that he had to do a job that he utterly disliked, added to the pressures of being responsible for his mother had something to do with this depression. Indicative of Borges's attitude toward "work" are the memories that he had about his grandmother. Rodríguez Monegal explains that after Borges's grandfather died his grandmother (Fanny Haslam), had to find the means to support her family: "She had two sons to care for and bring up. Undaunted, she opened her home to paying guests, young American women who came to Argentina to teach under an educational program conceived by President Sarmiento when he visited the United States." Borges does not tell this part of his grandmother's story in his 'Autobiographical Essay'; nor has he ever mentioned it in his interviews. He prefers to emphasize the less prosaic details of her life, the frontier adventures" (Rodríguez Monegal, *Literary Biography* 8). Borges probably saw in his own situation (working in the library to support himself) a reflection of his grandmother's.

them was a way of keeping the old separation between literature and profit alive. It is then no surprise that these writings are so close to the popular forms of literature in their aim: to provoke pleasure, to provide a certain amount of entertainment. There is definitely no place in his fiction for the modernist conception of literature as the result of a "long and laborious" process. He refused to turn creative writing into *more* work.

But Borges was still too close to Modernism, too influenced by the high/low culture division to attempt a complete rejection of Modernism, and even less a direct imitation of popular writing. What we are given in his stories in the same high cultural ideas present in all modernist literature: theories about time and about memory, a disbelief in a coherent self, the problem of the relativity of point of view. But in spite of all the emphasis on philosophy, theology, aesthetic theories, and so on, this "knowledge" is presented to us in a way that we can enjoy learning about it. This is so because the reader is not offered knowledge in Borges's stories but pseudo-knowledge. The question is not whether Borges employs real or false philosophical or scientific foundations as the basis for his fictions. Nor am I questioning the accuracy of the ideas employed but how those ideas are presented. It could be argued, quite properly, that Proust's meditations on time are equally without any scientific or philosophical rigor. However, what makes knowledge look like a commodity in Borges's case is not his lack of scientific evidence or method but the fact that, unlike what happens in modernists' works, in Borges's fictions the reader does not have to "work" to receive this knowledge.

In order to make knowledge or pseudo-knowledge attractive to the reader/consumer, the author must banish any notion of work from the process of acquiring knowledge so that the reader can enjoy directly and immediately the end-product of a thinking process. Work—and not only the representation of physical work, but thinking *as work*—is the most obviously absent element in Borges's fictions. Borges's readers no longer have to submit themselves to those tortuous and long hours (and days, weeks, and months) that the reading of high modernist works takes. Readers of modernist texts try to find out, with Proust, how memory works through multiple examples and situations, or they try to solve the problematics of time and history in Eliot's *Waste Land* or Rilke's *Notebooks*. Borges prefers to give a summary of a theory about memory or about time in a few lines. In classical modernist works, the writer wishes to represent the act of acquiring knowledge and how this new knowledge changes the characters' personality (this is the *Bildung* process that Lyotard refers to). In Borges, the process of acquiring knowledge, of thinking, has been obliterated, leaving us simply with its result, its product.

This leads us to a necessary revaluation of Borges's "poetics of briefness," his preference for summaries, for condensation and allusion. Unconditionally praised by most of his critics (Christ, Rodríguez Monegal, Alazraki, to mention only the better known ones), these "poetics" can also be shown to be a structural consequence of the elimination of "work" in Borges's writings. The connection between briefness and the absence of thinking/reading as work is best represented in his tales by the figure of the *Encyclopedia*: a place where an unmeasurable amount of ideas, theories, are given to a reader without the normal amount of work that usually intervenes in the process of acquiring the information—there is no work involved in their consumption for even reading (the work that the reader must do in order to consume the commodities—that is, the "philosophical ideas," the "theories," etc.) is reduced to the minimum.

Rodríguez Monegal has noticed some similarities between the form of the encyclopedia and that of Borges's writings:

> Even more interesting than the use Borges makes of encyclopedias, as a literary subject, or motif, [in "Tlön," "The Library of Babel," and "The Book of Sand"] is the fact that encyclopedias, as literary structures and as prototypes of a certain style of writing, serve as models not only for Borges' essays but for many of his most celebrated stories. Thus he generally begins an article or a story by summarizing the subject; he then moves to an analysis of the chief theme; finally, he offers conclusions that usually contradict (totally or partially) the starting point. The technique is like a reduction, by way of his skill at minimal art, of the structure of articles in the *Encyclopedia Britan-*

nica. Even the technique of including at the end a note with a basic bibliography corresponds to the model. The only difference (*the* difference) is that Borges's texts are not just a reduction of the model but also a parody. In parading his scholarship, Borges undermines it by introducing not only false leads but false sources, apocryphal books, misquoted texts. (*Literary Biography* 89-90)

But parody may not be Borges's only reason for producing false knowledge: he is also in need of more theories, more ideas than the ones that he can find in real sources. In writings where knowledge has been turned into a commodity, the more ideas, summaries, one-sentence theories given to the readers, the more entertaining the stories are. It does not matter if these theories contradict each other, as it often happens in Borges's writings, since it is the amount and the simplicity of the output that is important.

To a certain extent, one could argue that this tendency towards elimination of "work" was already part of the project that in the eighteenth century led to the creation of the first encyclopedia. Jean D'Alembert, in his *Preliminary Discourse* to Diderot's *Encyclopedia* explains that one of the main purposes of this project is to reduce unnecessary work for scientists and thinkers:

> [The means by which an individual may educate himself/herself] would be abridged even further if all man's discoveries in the sciences and the arts up to our time were reduced to a few volumes. This project (even if it comprised the facts of history that are of true utility) would perhaps not be impossible to execute. It should be hoped at least that someone would attempt it; today we claim only to make a rough sketch of it. It would free us at last of so many books whose authors have merely copied one another. What ought to secure us against the satirical attack on dictionaries is that the most estimable journalist might likewise be subject to the same ill-founded criticism. Is not their aim essentially to set forth in abridged form what our century is adding to the enlightenment of the preced-

ing centuries? Is it not to teach how to do without unabridged texts and consequently to tear out those thorns which our adversaries like to leave in our path? How much useless reading would be spared by good abstracts! (107-108)

But D'Alembert also condemns the use of dictionaries and encyclopedias to replace the real process of learning:

> It is contended that by multiplying the aids and the facility for self-instruction, dictionaries will contribute to extinguishing the taste for work and study. . . . At the very most such collections [dictionaries] serve to provide a little enlightenment for those who would not have had the courage to find it without their aid; but they will never replace books for those who wish to educate themselves. (107)

Diderot's encyclopedia was intended to be the answer to the emerging specialization of knowledge whose effects were already beginning to be felt by the eighteenth century. Built within the encyclopedic *form* there is, however, the danger that it could lead to a simplification of knowledge. It is exactly the adoption of this form that allows Borges to include all types of discourses in a simplified form. It makes possible for Borges to include popular forms of writing (detective stories, adventure tales) in his stories without turning them into popular literature.

The simplistic presentation of obscure or highly specialized knowledge is a feature that Borges's fiction has in common with the detective fiction.[22] Often in detective fiction, a case is initially confus-

---

[22]Sturrock believes that Borges would probably show no interest in today's highly specialized philosophy: "Professional philosophers these days care more than they once did that their philosophy should be true. After two thousand years of unsuccessful system-mongering they are anxious to establish incontrovertible laws of thought. The paradigm of modern philosophy is surely symbolic logic, which can be manipulated in complete security by those who have learnt its notation even if the results of its operations turn out to be elaborate tautologies. The wish

ing to both the detective and the reader because the criminal possesses some kind of skill related to a field of knowledge that is foreign to the average person. The solution of the mystery therefore requires that the detective (and the reader) "learn" as much as he or she can about this new field. In his book, *Delightful Murder*, Ernest Mandel explains the ever-increasing presence of specialized knowledge in the detective story as a result of the market forces:

> With the broadening of its market, the initial function of the genre [i.e., crime story] had to be broadened. It was no longer enough to thrill readers, to lull them into forgetfulness, or to help them to live vicarious lives that standardized work and a standardized existence would never allow them to live in reality. The novel was increasingly obliged to provide additional services. The growth of the market itself furnished the stimulus for a secondary function of the detective story. A mass market implied hard competition, but since this was monopolistic competition with rigidly fixed prices, and since production costs were about the same—and irreducible—throughout the industry, price competition was excluded. The only way to get the edge over competitors was to endow one's commodities with additional use-value, to provide additional services.
>
> The service the crime story could offer, aside from straight-forward "entertainment," was to provide condensed, standardized, specialist knowledge in innumerable fields of human endeavor. From the late thirties and early forties (the heyday of a Rex Stout) to the seventies and early eighties (the period of an Adam Hall), the list has been growing. The reader has been given a crash course in forensic medicine and courtroom procedure (Erle Stanley Gardner); orchid-growing and *haute cuisine* (Rex Stout); . . . gambling (Ian Fleming and oth-

---

for certainty makes for dullness and for secrecy. There is nothing, except for its often exquisite detachment from reality, which might stir Borges's enthusiasm for such die-hard empiricism." (21-22)

ers); cheating at cards; make-up and disguise; the conditions of existence of Soviet generals and KGB chiefs; the standing orders of the Spanish Communist Party's Central Committee meetings—and so on *ad infinitum*. (78-79)

It should be remembered that in "Death and the Compass" Borges's readers also get a "crash course" on Jewish Kabbala and on the controversy about the name of God (in one paragraph! [see *Obras* 1.500-501]). Although, as Mandel explains, the inclusion of specialized knowledge in detective fiction is a phenomenon of this century, one could argue that the question of specialization has always formed part of the detective story.[23] As was mentioned before, for the Great Detective to discover the central mystery of the story, s/he usually has to understand the inner mechanisms of a specialized sector of the society, which can be symbolically represented by an important family, a secret society etc. The detective will always act as an outsider whose knowledge of the "secret" or specialized laws is superficial yet sufficient to solve the mystery. In the case of the prototypical rich family that seals itself off from society, the highly complex relations among its members—which stand for the specialized "laws"—are ultimately reduced to a case (or cases) of basic feelings: hatred, jealousy, avarice, lust. Of course, we are perhaps simply pointing out a characteristic common to all popular literature, which is the simplification of information about characters, events, setting etc. Simplification of knowledge is a characteristic that Borges's stories share with popular forms of fiction.

The detective story can easily be incorporated into Borges's fiction thanks to a mutual interest in simplifying specialized knowledge. The adventure tale, however, cannot be equally or easily assimilated, mainly because the narration of adventures requires a length that is incompatible with Borges's poetics of briefness. The adventures of the

---

[23]On the relationship between specialization and the origins of the detective story, see Priestman's chapter on Poe (36-55; see also 148-50). He also has an interesting chapter on the similarities between Modernism and the detective story structure (136-50).

adventure tale must then be "reduced" before they can become part of the typical form of a Borges story. Borges's rewriting strategy in this case is to present the adventures in the form of summaries that can be blended with other summaries. One could argue that his famous tendency to reduce a character's adventures to a few "scenes" ("la reducción de la vida entera de un hombre a dos o tres escenas" (*Obras* 1.289; "the paring down of a man's whole life to two or three scenes" [*A Universal History of Infamy* 13]) is a formal necessity.

In one of the examples mentioned earlier, the adventures of an Englishwoman living among the Indians in "Story of the Warrior and the Captive," or rather, the summary of those adventures, is presented simply as more information given to the reader. Adventures are reduced to mere information about the characters, to "knowledge" that the reader can have about them. By suppressing the narration of the actual adventures and replacing it with summaries, Borges is separating action from adventures. Curiously, thanks to the elimination of action in adventures, Borges has also been able to overcome the incompatibility analysis and action. The reduction of action and knowledge to mere information that one happily and easily learns allows Borges to transcend the traditional conflict between thinking and acting, between the novel of adventure and the novel of analysis.

Scholars, learned men or "thinkers" appear more often than men of adventures in Borges's fiction. It should be noticed at the same time that the readers are given in Borges's stories a caricature of the "thinker" and of the real thinking process so that they may project on it their dream of a nonalienated type of work. "Thinkers" and "philosophers" do not have to work eight hours every day, they are not subjected to any schedule and their work appears to be definitely more interesting than that of a common reader. Labor, then, must be banished from the stories because hard work does not form part of the life-style that the readers think "thinkers" have. The best comparison between the real life of a thinker and the public perception (or folk dream) of it can be found in some comments made by Heidegger in his "Letter on Humanism." Heidegger first quotes an anecdote about Heraclitus in which the philosopher is visited by some strangers who are surprised to find him warming himself in front of a stove. Heidegger then explains:

> The group of foreign visitors, in their importunate curiosity about the thinker, are disappointed and perplexed by their first glimpse of his abode. They believe they should meet the thinker in circumstances which, contrary to the ordinary round of human life, everywhere bear traces of the exceptional and rare and so of the exciting. The group hopes that in their visit to the thinker they will find things that will provide material for entertaining conversation—at least for a while. The foreigners who wish to visit the thinker expect to catch sight of him perchance at the very moment when, sunk in profound meditation, he is thinking. The visitors want this "experience" not in order to be overwhelmed by thinking but simply so they can say they saw and heard someone everybody says is a thinker. (233-34)

It is precisely that which the disappointed visitors were expecting to find for their own "intellectual" pleasure, that Borges's undeniably entertaining fictions provide his readers—who, like the visitors, come to him looking for an interesting, but brief, "exchange" of ideas.

The problematic relation between specialization of knowledge and popular literature that we have been describing should now help us to cast some light on those aspects of postmodern literature that were our point of departure. Borges's mix of theology, philosophy, history, literature etc. is perhaps the most postmodern aspect of his work. His is a "discourse" that tries to include other, sometimes totally incompatible, "discourses." Our analysis of Borges's strategy to include and use in his fictions these immensely different fields of knowledge, however, tells us something very important about Borges's Postmodernism (and perhaps about Postmodernists in general): "overcoming" specialization of knowledge can only be achieved through a simplification of knowledge. Specialization is not merely a tendency or fashion in modern society of which one could easily get rid. An imaginary transcendence of specialization in literature only leads to a superficial treatment of the different "discourses" that the author wishes to cover. As in Borges's writings, in postmodern literature in general the influence of the Culture Industry may often result in an appropriation of only the most superficial elements of a specialized "discourse" or field of knowledge.

BETWEEN KRAZY KAT AND *BATTLESHIP POTEMKIN*

After spending part of his youth in Europe, Borges returned to Argentina in 1921, where he quickly became the leader of a group of young avant-garde artists. By December of the same year when this group published the first edition of their new magazine *Prisma*, Borges had fully immersed himself in the intellectual life of Buenos Aires. It is possible that he read at the time some of the articles about film that Horacio Quiroga was publishing during the 1920s in magazines and newspapers such as *El Hogar*, *Caras y Caretas*, *La Nación,* and *Atlántida*. So much had cinema impacted Quiroga that as early as 1919 his interest in films was already beginning to influence directly his fictional writings (Dámaso Martínez 1297). In an essay entitled "Los intelectuales y el cine" (Quiroga 1216-18) and published in *Atlántida* in 1922, Quiroga comments extensively on an article that he found in the French magazine *Clarté* about how intellectuals have failed to understand film as a new art. He probably saw in this article a vindication of his own efforts to get Argentine intellectuals to treat this art seriously. For Quiroga, however, the reaction of most intellectuals towards film was understandable since, he argues, when a person goes to a movie theater, he or she is very likely to see a low-quality production. In this and in other articles (see "Las cintas mediocres—efectos de la superproducción" [Quiroga 1213-14]), Quiroga blames the overproduction of films for the bad quality of most of the movies being made: "[la mediocridad de los films se debe] sin duda alguna a la superproducción de estos últimos años que exige libretos y asuntos con urgencia febril" (1214).[1] A surprising statement when one considers it from the standpoint of to-

---

[1] "their mediocrity is the result of the recent overproduction of films which demands that new plots and scripts be quickly produced."

day's massive production of films that now reaches quantities probably unimaginable in 1921. Obviously, Quiroga had problems understanding film as part of a culture industry phenomenon in which art is not only produced for the masses but also massively produced. In his article, Quiroga warns intellectuals that if they want to be able to appreciate the new art they will have to go frequently to the movie theater and they will probably have to watch an incredible amount of bad films before they can find one worthy of being called a work of art: "es menester que transcurra un mes entero—y tal vez un trimestre—, para hallar por fin un film que sea el exponente de este maravilloso arte" (1218).[2]

Of course, there is no evidence that Borges ever read this or any other of Quiroga's articles on film. In general, Borges never thought very highly of Quiroga's writings (Dámaso Martínez 1293 and 1301), whose fictional work he considered a bad imitation of Poe's. For the same reason it is surprising to discover that in 1939 Borges wrote a movie review in which he praised very highly an Argentine film that was based on some of Quiroga's short stories (Cozarinsky, *Cine* 66-7), calling it superior to many of the ones that Hollywood was producing during those years. Of course, the fact that his close friend Ulyses Petit de Murat was involved in the project probably had something to do with his favorable review of the film. In any case, even if the young Borges never read Quiroga's article "Los intelectuales y el cine," the frequency with which Borges attended movie houses after his return to Argentina—as if he were following Quiroga's advice—was exceptional in an intellectual climate in which, as Quiroga points out, films were commonly despised as another manifestation of the emerging mass culture (Quiroga 1217). The young Borges went so frequently to see films during this decade that when one looks at the articles and film reviews that he published between 1929 and 1945, what is most impressive about them is the expertise that he acquired about pre-1929 films. A sheer amount of movie references, mostly to films from the silent period, clutter these texts. For example, his first review published in *Sur* in

---

[2]"A month—perhaps three—has to go by before one can finally find a film worthy of representing this wonderful art."

1931 (although probably not the first one that he ever wrote; apparently he had published others in local newspapers before then), mentions twelve different films in a text that is less than three pages long (Cozarinsky, *Cine* 30-2). In other words, Borges had become a perfect example of the "new" intellectual that Quiroga wanted to see: someone for whom movie going was an essential part of his intellectual life and not an occasional distraction. Borges himself underscores the difference between his attitude towards films and that of the "traditional" intellectuals in a 1936 review of Allardyce Nicoll's book, *Film and Theatre*:

> Allardyce Nicoll, hombre versado en bibliotecas, docto en ficheros y absoluto en catálogos, es casi analfabeto en boleterías. Ha ido rara vez al cinematógrafo. Mejor dicho, hace pocos años que visita cinematógrafos. De la época muda, de la época anterior a 1929, no sabe casi nada. De la actual, poquísimo. Sólo así alcanzaremos a comprender, ya que no a perdonar o vindicar, la omisión de las obras y los nombres de Josef von Sternberg, de Lubitsch y de King Vidor. (Cozarinsky, *Cine* 49)[3]

On the one hand, Borges criticizes Nicoll for being the type of intellectual for whom going to the movies does not have the cultural importance that other intellectual activities do, while, on the other, he is also accusing Nicoll of having recognized only recently the status of film as art. For Borges, the defects of Nicoll's book come from the author not being able to make a genuine transition from the traditional

---

[3]"Professor Allardyce Nicoll, a man well versed in libraries, erudite in card catalogues, and sovereign in files, is almost illiterate in box-offices. He has rarely gone to the movies. To be more exact, he has been going to the movies only in the last few years. About the silent era, about the period before 1929, he knows next to nothing. About the present period, extremely little. Thus we can understand— but neither pardon nor defend—the omission of the works and names of Josef von Sternberg, Lubitsch, and King Vidor." (Cozarinsky, *On Film* 40)

to the "new intellectual" status. A reading of Nicoll's book would prove that Borges was not far from the truth in his characterization of the author as a "newcomer" to the field of film criticism. Nicoll's argument shows that he is judging films from the point of view of someone used to being in contact with high culture. Nicoll assigns himself the task of writing a book to defend film from those who consider it merely a manifestation of popular entertainment and not a "legitimate" form of art and he tries to accomplish this by asserting the artistic value of commercial film while, at the same time, pointing out the influence of commercialism on other forms of art such as Elizabethan theater (1-37). Yet in spite of the fact that he is trying to "elevate" film to the status of art, Nicoll also views film as a "developing" artistic form since it still has to produce works that are "as vividly arresting and as profoundly searching" as those created for theater (2). Although some of what are now considered masterpieces of early cinema had already been produced by the time that Nicoll is writing the book, his condescending attitude does not allow him to see this. The difference between Nicoll and Borges is not due to the former's shortsightedness, but to the fact that Nicoll feels the need to prove that film is a valid artistic medium, something that for Borges is never an issue.

Borges's interest in cinema was to a certain extent a reaction to the early attention that the film industry received in Argentina. In 1919, notes Beatriz Sarlo, *Imparcial Film*, the first magazine completely devoted to the film industry in Buenos Aires appeared, and in the following years others were soon going to begin publication: *Cinema Chat* and *Hogar y cine* (both in 1920), *Argos Film* (1922), *Los héroes del cine* (1923), *Film Revista* (1924) (*La imaginación* 29). That Borges became so early interested in the new artistic medium simply underlines the fact that the growing influence of mass culture was an important element of his aesthetic and ideological evolution. Although the relationship between Borges's interest in mass culture and the changes in his political ideology is an aspect of his work that I will address directly in my last chapter, it is necessary to notice that one of the problems with the existing studies on Borges and film is that the influence of the latter has always been analyzed in isolation from the emerging culture industry in Argentina. It is impossible not to see film in his work as related to his interest in other popular culture products, such as the adventure tale and the detective fiction. It was not by chance that when Borges wrote his stories in *A Universal History of Infamy*, cinema appeared mentioned in the preface to the book, alongside the names of Chesterton and Stevenson. Departing from previous studies on Borges's use of film, which traditionally focus on the influence of a specific technique (montage) or a film director (von Sternberg) I will study the function of cinema within a general Borgesean strategy to erase the boundaries between high and low culture. As in my preceding chapter on popular narrative, one of the central aims of my investigation will be to show how Borges tries to reproduce in his fictions the pleasure that one supposedly derives from entering in contact with commercial art.

Critics who have studied the influence of film on Borges's work have normally focused on how the technique of montage was decisive in the formation of his writing style. It has become almost a commonplace to say that Borges's fragmentary prose is somehow the result of his mimicking this technique in his stories (Cozarinsky, *Cine* 16; Christ 64). Let us turn our attention first to the two classical passages that form the basis of this theory of Borges's style as the literary representation of film montage. The first mention of cinema in his work in relation to writing appears as early as 1928 in a passage from his biography of the poet Evaristo Carriego in which, looking for the appropriate method to narrate the pre-history of the neighborhood of Palermo, its "mythological" foundation, Borges suggests that

> Lo más directo, según el proceder cinematográfico, sería proponer una continuidad de figuras que cesan: un arreo de mulas viñateras, las chúcaras con la cabeza vendada; un agua quieta y larga, en la que están sobrenadando unas hojas de sauce; una vertiginosa alma en pena enhorquetada en zancos, vadeando los torrenciales terceros; el campo abierto sin ninguna cosa que hacer; las huellas del pisoteo porfiado de una hacienda, rumbo a los corrales del Norte; un paisano (contra la madrugada) que se apea del caballo rendido y le degüella el ancho pescuezo; un

humo que se desentiende en el aire. Así hasta la fundación de Don Juan Manuel. (1.105-106)[4]

But after giving us here a specific example of how to translate montage to literature, he does not employ the technique again anywhere else in the book. By being so precise about how montage could be employed as a narrative technique, he establishes a distance between the style that he is using in *Evaristo Carriego* and literary montage. The latter is a style that *could be* used by Borges if he wanted to, but it is not the one that he is employing to write the book. Of course, when critics argue that montage is the origin of the "fragmentation" in Borges's style, they are not referring to the style of such early books as *Evaristo Carriego* or *Discusión* but to his narrative fictions. They are mostly thinking of his "mature" paratactic style from the late 1930s on. This passage is then taken to be an experiment with prose that will bear fruits only later and has no connection whatsoever with the prose of *Evaristo Carriego*. And yet, when one looks carefully at his style in *Evaristo Carriego,* it is obvious that even if it does not have many of the features of his mature style, it still shows a certain "fragmentation" in it. Clearly, Borges is already beginning to eliminate causative links and replace them for a comma, a period or a semicolon.

Whatever the source of his parataxis is—its origin in the baroque style is something I study in detail in my next chapter—it has nothing to do with montage. In the passage quoted before, literary montage is thus not presented as a model or the origin for his narrative

---

[4]"The best approach, if we were to adopt the techniques of film-making, would be to present a continuous flow of vanishing images: a mule train laden with wine casks, the less tame animals blinkered; a long, flat strech of water on which a few willow leaves float; a phantasmal wandering soul high on his horse, fording flooded streams; the open range, where absolutely nothing happens; the rentless hoofprints of a herd of cattle being driven to the Northside stockyards; a cowhand (silhouetted against the dawn) who dismounts from his spent horse to slit its broad throat; smoke from a fire dispersing into air. So it was until the arrival of Juan Manuel de Rosas." (*Evaristo Carriego* 38-39)

style, but as an artistic resource that fulfills a definite function within the text and that the author can easily employ because its fragmentation fits the already fragmented style that he is developing. I propose that Borges saw literary montage as a literary device and, like other literary techniques, this one is used with the purpose of creating an intended effect. I must explain that when I argue that Borges reduces montage to a literary technique, I am saying that instead of using montage to shape the form of the entire narrative, he has chosen to limit its usage to a very brief section and give it a specific function within the text. But what kind of effect is he exactly looking for when employing literary montage? From the citation above—where he uses it to narrate the mythical pre-history of Palermo—one can infer that Borges is employing literary montage to evoke a sense of "the epic."[5] I think that one can corroborate this by giving a quick look at how Borges uses the same technique—though more extensively—in *A Universal History of Infamy*. The same idea of presenting a series of images without connection among them that he mentions in *Evaristo Carriego* reappears in his 1935 preface to *Infamy*: these short stories, he says, "abusan de algunos procedimientos: las enumeraciones dispares, la brusca solución de continuidad, la reducción de la vida entera de un hombre a dos o tres escenas" (*Obras* 1.289).[6] Even the general organization of his tales in *Infamy*, it has been suggested, reflects the influence of montage, "with subtitles that divide each story into a frame-like pattern" (Accaria-Zavala 120).

There is no denying that montage had a strong influence in the composition of this book. One could even argue that even if montage was not the origin of Borges's paratactic style his experiments with it had the effect of intensifying an already fragmentary form of writing. The "tales of infamy" no doubt show more disconnection among their

---

[5]On Borges's view of Hollywood as the place where the epic tradition has been preserved, see Accaria-Zavala 75-77.

[6]They exploit certain tricks: random enumerations, sudden shifts of continuity, and the paring down of a man's whole life to two or three scenes. (*Infamy* 13).

parts than anything that Borges wrote before or after them. But even if we accept describing this book as an experiment with film techniques, it has to be admitted that Borges probably realized that it was impossible to structure an entire story employing literary montage. For that reason, film techniques in *Infamy* are once again reduced to devices ("procedimientos") that the author uses frequently but that do not interfere with, much less replace, the traditional linear ordering of the story. The epic intentions that we detected in *Evaristo Carriego* are present here too, since these are stories of adventures and, in some cases, such as in the opening paragraph of his rewriting of the legend of Billy the Kid, the connection with his use of montage to describe the epic origins of Palermo is very clear:

> La imagen de las tierras de Arizona, antes que ninguna otra imagen: la imagen de las tierras de Arizona y de Nuevo México, tierras con un ilustre fundamento de oro y de plata, tierras vertiginosas y aéreas, tierras de la meseta monumental y de los delicados colores, tierras con blanco resplandor de esqueleto pelado por los pájaros. En esas tierras, otra imagen, la de Billy the Kid. (*Obras* 1.316)[7]

But after this extremely visual or cinematic opening, the narrative abandons the literary montage technique and returns to a more "normal" or traditional narrative style. I have been arguing that Borges employs montage techniques to create a literary effect—which in these particular examples is an epic view of history—and that by turning montage into a literary device that can be employed by the author when he needs it, Borges incorporates film as part of his prose style. I will come back later in this chapter to this idea of assigning montage tech-

---

[7]"An image of the desert wilds of Arizona, first and foremost, an image of the desert wilds of Arizona and New Mexico—a country famous for its silver and gold camps, a country of breathtaking open spaces, a country of monumental mesas and soft colors, a country of bleached skeletons picked clean by buzzards. Over this whole country, another image—that of Billy the Kid." (*Infamy* 61)

niques specific functions within the text and analyze how it is the result of Borges's view of cinema. But I think that it was necessary to demystify the belief that Borges's style is the result of his passion for films. As for the use of "subtitles" in *Infamy*, when one compares these essay-like stories to, for example, Mark Twain's essays (I am thinking here of texts like "What Is Man?" [Twain 335-99]), the similarity in the use of subheadings to separate the sections in the text is striking. We are probably dealing here with an direct influence of Twain, whose book *Life on the Mississippi* Borges mentions as one of the "sources" of *A Universal History of Infamy*.

Diane Accaria-Zavala has written one of the most complete studies on Borges and film so far, and, like many critics before her, she pays a great deal of attention to the connection between montage and Borges's prose. Although her criticism also sheds new light on other areas of the complex relation between Borges and cinema, some of her conclusions, however, are not very convincing. For example, she unsuccessfully attempts to link Borges's past as a member of the avant-garde in Spain, and his early fascination with Expressionism, with his interest in film. Accaria-Zavala suggests that perhaps Borges and his Spanish friends imitated other European avant-garde artists, like Apollinaire, who used to "go in and out" of movie theaters only to see "bits and pieces of diverse films so as to grasp the intensity of fragmentation in life up on the screen" (43). We know little about Borges's Spanish period, but there are no proofs of his being interested in cinema during that stage of his career, whereas, on the other hand, it is evident that there were too many things that he profoundly disliked about Expressionist cinema, as recorded in a later film review: "la simbología lóbrega, la tautología o vana repetición de imágenes equivalentes, la obscenidad, las aficiones teratológicas, el satanismo" (Cozarinsky, *Cine* 30).[8] Had he been attracted to Expressionist cinema as the critic suggests, I suppose that not only would we find a more positive view of this style

---

[8]"lugubrious symbolism, tautology or meaninglessness repetition of equivalent images, obscenity, a propensity for teratology, and Satanism," (Cozarinsky, *Film* 23).

of filmmaking but references to Expressionist cinema would have appeared more frequently in his movie reviews. One of Accaria-Zavala's central concerns is to define a notion of "verisimilitude," which the critic claims is the key to understanding Borges's preference for certain film directors. Accaria-Zavala quotes an important paragraph from "The Postulation of Reality" (1931) in which Borges argues that "la impresición es tolerable o verosímil en la literatura, porque a ella propendemos en la realidad" (*Obras* 1.218).[9] He then goes on to explain that a person's mind does not register (or remember) every single detail that it perceives, only the most interesting ones: "El hecho mismo de percibir, de atender, es de orden selectivo: toda atención, toda fijación de nuestra conciencia, comporta una deliberada omisión de lo no interesante" (*Obras* 1.218).[10] I have already explained this rewriting of realism as a realism paradoxically based on the omission of reality that, with the purpose of finding an alternative to both Realism and Modernism, will later become a Borgesean strategy to incorporate Realism into a non-realistic prose. For Accaria-Zavala, Borges's version of verisimilitude (which she calls "mental editing") will influence his taste in films as he will feel attracted to the work of directors who present a "subjective view" of reality: "[Borges] will align himself to a cinema of stylized and poetic perception ('à la Sternberg') rather than to a cinema defined by nineteenth-century realism ('à la Griffith')" (64). Borges's rejection of Eisenstein and Welles, two directors whose departure from nineteenth-century realism should have attracted Borges according to this theory, present a problem for Accaria-Zavala; a problem whose solution only leads her to other problems. In her desire to justify the negative review of *Citizen Kane* that Borges wrote in 1941, for example, she says that Borges was disapproving of Welles's ideology and his critique of capitalism. "Borges' political views," the critic argues,

---

[9]"imprecision is tolerable or plausible in literature because we are always inclined to it in reality." (*Reader* 31)

[10]"The very act of perceiving, of heeding, is of a selective order; every attention, every fixation of our conscience, implies a deliberate omission of that which is uninteresting." (*Reader* 31)

"more so during this period of Peronism were always aligned to the right wing" (162). The explanation not only is historically inaccurate—Perón will not reach the presidency until a few years later—but it completely ignores the evolution of Borges's ideology, assuming that it remained constant throughout his entire life. In spite of its flaws, Accaria-Zavala's study points to the right direction since discovering why Borges gives preference to certain types of film (*not* film directors) and rejects others seems absolutely necessary if we want to establish a valid connection between cinema and his fictional prose. The first, elementary but critical step should be defining the characteristics of the movies for which Borges shows preference. For instance, as we are going to see, even though many critics have pointed out Borges's fascination with montage, they have consistently failed to notice that he was not attracted to *all* kinds of montage techniques, as it can be observed in the above mentioned review of *Citizen Kane*. In that review Borges's main objection to the film comes after a careful analysis of the director's editing technique:

> El procedimiento es el de Joseph Conrad in *Chance* (1914) y el del hermoso film *El poder y la gloria*: la rapsodia de escenas heterogéneas, sin orden cronológico. Abrumadoramente, infinitamente, Orson Welles exhibe fragmentos de la vida del hombre Charles Foster Kane y nos invita a combinarlos y a reconstruirlo. Las formas de la multiplicidad, de la inconexión, abundan en el film... Al final comprendemos que los fragmentos no están regidos por una secreta unidad: el aborrecido Charles Foster Kane es un simulacro, un caos de apariencias" (Cozarinsky, *Cine* 68-69)[11]

---

[11]"The procedure is the same as in Joseph Conrad's *Chance* (1914) and the beautiful film *The Power and the Glory*: a rhapsody of heterogeneous images, out of chronological order. Overwhelmingly, endlessly, Orson Welles shows fragments of the life of the man, Charles Foster Kane, and invites us to combine them and to reconstruct him. The film teems with forms of multiplicity, of incongruity. . . . At the end, we realize that the fragments are not governed by any secret unity: the

When comparing it to a book from one of Borges's favorite authors and to a film that apparently he enjoyed, both of which, he says, employ a similar heterogeneous structure, Welles's film is said to lack coherence: it is nothing but a collection of disconnected fragments, a chaos of images. It seems as if, for Borges, heterogeneity is acceptable only when a reader/spectator can transcend it by giving it a unified sense. However, when we look at other texts in which Borges deals with the problem of the representation of heterogeneity in literature, things get more complicated. I am thinking now of the *disjecta membra* case that Silvia Molloy studies and turns into the starting point of her analysis of Borges's prose in *Signs of Borges* [*Las letras de Borges* (1979)]. Borges mentions *disjecta membra* in "Sobre la descripción literaria," an article that he published in *Sur* in 1942. In that article Borges complains about the way the Spanish writer Gabriel Miró describes his characters, which, Borges says, are simply impossible to imagine by the reader: "Trece o catorce términos integran la caótica serie; el autor nos invita a concebir esos *disjecta membra* y a coordinarlos en una imagen coherente. Esa operación mental es impracticable: nadie se aviene a imaginar pies del tipo X y añadirles una garganta del tipo Y y las mejillas del tipo Z" (101).[12] As in his review of *Citizen Kane*, published a year before this article, Borges is annoyed because he cannot unite all the fragments into a single image. Molloy explains that what bothers Borges is that Miró's descriptions "are coordinated in an anthropomorphic image: a character not a text" (19). Thus implying that Borges did not have any objections to "textual" (meaning non-anthropomorphic to use Molloy's terminology) representations of heterogeneity. Molloy's problem, of course, consists in convincingly showing that there is really

---

detested Charles Foster Kane is a simulacrum, a chaos of appearances." (Cozarinsky, *On Film* 55)

[12]"Thirteen or fourteen elements make up the chaotic series; the author invites us to conceive those disjecta membra and coordinate them in a single, coherent image. Such a mental operation is impracticable: no one is able to imagine type X feet, add them a type Y throat, and then type Z cheeks." (trans. in Molloy 18)

a difference between the textual and the anthropomorphic image. Miró's descriptions are, after all, also textual, that is, "made up of words." To support her point, the critic quotes an example of *disjecta membra* that was praised by Borges in an earlier text, the title essay of *Historia de la eternidad* (1936):

> Oír la descripción de una reina—la caballera semejante a las noches de la separación y la emigración pero la cara como el día de la delicia, los pechos como esferas de marfil que dan luz a las lunas, el andar que avergüenza a los antílopes y provoca la desesperación de los sauces, las onerosas caderas que le impiden tenerse de pie, los pies estrechos como una cabeza de lanza—y enamorarse de ella hasta la placidez y la muerte, es uno de los temas tradicionales en las 1001 Noches. (*Obras* 1.358)[13]

Although Borges's description of the Oriental queen looks no different from Miró's characters (at least Borges's perception of them) Molloy argues that in Borges's text the author has rendered the description impersonal by means of rhetorical devices (19). Borges himself explains that with this description he wants to give an example of how "lo genérico (el repetido nombre, el tipo, la patria...) prima sobre los rasgos individuales, que se toleran en gracia de lo anterior" (*Obras* 1.358).[14] The queen's characteristics are supposedly fused together by "generic traits (Molloy 20) that turn what would have been an anthro-

---

[13]"To hear the description of a queen—hair like nights of flight and exile but a face like a dawn of delights, breasts like ivory spheres lending their light to the moons, a walk that would shame the antelopes and make the willows rage, hips so ample that she cannot stand, feet as narrow as the tip of a spear—and to fall in love with her unto pleasure and unto death, is one of the traditional themes of the Thousand and One Nights." (trans. in Molloy 20)

[14]"generic traits (the commonplace, the type, the fatherland . . .) take precedence over individual traits, which are tolerated thanks to that precedence."

pomorphic *disjecta membra* into a textual one and in the process give the image a coherence that it otherwise would lack. "The text cancels the individual it describes," explains Molloy, "an individual impossible to represent in a single image" (20). Conventional signs create a "mask" that erases the original heterogeneous traits. In other words, according to the critic, Borges favors textual *disjecta membra* because it permits him to hide the fragmentation of his representations. Armed with this distinction between Miró's and Borges's use of *disjecta membra*, Molloy develops a theory about how the characters in *A Universal History of Infamy* gain coherence through "masks" (although very unstable ones) which conceal the heterogeneity of the images. Yet when Molloy discusses examples of *disjecta membra* from Borges's mature work, the desire to give them coherence, which was one of the characteristics that he found lacking in Miró's writings, has disappeared. If Molloy is right and Borges was trying to conceal heterogeneity in his early texts, how could one explain the heterogeneous descriptions in his later *ficciones,* which are obviously intended to represent the absence of coherence? Molloy does not clearly explain this transition, except that in her book there is a suggestion that Borges realized that his early strategies to avoid heterogeneity were unsuccessful, and that for that reason the "mask" comes off in his later texts. However, suddenly dropping the desire for textual coherence as a determining factor in Borges's search for an alternative *disjecta membra* erases part of what made the textual and the anthropomorphic different from each other. What, if it is no longer coherence, would be the purpose for transforming an anthropomorphic description into a textual one?

I wish to introduce now an element that Molloy completely ignores when she contrasts the Oriental queen passage with Borges's opinion of Miró's descriptions: *pleasure.* The ability to imagine a coherent image from the description given in a text (even if it is necessary to believe in the "masks" created by the author) gives the reader a pleasure that, on the other hand, Miró's *disjecta membra* denies him or her. Considering the problem of heterogeneity in relation to pleasure, we can see that the distinction between textual and the anthropomorphic descriptions ceases to matter. Whether one or the other is being employed, the lack of coherence has the same result, that is, the elimination of pleasure, even if it is for a brief moment. This is even more clear when we look at another example discussed by Molly, this time a well-known story from *Ficciones*, "Pierre Menard, Author of the *Quixote,*" in which the anthropomorphic and the textual are curiously intertwined. Although the entire story revolves around a description of the main character, the *disjecta membra* that one finds here is not anthropomorphic—or so Molloy's argument goes—because what is being given to us is not a physical description, but that of Menard's mental history (27-32). Curiously, this "textual" description lacks as much coherence as the "anthropomorphic" ones. The story contains the bibliography of Menard's visible work, and while reading it the reader discovers that it is composed of such disparate elements that the same person could not have possibly produced all of them. In other words, it is impossible to imagine Menard's "mind," and this Molloy finds "disquieting," a comment that is intended as an allusion to the now well-known reaction that Michel Foucault had when faced with a similar textual *disjecta membra* in another of Borges's writings. In Foucault's case, he felt a "disquieting" feeling after reading Borges's description of an improbable Chinese encyclopedia in which animals were classified into several absurd categories (e.g., belonging to the Emperor, embalmed, fabulous, innumerable):

> That passage from Borges kept me laughing a long time, though not without a certain uneasiness that I found hard to shake off. Perhaps because there arose in its wake the suspicion that there is a worse kind of disorder than that of the *incongruous*, the linking together of things that are inappropriate; I mean the disorder in which fragments of a large number of possible orders glitter separately in the dimension, without law of geometry, of the heteroclite . . . in such a state, things are "laid," "placed," "arranged" in sites so very different from one another that it is impossible to find a place of residence for them, to define a *common locus* beneath them all. (xvii-xviii)

Foucault's uneasiness, Molloy's disquieting feeling can no doubt be subjected to very complex analysis, such as the one that Foucault undertakes in the preface to *The Order of Things*, but for Borges they would be on a basic yet important level also the result of the "absence of pleasure" that these critics experience as readers. It is the same feeling that Borges discovered when he was reading Miró and found himself unable to create a coherent image out of what it was being described in the text, and the same feeling that makes him unable to enjoy *Citizen Kane*: the film is for him nothing but a collection of fragments that "no están regidos por una secreta unidad" (69).[15] His inability to enjoy *Citizen Kane* has nothing to do with his judgment about the movie, which he thought was a brilliant work of art: "No es inteligente, es genial" (69).[16] But it is one that he would prefer not to see again. His review of the film (entitled "An Overwhelming Film") simply seeks to register the reaction of a member of the audience who was unable to enjoy a movie, and it is in the extreme heterogeneity of the narration that Borges finds the cause of his reaction. Since Borges appears to be so aware of the effect that narrative heterogeneity has on the reader/spectator, one is forced to conclude that the presence of *disjecta membra* in his texts is often a conscious recreation of the same lack of coherence that he criticized in Miró's books or Welles's films. Only that what he saw as a defect in them, is now carefully employed to produce—if we choose to believe Molly and Foucault—discomfort or at least to disrupt the enjoyment of the reading experience. The purpose of that disruption, of course, varies from story to story and it would be impossible to totalize them with a single interpretation. Although it is important for my conclusions in this chapter to notice that *disjecta membra*, like montage, becomes a literary technique and it is thus incorporated into the Borgesean discourse, for now I simply wish to note that just as Borges discovers that heterogeneity produces "displeasure," symmetry and order will be given the task of producing pleasure. For that

---

[15]"are not governed by any secret unity." (Cozarinsky, *On Film* 55)

[16]"It is not intelligent, it is a work of *genius*." (Cozarinsky, *On Film* 56)

pleasure," symmetry and order will be given the task of producing pleasure. For that reason, the ability to organize coherently in one's mind all the images seen on the screen, I will argue, was more important than Accaria-Zavala's idea of "verisimilitude" in determining whether Borges liked or disliked a film.

The use of an excessive order or symmetry to shape the plot has always been recognized as one of the most distinctive characteristics of Borges's fiction, and also one that has often been celebrated. In fact, one of the great contributions of Silvia Molloy's study was that it attempted to prove that Borges's writings were constantly subverting their apparent orderly nature. It is for the same reason not surprising that she tried to show that, for Borges, one can obtain pleasure from strategies to subvert order (Molloy 100-105), paying less attention to the undeniable attraction that "order" in art has for him. From Borges's film reviews one can infer that in a movie theater nothing seems more enjoyable to him than a well-constructed film in which no image is wasted. This is evident in his review of *La fuga*, a 1937 Argentine film, in which Borges complains again about the lack of unity of certain films, especially European ones. "Hay numerosos films que no pasan de meras antologías fotográficas, acaso no hay un solo film europeo que no sufra de imágenes inservibles . . . *La fuga*, en cambio fluye límpidamente como los films americanos" (Cozarinsky, *Cine* 57).[17] Borges's preference for Hollywood movies is a constant in his writings about cinema. In the same review in which he criticized German Expressionist cinema, he also attacked French movies for their highbrow approach to filmmaking: "De los franceses no hablo: su mero y pleno afán, hasta ahora es el de no parecerse a los norteamericanos—riesgo que les pro-

---

[17]"There are numerous films that never go beyond mere photographic anthologies . . . and perhaps there is not a single European film that does not suffer from pointless images. In contrast, *La Fuga* flows limpidly, the way American films do." (Cozarinsky, *On Film* 47)

meto no corren" (30).[18] It is interesting that Borges disagrees here with what he sees as a general rejection of Hollywood movies within the intellectual community. What for the French directors is a positive quality, that is, not to create popular films such as the ones being produced in the United States, for Borges becomes a negative one. What he "promises" them here is that they will never be able to match the higher quality of North American films. In his film reviews Borges became an unconditional supporter, one could also say a fan, of Hollywood style of cinema.

The introduction of new means of communication in Argentina at the turn of the century immediately attracted the attention of large groups of people fascinated with the possibilities that new inventions such as radio and television offered. In *La imaginación técnica*, Beatriz Sarlo has showed how the introduction of the radio in the 1920s created a legion of followers that were initially attracted to the technical aspects of the medium (building, repairing, inventing), and it was only later in that decade that a different group emerged, one composed of people only interested in being listeners and for whom the radio represented simply a new form of entertainment. The creation of a radio audience was the result of the sudden availability of radios at a lower cost and of the establishment of new broadcasting stations. The story of the reception of film in Argentina was somewhat different. Unlike what happened with the radio, the higher prices of movie making and the small amount of technical information available, turned the great majority of those interested in films into mere *spectators* from the very beginning (Sarlo, *La imaginación* 109-28). The possibility or at least the illusion of intervening in the development of the technical means of film creation was never there; only a few inventors in Argentina tried to contribute to its development. From spectators, many movie goers quickly moved to the category of *fans*. It was under the impact of the early culture industry in Argentina, then, that Borges, as so many other mod-

---

[18]"I will not even mention the French: thus far their one and only desire has been not to resemble the Americans—a risk, I assure them, they do not run." (Cozarinsky, *On Film* 23)

ern subjects in the Argentina of the 1920s, became a movie *fan*. Borges was not of course a fan interested in the studio-produced life of the movie stars, but one could say that he became a fan of film directors, to the point of attributing to them the failure or success of each film. We can thus legitimately read his review of von Sternberg's *Crime and Punishment* (Cozarinsky, *Cine* 41-2) as the disappointment of a fan before the latest movie of his idol when his work does not live up to the fan's expectations. The review begins by telling us about the author's disappointment after noting a change in   von Sternberg's style in *Crime and Punishment* (1935): "Yo aguardaba...la normal pesadilla de Sternberg. Yo esperaba la asfixia y la locura. ¡Vana esperanza!" (Cozarinsky, *Cine* 41).[19] But the reviewer is not disappointed because of the change in itself but because von Sternberg has not replaced his previous style with anything new: "[von Sternberg] ha pasado del estado alucinatorio...al estado tonto" (42).[20] The review ends with the reviewer/fan asking the readers "not to despair" because perhaps not everything is lost, perhaps making this bad film is a sort of purification that the beloved director has to go through and after which von Sternberg will once again surprise his followers with his "talents," and start making again the quality films that he used to make. The short review contains the normal reactions that we attribute to fan's resistance to accept the evolution of his or her idol's art, complete with the remembrance of the idol's earlier work (his "masterpieces") and the closing hope for a return to his former glory days. Borges was not only a fan of film directors but also one of what today one would call action films: "Yo he sido ¿cuál de mis amigos lo ignora? cliente insaciable y fervoroso de Milton Sills, de Kohler y de Bancroft," directors of "sanguinarias

---

[19]"I was expecting the usual von Sternberg nightmare. I was waiting for the suffocation and the madness. In vain!" (Cozarinsky, *On Film* 33)

[20]"[von Sternberg] has merely passed from the state of hallucination . . . to the condition of foolishness." (Cozarinsky, *On Film* 33)

películas" (Cozarinsky, *Cine* 67).[21] More than anything, as can be noticed in his review of *La fuga*, Borges is a fan of Hollywood's films in general and, more precisely, of the artistic harmony that he finds in Hollywood's films and that in his opinion European modes of filmmaking lack.

Borges also celebrates the perfect geometry of Hollywood films in "Narrative Art and Magic," this time in relation to his defense of the adventure novel and the carefully constructed plot that I studied in the previous chapter. In his attack against the psychological novel, Borges presents as an alternative to this writing style the geometrical plot construction that he discovers in the adventure and detective fiction and also in "la infinita novela espectacular que compone Hollywood con los plateados *ídola* de Joan Crawford y que las ciudades releen" (*Obras* 1.230).[22] Hollywood films thus become another example of a narration controlled by a rigorous scheme of "vigilancias, ecos y afinidades" (*Obras* 1.231).[23] Although, I think that it is important to insist that a well-ordered plot is not a special attribute of popular cultural expressions and that Borges will also find examples in high cultural products (e.g., Joyce's and Dante's writings) to support this view of literature, it is noteworthy that he is bringing together in this essay his interests in popular fiction and Hollywood films. Given that this text is one of his earliest theoretical essays (from 1932), it is significant that examples from popular culture predominate in it. Also from 1932 is a critique of Eisenstein and the Soviet cinema, in which Borges once again prefers the orderly composition of the Hollywood movies to the Soviet school's experimental montage sequences:

---

[21]"I have been—which of my friends doesn't know it?—an insatiable and fervent patron of Milton Sills, of Kohler, and of Bancroft." (Cozarinsky, *On Film* 53)

[22]"the endless spectacular fictions made up in Hollywood, with the silvery images of Joan Crawford, that are read and reread the whole world over." (Borges, *Reader* 37)

[23]"attentions, echoes and affinities." (Borges, *Reader* 38)

[Los descubrimientos de los soviéticos] fueron propuestos a un mundo saturado hasta el fastidio por las emisiones de Hollywood. El mundo los honró, y estiró su agradecimiento hasta pretender que la cinematografía soviética había obliterado para siempre la americana... Se olvidó, o se quiso olvidar, que la mayor virtud del film ruso era su interrupción de un régimen californiano continuo. Se olvidó que era imposible contraponer algunas buenas o excelentes violencias (*Iván el Terrible, El acorazado Potemkin*, tal vez *Octubre*) a una vasta y compleja literatura. (Cozarinsky, *Cine* 35-36)[24]

German and French styles of filmmaking, Borges dismissed quickly as inferior to Hollywood films, and never paid too much attention to them, which explains why he very rarely made references to these schools in his reviews. Of the fifty-eight films mentioned—some of them more than once—in the reviews collected by Cozarinsky, forty-one are American, six British, five Soviet, three Argentine, two French and one German. Unlike the German and the French modes of film production that he feels that he can easily reject, the Soviet school presents other problems for him, given the extraordinary quality of the films that it was producing, a fact that Borges feels compelled to recognize. And as a fan of movies about "violence," Borges had to admire Eisenstein's work (author of "excelentes violencias"). On the other hand, although it is not mentioned in this article, elsewhere Borges employs again the argument of lack of coherence as the reason for rejecting Soviet cinema, describing the movies coming from this school as having the defect of being nothing more than an "anthology of images" ("antología fotográfica" [Cozarinsky, *Cine* 30]). This attitude signifies a rejection of a very

---

[24]"[The Russians' discoveries] were proposed to a world satiated to the point of disgust with Hollywood productions. The world respected these discoveries and extended its gratitude to the point of pretending that Soviet cinema had wiped out American cinema forever. . . . The world forgot that it was impossible to contrast some good, even excellent acts of violence (*Ivan the Terrible, Battleship Potemkin*, perhaps *October*) with a vast and complex literature." (Cozarinsky, *On Film* 27)

specific notion of montage that Eisenstein and other Soviet directors were promoting and that I plan to study later. Suffice it to say for the moment that if one is going to analyze Borges's prose in relation to montage, then, it would be necessary to specify the type of montage that Borges is trying to imitate and in which way it was different from the intellectual montage that Eisenstein was creating. This is exactly what I will try to do but not before looking for a clearer definition of the characteristics of Hollywood films that Borges thinks are absent from the French, German, or Soviet modes of film production. In the article quoted above, Borges's argument for preferring Hollywood films to the Soviet school is tradition. He seemed to be attracted to the idea that there is a tradition of film practice that is handed down from one generation of Hollywood directors to the next, whereas the Soviet school—like modernist artistic movements in general—represents for him a group of filmmakers whose originality is based on breaking with the past, on a negation of tradition. It is the exact nature of that Hollywood tradition that Borges is defending that I wish to explore now.

The North American mode of film production that Borges so much admires and even describes as a vast and complex "literature," has been given the name of "classical Hollywood cinema" by film theorists, who have defined it as a standard form or style that "reigned supreme between 1915 to 1938 and which is still influential today" (Andrew 174). Although some critics have challenged these dates and argued that the period of classical cinema lasted longer, a fact that cannot be contested, however, is that Hollywood created a powerful and unique mode of film practice composed of a set of norms about how films should look like. André Bazin was one of the first film theorists who made serious contributions to understanding the characteristics and appreciating the value of the classical Hollywood film. Although he was not the first critic to use the expression "classical film" in reference to Hollywood movies (Bordwell, Staiger, and Thompson 3), Bazin popularized the term and helped to define it. For Bazin, classical cinema was as much the result of the studio system as that of the personality of the film director:

> What makes Hollywood so much better than anything else in the world is not only the quality of certain directors, but also the vitality and, in certain sense, the excellence of a tradition. . . . The American cinema is a classical art, but why not then admire in it what is most admirable, i. e., not only the talent of this or that filmmaker, but the genius of the system, the richness of its ever-vigorous tradition, and its fertility when it comes into contact with new elements? (Qtd. in Bordwell, Staiger, and Thompson 4)

It is this idea of a tradition to which filmmakers adhere that Borges is alluding to when he talks about Hollywood being a vast and complex literature. David Bordwell, Janet Staiger and Kristin Thompson have meticulously explained the specificity of this tradition in their monumental study *The Classical Hollywood Cinema*. My own analysis of the influence of film on Borges will depend greatly on their (as well as Bazin's) attempt to define classical cinema and understand its evolution. Following Bazin, Bordwell describes the Hollywood style as a "fairly coherent aesthetic tradition which sustains individual creation" (4). However, this is not a system of movie making that imposes an inflexible formula on film directors; it is more precisely a "group style" and with as any group style there are always several alternatives available for achieving the same results: "there is always another way to do something," notices Bordwell, "a group style . . . establishes what semiologists call a paradigm, a set of elements which can, according to rules, substitute for one another" (5). In an exhaustive analysis, Bordwell studies the norms that control the narrative logic and the representation of time and space in classical film. I will not try to summarize his conclusions because I am less interested in the specifics of those norms (e.g., the happy ending, continuity editing, the subordination of time to causality, the fact that a typical Hollywood film lasts between 80 to 120 minutes) than in the idea of a system or tradition within which the film creator must work. Borges seemed to have understood perfectly well the advantages and disadvantages of being tied to a cinematic tradition:

[Hace] muchos años que Hollywood (a semejanza de los trágicos griegos) se atiene a diez o doce argumentos: el aviador que, mediante una conveniente catástrofe, muere para salvar al compañero de quien su mujer está enamorada; la falaz mecanógrafa que no rehusa donaciones de pieles, departamentos, diademas y vehículos, pero que abofetea o mata al dador cuando éste "se propasa"; el inefable y alabado repórter que busca la amistad de un *gangster* con el puro propósito de traicionarlo y hacerlo morir en la horca (Cozarinsky, *Cine* 74).[25]

The passage is at the same time a condemnation and a celebration of the limitations imposed by the studio system. Borges ridicules the typical Hollywood argument, especially those aspects where it reveals its origins in the nineteenth-century melodrama, but praises the idea of a set of themes that are constantly revisited, comparing it to the Greek tragedy. As it happened with the spectators of Greek tragedies, the audience of a Hollywood movie "already know" what they are going to see. It is the variations of the old paradigm that attracts them to the movie theater. By drawing a parallel between high culture and popular art, the implication is that even if the content of Hollywood movies cannot be compared to the plots of the Greek tragedies, in both artistic forms one can find the same idea of a paradigm that offers the authors a limited number of alternatives within which they have to work. For Borges, the challenge comes in creating an "original" work with such a limited range of possibilities. While making fun of the typical plots of Hollywood classical cinema by emphasizing its melodramatic elements, Borges lets us know that he is interested in a film form

---

[25]"For many years, Hollywood (like the Greek tragedians) has stuck, in effect, to ten or twelve plots: the aviator who, by means of a convenient catastrophe, dies in order to save the friend whom his wife loves; the deceitful typist who does not refuse the gifts of furs, apartments, tiaras, and cars but who slaps or kills the giver when he "goes too far"; the unspeakable and renowned reporter who seeks the friendship of a gangster with the sole motive of betraying him and making him die on the gallows." (Cozarinsky, *On Film* 59)

that is a consequence of this cinematic tradition and not in claiming that Hollywood produces high art, which is what for him Soviet cinema is trying to achieve in both form and content. Precisely because he is not interested in "content," Borges can assert that the tradition that he is defending is "ejercitada con desempeño feliz en todos los géneros, desde la incomparable comicidad (Chaplin, Buster Keaton y Langdon) hasta las puras invenciones fantásticas: mitología de Krazy Kat y de Bimbo" (Cozarinsky, *Cine* 36).[26] What matters is the general classical paradigm and not how artistically weak some of the elements (like the predictable plot with its also predictable happy ending) that form it are. Is Borges preferring Krazy Kat to *Battleship Potemkin*? We are obviously posing the wrong question because what Borges is comparing are ways of structuring art, not individual achievements. I consider it crucial to stress that in addition to choosing to "go to the movies" during the 1920s, a time when apparently (if we believe Quiroga) intellectuals in Argentina despised cinema as a form of popular entertainment, when Borges noticed that within the film industry began to emerge a new division between "high culture" (Soviet cinema) and popular culture (Hollywood movies, especially those with the kind of plot that he ridicules, but that nonetheless recognizes as an essential part of the Hollywood tradition), he again preferred popular culture to "high art."

Understanding the interplay between a film tradition and the individual films that make it possible, entails that we revisit Borges's important essay on tradition, "The Argentine Writer and Tradition." It is in this essay where Borges presents a coherent theory about the function of tradition in art. I have already studied a different aspect of this essay in my first chapter, but I would like to come back to it to show how Borges's perception of the importance of tradition for artistic creation motivates his interpretation of Hollywood art. Since the essay's main theme is that Argentine writers should not limit themselves to

---

[26]"brought to happy fulfillment in all genres, from the incomparable comic (Charlie Chaplin, Buster Keaton, and Harry Langdon) to the purely, inventively fantastic: the mythology of Krazy Kat and Bimbo." (Cozarinsky, *On Film* 27)

work with local topics for the composition of their works but rightfully consider the entire Western tradition as their own and feel free to use it, it may look as if Borges were really saying that no limits whatsoever should be imposed on a writer, as if he were arguing for total freedom of expression. The opposite, however, is true. Let us retrace his argument. In his search for the answer to the question of which tradition should the Argentine writer belong to, he rejects first the local tradition as having too narrow a scope, and then the Spanish one because Argentines do not feel particularly close to Spanish culture. A last option, which he also discards, would be that Argentines have no tradition, that they are "alone." In rejecting the possibility that "nosotros, los argentinos, estamos desvinculados del pasado" (*Obras* 1.272)[27] and asserting that the tradition of the Argentine writer is the totality of Western culture, Borges is refusing to consider the idea that a writer could completely break from tradition. This notion of a complete break with what came before was one of the main characteristics of Modernism, which regarded a violent break with the past as a necessary step to create an original work of art. In opposition to that view of literature Borges is proposing that it is the existence of a tradition and the limits that tradition imposes on a writer that allow innovation to take place in the first place. Borges's argument is that Argentine writers, like Jewish or Irish, artists, can use the Western tradition with freedom and create innovative works. The creation of unique works in the Jewish and Irish examples is not the result of having total freedom but of coming from marginal cultures subordinated to the Western one. To Irish writers such as Shaw and Swift "les bastó el hecho de sentirse irlandeses, distintos, para innovar en la cultura inglesa" (*Obras* 1.273).[28] They did not have to reject tradition to be able to change it. Likewise the Jews "actúan den-

---

[27]"that in Argentina we are cut off from the past, that there has been something like a dissolution of continuity between us and Europe." (*Labyrinths* 177)

[28]"it was sufficient for them to feel Irish, to feel different, in order to be innovators in English culture." (*Labyrinths* 184)

tro de [la cultura occidental],"[29] but feel free to modify it because it is not their main tradition. Borges grants Jewish, Irish and Argentine writers the right to partial freedom; the right to partial difference as opposed to the absolute difference that, he argues, nationalist Argentines proclaim for themselves when they reject Western tradition. Although Borges does not pay enough attention to the role of individuals within their primary tradition (he is interested in emphasizing the relation between traditions), we will see that the topic will indirectly come up in his comments on the relationship between individual filmmakers and classical cinema.

The same interplay between tradition and innovation that Borges observes in literature is valid for that other "literature" that Hollywood creates. A corollary of Borges's axiom that one must work within tradition in order to innovate, to change tradition, is that challenging tradition from the outside, a complete break with tradition as the modernist artists wanted to do, is ineffective in bringing about any changes. Whether one accepts this view or not, it certainly seems to apply to classical film tradition. As Bordwell notices, the Hollywood paradigm is so powerful that one can only realistically attempt to change it from within the system itself:

> In Hollywood cinema, there are no subversive films, only subversive moments. For social and economic reasons, no Hollywood film can provide a distinct and coherent alternative to the classical model. . . . Even the most deviant Hollywood films, however, must ground themselves in the external norms of group style. . . . Really problematic Hollywood films become limit-texts, works which, while remaining traditionally legible, dramatize some limits of that legibility. They do not, however, posit thoroughgoing alternatives. So powerful is the classical paradigm that it regulates what may violate it. (81)

---

[29]"they act within [Western] culture." (*Labyrinths* 184)

An example of what Bordwell means by "limit-texts" is Hitchcock's *Psycho*, which although it is considered a film that challenged many of the classical norms, especially about the psychology of the characters, still had more in common with other Hollywood films than with alternative film styles. On the other hand, those films that proposed a different mode of film practice, one not bound by Hollywood rules, have been ineffective in defeating the latter. This was the case of the experimental cinema that was produced in Europe from the 1920s to the 1950s, which created new artistic techniques that initially seemed totally incompatible with classical cinema style of filmmaking. Hollywood, however, was always quick to assimilate—and neutralize—alternative styles and it achieved this by selecting those elements from avant-garde movements, in film and other media, that could be more easily incorporated into the classical paradigm. Bordwell mentions avant-garde music as an example of a movement whose product Hollywood appropriated. Although initially dissonant music may look incompatible with our conception of classical cinema, Hollywood learned to combine atonality with the "normal" music used in films for scenes that expressed disturbed states of mind. In other words, it became a signal for the spectators to recognize when there was something not "normal" happening on the screen (Bordwell, Staiger, and Thompson 72). Among the avant-garde movements in cinema that were also assimilated, one that quickly caught Hollywood's attention was the German Expressionist cinema. Once again, as it happened with atonal music, the artistic elements that were most compatible with classical cinema were selected and incorporated with the task of producing specific effects: "low-key lighting for mystery, distorted perspectives for horror, odd angles for shock effects" (Bordwell, Staiger, and Thompson 73), were among the techniques appropriated by Hollywood. But even more interesting, especially in relation to Borges, is the case of Soviet cinema, which presented a powerful challenge to the classical cinema in terms of narrative unity, narrational voice, point of view, and spatial and temporal continuity (Bordwell, Staiger, and Thompson 73-74). In his critique of Soviet cinema mentioned before, Borges noticed that one of the main challenges of this school to the Hollywood paradigm was an innovative use of camera shots and montage techniques: "Los rusos descubrieron que la fotografía oblicua (y, por consiguiente, deforme) de un botellón, de una cerviz de toro o de una columna, era de un valor plástico superior a la de mil y un *extras* de Hollywood, rápidamente disfrazados de asirios y luego barajados hasta la total vaguedad por Cecil B. DeMille" (Cozarinsky, *Cine* 35).[30] The plastic quality that Borges mentions is the result of a use of montage that sees every shot in the film as raw material with which the director can build his or her work of art. In fact, Eisenstein liked to compare film directors to painters or sculptors. However, if Borges understood perfectly well the intentions of Soviet directors for breaking away from other forms of movie making, he was not attracted to their experiments and, as I mentioned before, went as far as describing Soviet films as anthologies of images, thus suggesting that they lack the coherence that Hollywood films have. He also disliked what became one of the most influential forms of montage created by the Soviets, Eisenstein's intellectual montage. Although Eisenstein's ideas about film form were always evolving, we will simplify his theory and say that intellectual montage occurs when two opposing shots collide with each other creating a juxtaposition of images. The consequence of that juxtaposition is the creation of a new image or idea (different from the two that initially collided) in the mind of the spectator (Eisenstein, *Film Form* 238). It was Eisenstein's study of the Japanese language and of haiku poetry that gave him the idea for this conception of montage. In a haiku poem ideograms with no apparent links among them are brought together, forcing the reader to find the missing connection, to give them a unified sense. Eisenstein went even further and claimed that even in every ideogram that composes the haiku there is already present a collision of ideas, similar to the one that he wanted to create with intellectual montage. But these attempts to create visual metaphors in cinema did not impress Borges, as his criticism of Chaplin's use of intellectual montage shows:

---

[30]"The Russians discovered that the oblique shot (and, consequently, the distorted shot) of a bottle, a bull's neck, or a column had greater esthetic value than Hollywood's thousand and one extras, quickly gotten up as Assyrians and then shuffled into total confusion by Cecil B. DeMille." (Cozarinsky, *On Film* 27)

Chaplin exhibe unos apretados obreros que entran en una fábrica; después una segunda muchedumbre, pero de ovejas, que entran en el corral. "Ah! el rebaño humano", murmura embelasada la gente, muy satisfecha de haber percibido en el acto ese audaz avatar cinematográfico de un lugar común literario. (Cozarinsky, *Cine* 51)[31]

One could try to link Borges's well-known aversion towards metaphors (see his writings about the Icelandic sagas) with his lack of enthusiasm for intellectual montage, but what seems to me more intriguing is that the view of montage promoted by Eisenstein is closer to Borges's own aesthetics than Hollywood's editing technique is. Eisenstein theories went against the creation of films that faithfully mimic reality. Even if the director had the power to choose what to record in a film, it seemed to Eisenstein that he or she was still at the mercy of nature. If the director was going to create a work of art, he or she had to be able to fashion reality at will, not let reality be in control. His technique of montage (exaggerated close-ups, the unusual camera angles that Borges mentions in his article) constantly reminded the spectator of the artistic character of film.

Completely different from Soviet montage in form and purpose were the classical editing techniques of Hollywood, which were designed to "give us the illusion of being present at real events unfolding before us as in everyday reality" (Bazin, *Welles* 77). André Bazin gave the name of *découpage* or shot breakdown to this technique, by which he meant that the shots in the film are ordered in such a way as to have a dramatic or psychological effect (Bazin, *Cinema 1* 32; *Welles* 77-78). If there is a corpse lying on the floor, for example, a close-up of the murder weapon that has been left next to the corpse would follow so that the audience can infer a cause/effect relationship from both imag-

---

[31]"Chaplin shows a crowd of workers entering a factory; then a second horde, this time of sheep, entering a pen. 'Ah, the human flock!' the enraptured audience murmurs, quite satisfied with having recognized this daring cinematic avatar of a literary commonplace." (Cozarinsky, *On Film* 42)

es. Similarly, a shot of a character anxiously waiting for someone, followed by a shot of a hand knocking on the door and then the same hand turning the doorknob is an example of a series of shots composed to follow the thoughts of a character or of the audience. The main characteristic of classical narration is that both time and space are subordinated to the story line. Most of the time the audience is not aware of this technique. One is more interested in what is going to happen than in how the story is being told. The spectator gets caught up in the drama and the logic of the narration. It is for this reason that Hollywood's classical narration has been called "invisible," although perhaps the adjective is not entirely appropriate (Bordwell, Staiger, and Thompson 25). If the form of Eisenstein's films constantly calls attention to its own status as a fictional work of art, Hollywood films pretend to be realistic by making the audience believe that they are witnessing real events. How is this kind of "realism" achieved? Bazin bears quoting at length here:

> This illusion [i.e. the illusion that real events are taking place on the screen] involves a fundamental deceit, for reality exists in a continuous space, and the screen in fact presents us with a succession of tiny fragments called "shots.". . . If, through a deliberate effort of attention, we try to see the ruptures imposed by the camera on the continuous unfolding of the event represented, and try to understand clearly why we normally take no notice of them, we realize that we tolerate them because they nevertheless allow an impression to remain continuous and homogeneous reality. In reality we don't see everything at once either. Action, passion or fear makes us proceed to an unconscious *découpage* of the space surrounding us. Our legs and neck didn't wait for the cinema to invent the tracking shot and the pan, nor our attention to contrive the close-up. This universal psychological experience is enough to make us forget the material lack of verisimilitude of *découpage*, and enables the spectator to participate in it just as he does in a natural relationship with reality. (*Welles* 77)

The explanation for why the "false" verisimilitude of classical cinema woks, according to Bazin, is that Hollywood editing style mimics the way the human mind perceives reality. Our mind focuses on those aspects of our surroundings that we find interesting and tends to ignore unimportant details. It should be noticed that Bazin's description of how human psychology becomes the basis of *découpage* is uncannily similar to the definition of verisimilitude given by Borges in "The Postulation of Reality." This similarity is probably what Accaria-Zavala saw when she claimed that Borges's idea of verisimilitude was the key to interpreting his cinematic preferences. It now becomes clear that her study would have gained considerable depth had she been able to identify this form of editing as an aspect of classical cinema. One would think that Borges, whose short stories are always laying bare the device, would feel affinity towards the Soviet editing style and its continuous disruptions of the spectator's suspension of disbelief. This is not to say that Hollywood movies do not have moments of self-referentiality; these, in fact, are more common than one would expect. But in classical narration causality is so important that baring the device constantly cannot be allowed because it would interfere with the story being told and, perhaps more importantly, with the capacity of the film to entertain the audience.

In spite of the radically different use of montage that the Soviet cinema was practicing, Hollywood was able to assimilate it, much in the same way that it assimilated other avant-garde movements. "Cundió la alarma rusa," says Borges about classical cinema's reaction to the Soviet challenge, "Hollywood reformó o enriqueció alguno de sus hábitos fotográficos y no se preocupó mayormente" (Cozarinsky, *Cine* 36).[32] Just as the dissonance of modern music became a disruption of the "normal" music of the film, Soviet as well as German montage techniques were employed when the "normal" editing of Hollywood needed to be disrupted for any reason. As with atonal music, Hollywood ini-

---

[32]"Alarm over the Russians grew. Hollywood reformed or enriched some of its photographic habits, and did not bother itself greatly." (Cozarinsky, *On Film* 27)

tially used a Soviet-style montage to represent character psychology but later also employed it, for dramatic and economic reasons, to summarize long periods of time in a few seconds. In other situations, montage was suited to represent natural disruptions like an earthquake or other natural disasters. But using avant-garde montage as a deviation of "normal" classical editing nullified the effectiveness of the technique, it became codified "as a symbolic shorthand, not a new way of seeing" (Bordwell, Staiger, and Thompson 74). Hollywood thus reduced an extremely original narrative structure to just another artistic technique.

This takes us back to the question of how montage "influenced" Borges's prose. So far, the studies realized about this topic have been very uncritical in the use of the term montage, never differentiating clearly between the avant-garde's and Hollywood's versions of the same technique. Even if, as a member of the audience in a movie theater, Borges shows preference for the classical cinema's *découpage*, I think that it would be difficult to prove that Borges consistently edited his stories following a similar technique. The self-referential nature of Borges's prose makes this impossible. This in no way means that one cannot find in his short stories sections that are structured in direct imitation of Hollywood's *découpage* sequences. Such is the case of the description of Juan Dahlmann's accident in "The South," a story whose relation to film I will study in detail later: "[A]lgo en la oscuridad le rozó la frente un murciélago, ¿un pájaro? En la cara de la mujer que le abrió la puerta vio grabado el horror, y la mano que se pasó por la frente salió roja de sangre" (*Obras* 1.525).[33] There are other uses of montage that Borges learned from watching Hollywood films, such as the summarizing of a character's life in a few sentences (see his preface to *A Universal History of Infamy*). But the greatest similarity between classical cinema's film form and Borges's use of montage has to do with the disruption of the "normal" or linear narration. Whether it is

---

[33]"In the obscurity, something brushed by his forehead: a bat, a bird? On the face of the woman who opened the door to him he saw horror engraved, and the hand he wiped across his face came away with red blood." (Borges, *Ficciones* 167-68)

used to summarize a character's adventures, to provoke a desired reaction in the reader (the "epic feeling" discussed earlier or the disquieting effect of *disjecta membra*) or to describe the indescribable ("The Aleph," "The God's Script"), Borges incorporates montage into his prose by assigning it specific functions in a move that is similar to Hollywood's appropriation of competing film modes. The story "The Aleph" provides us with a perfect example of this narrative strategy: when we reach the paragraph of the description of the aleph, we read it as a glimpse of the fantastic, as that which does not belong to the normal world, which justifies the use of a different narrative technique by the author. And when the description is over, both reader and narrator return to the "normal" world—and to a more "normal" and linear style of narration.

It is interesting that Borges never notices the obvious connection between classical cinema's ability to survive by appropriating alternative film practices and the survival tactics that any industry has to adopt in a capitalist economic system. For the Hollywood tradition that he admires to survive, it has to neutralize competing film modes. It is by bracketing the commercial reasons that underlie the creation of Hollywood artistic norms that the Borgesean discourse can represent this tradition as something that should be "venerated" and that makes originality possible and never as an impediment for innovative individual creation. Borges's favorite directors were those who, from this perspective, helped to preserve this tradition because they limited their innovations to only making slight changes to the classical paradigm. Within this view of the role of the film creator as a protector of tradition Borges is trying to place himself in the preface to the 1951 publication of two scriptfilms that he wrote in collaboration with Bioy Casares, *Los orilleros* and *El paraíso de los creyentes*. The preface was authored by both Borges and Bioy Casares, but we will see that it contains many of the ideas that Borges had already expressed in his film reviews:

> Los dos *films* que integran este volumen aceptan, o quisieron aceptar, las diversas convenciones del cinematógrafo. No nos atrajo al escribirlos un propósito de innovación; abordar un género e innovar en él nos pareció excesiva temeridad. El

José Eduardo González

lector de estas páginas hallará previsiblemente, el boy meets girl y el happy ending...las peripecias arriesgadas y el feliz descenlace. Es muy posible que tales convenciones sean desleznables; en cuanto a nosotros, hemos observado que los films que recordamos con más emoción—los de Sternberg, los de Lubitsch—las respetan sin mayor desventaja. (Cozarinsky, *Cine* 82-83)[34]

Once again, as he did in his film reviews, in this preface Borges recognizes the limitations of the conventions that make up Hollywood tradition ("boy meets girl, the happy ending"). Elsewhere, in the short article on Soviet cinema that I have mentioned several times before, he had compared these conventions with the new "norms" that Soviet filmmakers were following, showing that he recognized the complete artificiality of the rules of classical cinema's paradigm—and that therefore they could easily be replaced by others—, which he nonetheless prefers to the ones proposed by Soviet cinema: "[Los soviéticos] descubrieron," says a Borges completely aware of the arbitrary nature of artistic rules, "que las convenciones del Middle West—méritos de la denuncia y del espionaje, felicidad final y matrimonial, intacta integridad de las prostitutas...—podían ser canjeadas por otras no menos admirables" (Cozarinsky, *Cine* 35).[35] What is interesting about the

---

[34]"The two films that make up this book accommodate—or tried to accommodate—the diverse conventions of filmmaking. We were not drawn into writing them with an eye toward innovation. To take up a genre and to make innovations within it seemed excessively rash to us. Predictably, then, the reader of these pages will find the *boy-meets-girl* and the happy ending . . . the perilous reversal and the happy denouement. Quite possibly, such conventions are feeble. In our case, however, we have noticed how the films that we recall with greatest emotion—those by von Sternberg and Lubitsch—respect those conventions to no great disadvantage." (Cozarinsky, *On Film* 69)

[35]"They also discovered that the conventions of the Midwest—the merits of accusation and spying, of everlasting wedded bliss, the untarnished purity of prostitutes. . .—could be changed for other, no less

1951 preface is that Borges calls classical film's conventions "cinema's conventions" as if alternative cinematic practices, of which he was well aware, did not exist. It is as if Borges had already proclaimed the triumph of the Hollywood paradigm over any other competing mode of filmmaking. Ignoring the existence of other traditions, however, does not seem to follow the logic of the theory of tradition that we found in "Tradition and the Argentine Writer." In his essay on tradition he was granting a degree of autonomy to national cultures from the influence of Western culture. It was that semi-autonomy that allowed writers from marginal cultures to innovate. However, when Borges transports this view of tradition to the realm of film, not only does he not grant "autonomy" to other film traditions in relation to Hollywood, he completely denies their existence. The partial autonomy is now transferred from local cultures to individual creators. The fact that the other film traditions were based on a complete opposition to classical cinema's form and did not have the same relation of dependence to Hollywood that national cultures have in relation to Western tradition, might help explain why the emphasis is now placed on individuals (filmmakers or scriptwriters such as Borges and Bioy Casares) and their handling of "tradition" rather than on relations between traditions.

The 1951 preface shows the contrast between two views of innovation in art. Although the authors say that they have chosen not to innovate, not only is the door left open to innovate in the future—the excuse for not daring to do it is that they are newcomers to the field—but there is also a suggestion that just because their scripts are following the rules that the Hollywood paradigm demands, this does not mean that they are not also being original. Von Sternberg and Lubitsch also "respected" this cinematic tradition, Borges and Bioy Casares argue, and that was not an impediment for creating original works. They are replacing the modernist concept of originality, a search for the New that implies a complete rejection of the past, with the only originality that Hollywood can allow, a modification of the all-powerful paradigm that does not threaten its existence. Borges's position about the possibil-

---

admirable conventions." (Cozarinsky, *On Film* 27)

ity of challenging the classical paradigm is, then, no different from the one taken by Bordwell. Both agree that creating a completely original film mode is, if not impossible, ineffective in challenging Hollywood tradition.

Like André Bazin, Borges believed that the best movies produced by classical cinema were the result of a combination of the studio system and the imagination of individual creators. Although, as can be seen in his movie reviews, especially the ones that he wrote on von Sternberg's work, Borges placed most of the responsibility for the success or failure of a film on the director's shoulders, he did not make the mistake of overemphasizing the individuality of Hollywood directors, as much later the *Cahiers du cinéma* group would do in France with their *auteur* theory. As Bordwell reminds us, after the studio system declined, many of the directors admired by the *Cahiers*'s writers could only produce mediocre films. "We said that the American cinema pleases us," remarked a prominent member of this group, François Truffaut, "and its filmmakers are slaves; what if they were freed? And from the moment they were freed, they made shitty films" (Qtd. in Bordwell, Staiger, and Thompson 4).

Given Borges's preference for the film directors who "respected" the tradition of the classical cinema, it is understandable that he rejected Eisenstein's and Welles's challenges to the established paradigm. Eisenstein belonged to a group of filmmakers who were trying to replace Hollywood norms with new ones, while Orson Welles's *Citizen Kane* was identified by André Bazin as one of the films that started a new era by subverting the *découpage* editing techniques of classical cinema (Bazin, *Welles* 75-82; Andrew 160-4). Welles's deep focus was going against Hollywood's desire to give the spectators the illusion that they were seeing real events unfolding before their eyes. No longer was the camera assisting the spectator, selecting beforehand the most important objects in a scene and focusing on them. Instead, in Welles's film it was the spectator who had to try to make sense out of the image projected on the screen. By forcing the spectator to participate in the meaning of the film, Welles created a style that was the opposite of the "invisible" style that Hollywood filmmakers were striving to achieve and that for Borges was one of the most laudable characteristics of classical cinema. Outside the unsuccessful film scripts that Borges co-wrote with Bioy Casares and his early "tales of infamy," which include gangster and cowboy stories inspired by von Sternberg's and King Vidor's films, respectively, it is useless to try to find a consistent reproduction of Hollywood's plot conventions in his work. Among later stories perhaps the one in which Borges comes the closest to imitating the art of classical cinema is "The Dead Man," which seems to have the Western genre as an aesthetic model. In an interview with Richard Burgin, when talking about the possibility of this short story being turned into a movie, Borges even mentioned that it should be filmed as an American Western (see Accaria-Zavala 182). More interesting than directly comparing Borges's stories to Hollywood films, I found the possibility that, like Hollywood and Soviet cinemas, Borges had created his own "paradigm," his own "conventions." One could argue that he learned this creative strategy during his years as a film reviewer (the bulk of Borges's writings on film was produced between 1931 and 1936) and then began to apply it to his literary work after the late 1930s. We could then read his constant return to certain topics and symbols—e.g. the Other, pantheism, mirrors, labyrinths—as Borges's "conventions." In fact, Borges's constant reworking of certain topics in his work gives his stories such an unmistakable "look" that Paul de Man, still in his pre-deconstructionist phase, went as far as saying that "for all their variety of tone and setting, [Borges's stories] all have a similar point of departure, a similar structure, a similar climax, and a similar outcome" (De Man, "Master" 57). I believe that there is still another way in which the form of classical cinema influenced Borges, one that his critics have always overlooked because of their tendency to focus exclusively on literary montage.

  In my second chapter I concluded that the strongest connection between Borges's writings and the culture industry is located at the level of form and not content. And in the case of Hollywood's influence on Borges we seem to find a confirmation of this theory. But if Borges is not interested in Hollywood's conventions nor in using movie plots as inspiration, and if the *découpage* technique, no matter how much it contributes to Borges's enjoyment of these movies, is not widely reproduced in his fiction, and the avant-garde versions of montage are reduced to literary devices to be used sporadically, where in the form of his stories can we detect the presence of classical cinema? Here I wish to go back to an essay that I mentioned earlier, "Narrative Art and Magic," specifically to a second reference to Hollywood movies that appears in that text. It is a passage often quoted in the critical literature dealing with Borges's use of cinematic techniques, but one that I have intentionally not mentioned before in the belief that a full appreciation of its meaning depended on first identifying Borges's preference for classical cinema and providing a clear definition of that style of filmmaking. Towards the end of the aforementioned essay Borges gives another example of the orderly structure that attracted him to this particular mode of movie making:

> Esa teología de palabras y episodios es omnipresente también en los *buenos* films. [My emphasis] Al principiar *A cartas vistas* (*The Showdown*), unos aventureros se juegan a los naipes a una prostituta, o su turno; al terminar, uno de ellos ha jugado la posesión de la mujer que quiere. El diálogo inicial de *La ley del hampa* versa sobre la delación, la primera escena es un tiroteo en una avenida; esos rasgos resultan premonitorios del asunto central. En *Fatalidad* (*Dishonored*) hay temas recurrentes: la espada, el beso, el gato, la traición, las uvas, el piano. (*Obras* 1.232)[36]

---

[36]"This teleology of words and episodes is also omnipresent in good films. At the beginning of *The Showdown*, a pair of adventurers play cards for a prostitute, or a turn at her; at the end, one of them has gambled away the possession of the woman he really loves. The opening dialogue of *Underworld* concerns stool pigeons, the opening scene is a gunfight on an avenue; these bits foreshadow the whole plot. In *Dishonored*, there are recurring themes: the sword, the kiss, the cat, betrayal, grapes, the piano." (Borges, *Reader* 38)

The bringing together of the beginning and the ending of a film is in fact a common trait of classical cinema (Bordwell, Staiger, and Thompson 36). But it is in the use of motifs that are repeated and echoed throughout a film, not only at the beginning and the end, that the connection between Borges's writings and classical cinema is more obvious. Clearly, Hollywood films were an early and important influence on Borges's developing the idea that in fiction one event should prefigure another, that a work of art should be composed of internal analogies and symmetries. In their book *Film Art*, Bordwell and Thompson give an example of how the use of parallelism (as they call the narrative technique that Borges has "discovered") works in a typical Hollywood movie:

> Film form utilizes general similarities as well as exact duplication. To understand *The Wizard of Oz*, we must see the similarities between the three Kansas farmhands and the three figures Dorothy meets along the Yellow Brick Road; we must notice that the itinerant Kansas fortune teller bears a striking resemblance to the old charlatan posing as the Wizard of Oz. The duplication is not perfect, but the similarity is very strong. This is an example of *parallelism*, the process whereby the film cues the spectator to compare two or more distinct elements by highlighting some similarity. (Bordwell and Thompson 37)

One can probably trace back the origins of parallelism in film to the pre-classical period. Kristin Thompson has noticed that in the transition from primitive cinema to the classical mode there were two narrative models available to filmmakers. One of them, the one that was going to be adopted by classical cinema, was linear causality and the other was a parallel narrative, "which [used] contrasting lines of actions to create a conceptual point" (Bordwell, Staiger, and Thompson 176). A well-known example of parallel editing as a way of organizing a film's narrative is Griffith's *Intolerance* in which different periods of time (and civilizations) are contrasted against one another. "The parts thrown together by parallel montage," says Gilles Deleuze, explaining how this film is constructed, "are the civilizations themselves . . . the convergent actions are not just the duels proper to each civilisation—the chariot-race in the Babylonian episode, the race between the car and the train in the modern episode—but the two races themselves converge through the centuries in an accelerated montage which superimposes Babylon and America" (31). By 1916, when *Intolerance* is released, this alternative narrative mode is no longer being used. In the end, linear narrative won out easily over parallelism as the preferred system to organize film images probably because it was an easier way to present complex plots to an audience (Bordwell, Staiger, and Thompson 177). Parallel narrative apparently disappeared. However, Borges's (and Bordwell and Thompson's) comments about the use of parallelism by Hollywood cinema to organize a story makes us realize that parallel editing did not go away, it was "absorbed," integrated into the inner form of the typical Hollywood film. The two narrative models coexist side by side in classical cinema, though obviously one is subordinated to the other. One could go as far as adding that Hollywood's extensive use of parallelism in the construction of the plot was a possibility latent within the original concept of parallel montage. Borges was in reality less attracted to Griffith's parallel montage or parallel narrative actions (he apparently disliked Griffith's films [see Cozarinsky, *Cine* 56]), than to the internalization of parallelism by classical cinema.

In their example from *The Wizard of Oz*, Bordwell and Thompson tell us that in order for the members of an audience to *understand* the film they have to see the similarities among different events, they must perceive the presence of parallelism. Presumably, what the audience must understand is that the main character's visit to the land of Oz is nothing but a dream and that, as it supposedly happens when one dreams, she has transposed to it elements from her real life; hence the similarities between the people she meets during her travel and people that she knew in Kansas. I think a comparison it is unavoidable between the use of parallelism in *The Wizard of Oz* and Borges's version of the same dream/reality topic in "The South." In this semi-autobiographical story Juan Dahlmann is a librarian who all his life has bemoaned the fact that he was not going to have a heroic life similar to that of some of his ancestors. After suffering an accident at the beginning of the story, he is taken to a hospital and there, while dying in bed, he dreams of a romantic death in the pampas, having a knife duel with a gaucho. As in Dorothy's dream, elements from Dahlmann's real life reappear in his dream/hallucination though in a different context. In the same way that the fortune teller reappears as the Wizard of Oz in Dorothy's dream, one of the hospital employees becomes the owner of a bar in Dahlmann's. The reader then has to be able to see this parallelism (or any of the other ones in the story) in order to understand that Dahlmann is really dreaming and that the last scene only takes place in his mind before he dies in the hospital.

The use of parallelism to organize the structure of his short stories is one of Borges's most characteristic writing strategies. In some cases Borges even employs the type of historical parallelism favored by Griffith in *Intolerance* ("Cuéntase que Alejandro de Macedonia vio reflejado su futuro de hierro en la fabulosa historia de Aquiles; Carlos XII de Suecia, en la de Alejandro" [*Obras* 1.562]).[37] I will not go on to describe in detail the different meanings produced using parallelism in Borges's stories; these could be numerous and the blurring of the distinction between dream and reality in "The South" is just one of them. Borges's peculiar brand of pantheism is another characteristic that comes to mind now and that I will study in a moment in relation to "The Theologians." Instead of going through all of Borges's stories, finding and classifying examples of parallelism, I wish to analyze the process of interpretation that goes on when we as readers recognize a parallelism between two different events or fictional characters and draw conclusions about its meaning. As members of an audience in a movie theater, Thompson and Bordwell say, we are "supposed" to notice the presence of parallelism: the film "cues" us by "highlighting" some similarity. From their statement one gets the impression that part of our enjoyment of the film depends on our capacity to find parallelisms. In this context one can see Borges's negative evaluation of Chaplin's use

---

[37]"It has been said that Alexander the Great saw his iron future in the fabled story of Achilles, and Charles XII of Sweden,   in the story of Alexander." (Borges, *The Aleph* 83)

José Eduardo González 139

of intellectual montage that I quoted earlier as an example of his awareness of the pleasure that an audience derives from "discovering" a parallelism, even if he disliked this particular use of it. Let us remember Borges's comment. He tells us that the spectators first see a crowd of workers going inside a factory and immediately after that they connect it to the following image of the sheep entering a pen. The audience is "satisfied," Borges says, with their discovery. They *enjoy* the act of discovering it. Because, as he sees it, it is not difficult for the members of the audience to discover this analogy (after all, it is only "a cinematic avatar of a literary commonplace"), one can conclude that Borges is accusing Chaplin of manipulating the audience. A similar negative reaction to a film director's attempt to manipulate the audience appears in his review of Archie Mayo's *The Petrified Forest*: "No dejan de molestarme dos o tres fatuidades o pedanterías del diálogo: [el resumen] de un poema de Eliot, las forzadas menciones de Villon, de Mark Twain y de Billy the Kid, para que el público se sienta erudito al reconocer esos nombres" (Cozarinsky, *Cine* 44).[38] The review is from 1936. That same year he writes "The Approach to al-Mu'tasim," the first one of his fictions in which he parodies scholarly writings. This story includes footnotes, learned quotations, and references that are sometimes obscure, sometimes imaginary, sometimes easily recognizable. Part of the pleasure of reading Borges's texts, Molloy reminds us, comes from being able to identify a citation or reference among all the unrecognizable ones, but also from reading the "exotic" ones, whose function in the texts we are tempted to decipher: "because such references come from the most unexpected sources, the reader feels (or think that he or she is expected to feel) that they are held together by a critical argument whose mystery is unfathomable" (Molloy 108). If the Chaplin passage was an example of how parallelism produces pleasure, this one is an example of how to use citations with a similar purpose. It should not

---

[38] "Two or three weaknesses or pedantries in the dialogue continue to annoy me: [the summary] of a poem by T.S. Eliot, the forced allusions to Villon, Mark Twain, and Billy the Kid, contrived to make the audience feel erudite in recognizing those names." (Cozarinsky, *On Film* 35)

come as a surprise to anyone that the narrative strategies that he criticizes in Chaplin's and Mayo's movies are similar to the ones that he will employ in his fictions. Was not that what happened with Miró's *disjecta membra*? But what is then the purpose of Borges's imitation of Hollywood's technique of parallelism? Is it to give pleasure to the reader by allowing him or her to discover "hidden" connections among the different parts of a story? "Any" reader should be able to discover them in his short stories, just as "any" moviegoer should be able to see them in *The Wizard of Oz*. Is Borges trying to make the reader, paraphrasing what he said about Mayo, "feel erudite," by flattering his or her basic cognitive abilities, that is, the capacity to contrast and compare?

A brief reading of "The Theologians" would demonstrate that Borges uses parallelism to allow the reader to derive pleasure from discovering apparently hidden connections in his short stories. "The Theologians" is the story of the intellectual rivalry between two theologians, Aureliano and Juan de Pannonia, at the end of which Aureliano is hit by lightning and, in this way, his death is similar to that of his rival who had earlier been burned alive after being accused of heresy. They are both the same person, we are told by a narrator who calls our attention to the parallelism between the two theologians. The same narrator, however, "forgets" to tell us (he lets us discover it in the same way the audience of Chaplin's film discovered the human flock metaphor) that Juan's fate is also similar to that of Euforbo, the heresiarch whom both Aureliano and Juan de Pannonia were combating at the beginning of the story, and who was also burned alive. In fact, because this parallelism is so much more obvious than the one the narrator is pointing out to us (Euforbo and Juan are both burned at the stake for their heretical beliefs), we *cannot* fail to see it. After noticing that, one could then interpret this series of parallelisms as meaning that all the characters are all the same person, that "all men are one man," as Borges would say. And the intellectual "pleasure" of having the correct interpretation increases when we notice small details that support our theory and that were not seen in the first reading: for example, the only sentence preserved from Juan de Pannonia's writings is found quoted in Aureliano's (who is also Pannonia, therefore all of Aureliano's writings are also Pannonia's), and the sentence was addressed to Euforbo. Once again we are able to find a link among the three characters that confirms our initial pantheistic interpretation. I guess that one could continue finding more symmetries and analogies; the problem with this type of interpretation is that, no matter how much "pleasure" can bring to the reader, it adds very little to the historical understanding of the text. This is the type of Borgesean criticism that even though it was more characteristic of the first period of Borgesean criticism in the United States, especially during the 1960s and 1970s under the influence of New Criticism, has perhaps not disappeared completely from literary reviews:

> [Borges's] fictions conceal nothing. As in tight rope walking the skill is visible to all. Any reader (any reader with "competence") can pick up some of the clues, for they are meant to be deciphered. Much Borges criticism, for this reason, tends to become a second level demonstration of the skill and mastery of the fictions. (Franco 53)

The suggestion is that the very form of the stories encourages this kind of interpretation, that Borges is (unconsciously?) "manipulating" his readers. Under the appearance of interpretation, these readings of Borges simply try to reproduce the pleasure of finding the "echoes" and symmetries that the critics experienced when reading the text. The very form of the text (and the pleasure of reading it) is preventing the readers from venturing outside its limits in search for other kinds of interpretations. One would think that by now Borges critics should have learned the lesson that Lönnrot learned only too late in "The Death and The Compass," in which the "natural" inclination of his mind to look for symmetries and analogies was easily manipulated by Red Scharlach and eventually led him to the "wrong" interpretation.

LA PEINTURE DE LA PENSÉE

As Borges became popular in the United States and France during the sixties, more critical analyses of his writings began to appear. An aspect of Borges's work that received a great deal of attention then was his extremely original style of writing. Both James Irby in *The Structure of the Stories of Jorge Luis Borges* (1962) and Jaime Alazraki in *La prosa narrativa de Jorge Luis Borges* (1968), among others, dedicate entire sections of their studies to an analysis of Borges's prose style.[1] The stylistic studies that appeared during the sixties did not obey the logic of the old stylistics of Spitzer, Alonso, and Auerbach. The latter always understood style as somehow related to the psychology of an author or to a specific historical situation.[2] By the 1960s, however, New Criticism had already been institutionalized in the United States and was generally considered the equivalent of "criticism." That explains why for both Alazraki and Irby, "style" is merely another component of the organically structured literary work, whose function is to reflect, at a microscopic level, the main topics of the text (Alazraki, *La prosa* 6, 11).[3]

---

[1]Other important books published during this period are Ronald Christ's *The Narrow Act* (1969) and Carter Wheelock's *The Mythmaker* (1969), which I will discuss later.

[2]Amado Alonso was the first critic to analyze Borges's style in his well-known review of *A Universal History of Infamy*. But by the time Alonso wrote the review (1936), Borges had not written yet the fantastic stories that made him famous. Alonso's analysis was not a "serious" one, he simply pointed out the emergence of a new style in Borges's prose writings.

[3]From the sixties on, Borgesean criticism will be linked to the American literary establishment. The latter will promote symposiums on his work, popularize his writings, and, to a certain point, will even dic-

Carter Wheelock's book, *The Mythmaker* (1969), was part of that wave of critical works that popularized Borges studies in the United States during the sixties. Like all the other studies mentioned, *The Mythmaker* is also very much within the New Critical tradition. But, unlike Irby's and Alazraki's studies, which have become classics in Borges criticism, Wheelock's book has received little attention. I intend to take *The Mythmaker* as a starting point for a different kind of analysis of Borges's style. My investigation will focus on how Borges's historical situation shaped and determined his "unique" way of writing. In order to achieve this, I will first attempt a revaluation not of Wheelock's analytical method but of some truly important insights that constitute the base of his study. In spite of Wheelock's emphasis on the organic nature of literary works, his interpretation makes Borges look to us very "postmodern" (even though Postmodernism was an unknown term to Wheelock at the time). Wheelock argues that Borges's stories are characterized by a radical skepticism toward the possibility that the human mind can understand the world. This position leads Borges to reject any systematic search for true knowledge. On the one hand, Borges is convinced that it is impossible to find a logical explanation of the universe, but, on the other, he is also fascinated by the ability of the human mind to invent new theories and explanations. The mind cannot understand the outside world, it can only understand itself, that is, understand how the thinking process occurs. In the end, for Borges the human mind is an utterly useless instrument that can only turn upon itself and reflect about the very process of thinking, about the creation

---

tate the theoretical approaches to be used in the study of his fiction. The fact that this generation of Borges critics was writing within this tradition is not without its importance to contemporary critics in the field. There was an emphasis being put then on theoretical generalizations (the "abstract formalism" of the New Critics) as opposed to "the more descriptive discourse of traditional empirical historism" (Clark 230). This will later allow many of Borges scholars (like Rodríguez Monegal and Alazraki) to pass to a post-structuralist style of criticism without noticing any ideological conflict between this new practice and their old aesthetic position.

of thought. Borges's stories portray this extreme solipsism by deliberately describing the behavior of the mind as if it were an objective reality. In other words, according to Wheelock, in Borges's stories what look like objects in the outside world are in reality literary representations of the contents of the mind (ideas, concepts). Borges's stories are allegories of the reasoning process by which the human mind hypostatizes one idea and subordinates all aspects of reality to it (Wheelock 3-17). They are self-reflexive because Borges is not interested in reproducing reality but in analyzing the way the mind thinks. This self-reflexive characteristic is one of the reasons why Borges's stories look postmodern to us today.

But let us not try to elaborate postmodern "theories" about the metafictional or self-reflexive character of Borges's work before looking closely at Wheelock's argument. It is important to notice that Wheelock's theory about the self-referential nature of the Borges texts is based on a very obscure quotation. The quotation comes from the preface to Borges's *Personal Anthology*, originally published in 1961. In the "Prologue" Borges loosely compares literature to a "mental process":

> Croce held that art is expression; to this exigency, or to a deformation of this exigency, we owe the worst literature of our time. True enough, Paul Valéry was able to write with felicity:
>
>> Comme le fruit se fond en puissance,
>> Comme en délice il change son absence
>> Dans une bouche où sa forme se meurt
>
> and Tennyson could write:
>
>> . . .and saw,
>> Straining his eyes beneath an arch of hand,
>> Or thought he saw, the speck that bore the King,
>> Down that long water opening on the deep
>> Somewhere far off, pass on and on, and go
>> From less to less and vanish into light.

> These are verses that reproduce a mental process with precision; but such victories are rare and no one (I believe) will judge them the most lasting or necessary words in literature. Sometimes I, too, sought expression. I know now that my gods grant me no more than allusion or mention. (*Personal Anthology* ix-x; *Antología personal* 7-8)

Wheelock argues that Borges is attempting a similar project in his short stories. In other words, Borges is supposedly trying to represent in his short stories the way the mind thinks. The fact is that it is not even clear in the text quoted by Wheelock whether Borges is claiming there that his own texts try to reproduce a "mental process." However, it is by no means my intention to "deconstruct" Wheelock's interpretative method by calling into question the validity of the text chosen by the critic. Instead, I wish to point out the existence of other texts that, in part, vindicate Wheelock's observations but that, at the same time, force us to reevaluate his theory. In contrast to Wheelock's obscure (and ambiguous) citation, I will now quote a well-known text that will provide us with a better understanding of Borges's notion of a mental process:

> He dicho que los hombres de ese planeta [Tlön] conciben el universo como una serie de procesos mentales, que no se desenvuelven en el espacio sino de modo sucesivo en el tiempo. Spinoza atribuye a su inagotable divinidad los atributos de la expansión y del pensamiento; nadie comprendería en Tlön la yuxtaposición del primero (que sólo es típico de ciertos estados) y del segundo—que es un sinónimo perfecto del cosmos—. Dicho sea con otras palabras: no conciben que lo espacial perdure en el tiempo. La percepción de una humareda en el horizonte y después del campo incendiado y después del

cigarro a medio apagar que produjo la quemazón es considerada un ejemplo de asociación de ideas. (*Obras* 1.436)[4]

Wheelock understood "mental process" as the narration of a homogeneous and unending process by which ideas are created by the mind. To be more precise, the mind gives priority to one idea and all the others are subordinated to it. Other ideas or concepts can only be explained in relation to the central one. If the mind discovers that the central idea cannot explain certain phenomenon, then it replaces it with a new one. Wheelock saw Borges's stories as symbolic narrations of this process. Borges's fictions, Wheelock says, are about how ideas constantly displace each other from the central position:

> Two ideas, two aspects of reality, two attributes or "beings" vie for the attention of the consciousness; one must be victorious over the other; so Scharlach kills Lönnrot [in "Death and the Compass"], the Negro kills Martin Fierro [in "The End"], Bandeira kills Otarola [in "The Dead Man"], and so on . . . although the victory of one is necessary, it is nevertheless deplorable because the victor is only a perspective, a partial image of reality. (Wheelock 16)

---

[4]"I have remarked that the men of that planet [Tlön] conceive of the universe as a series of mental processes, whose unfolding is to be understood only as a time sequence. Spinoza attributes to the inexhaustibly divine in man the qualities of extension and of thinking. In Tlön, nobody would understand the juxtaposition of the first, which is only characteristic of certain states of being, with the second [i.e., thinking], which is a perfect synonym for the cosmos. To put it another way—they do not conceive of the spatial as everlasting in time. The perception of a cloud of smoke on the horizon and, later, of the countryside on fire and, later, of a half-extinguished cigar which caused the conflagration would be considered an example of the association of ideas." (Borges, *Labyrinths* 24)

However, Borges's conception of a mental process seems to be very different inasmuch as it does not consist of a single and constant process but "a series of mental processes." In fact, Borges did not get his idea of "mental processes" from literary texts, as Wheelock's quotation from Borges's *Anthology* suggests. Borges borrowed the idea from a seventeenth-century philosophy, British Empiricism, whose notion of knowledge is based on mental processes (Rorty 3-4; 139-47). It is no surprise that the main exponents of this philosophical system (Locke, Hume, Berkeley) were authors frequently read and quoted by Borges. The faculty of understanding or knowing was, for these philosophers, "something like a wax tablet upon which objects make *impressions*" (Rorty 142). To have an impression is to know already, to represent. Once the mind has received the impressions, it proceeds to combine them to create complex ideas. It is this series of raw impressions received by the mind that Borges—using one of Locke's expressions—calls mental processes.[5] I will not give here a full and rigorous account of British Empiricism and the differences among its theoreticians, since it is not my intention to investigate how faithfully Borges represents the idealist concept of the mind. To do so will be to repeat the mistakes that most criticism on Borges has been doing for decades: to take some relevant or irrelevant influence or "source" of his fictions and turn it into a governing principle that is, in one way or another, present at all levels of his texts. Borges's "sources" are important, not because they will provide us useful information regarding his narrative techniques, but because by restoring Borges's quotations and literary allusions to their original context we may be able to see how he has transformed and adapted them to his ideology. Thus, what is interesting and, as we will see, important for the understanding of Borges's style, is the interpretation that Borges himself makes of philosophical idealism and the conclusions that he draws from it:

---

[5]On British Empiricism, see Priest's *The British Empiricist* and Woolhouse's *The Empiricists*.

No hay otra realidad, para el idealismo, que la de los procesos mentales; agregar a la mariposa que se percibe una mariposa objetiva le parece una vana duplicación; agregar a los procesos un yo le parece no menos exorbitante... Ahora bien, si cada estado psíquico es suficiente, si vincularlo a una circunstancia o a un yo es una ilícita y ociosa adición, ¿con qué derecho le impondremos después, un lugar en el tiempo? Chuang Tzu soñó que era una mariposa y durante aquel sueño no era Chuang Tzu, era una mariposa. ¿Cómo abolidos el espacio y el yo, vincularemos esos instantes a los del despertar y a la época feudal de la historia china? (*Obras* 2.147)[6]

Wheelock's idea of a single mental process implies the existence of a temporal continuum that Borges sees as incompatible with philosophical idealism. In contrast, Borges's notion of multiple mental or "psychic" processes turns that continuous time into a series of autonomous instants: "Cada instante es autónomo... cada momento que vivimos existe, no su imaginario conjunto" (*Obras* 2.140).[7] Each mental process exists as an independent event in itself, as a fragment that can

---

[6]"There is no other reality, for idealism, than that of mental processes; adding an objective butterfly to the butterfly that is perceived seems a vain duplication; adding a self to these processes seems no less exorbitant. . . . Now if each psychic state is self-sufficient, if linking it to a circumstance or to a self is an illicit and idle addition, with what right shall we then ascribe to it a place in time? Chuang Tzu [main character in Chinese tale from the fifth century B.C.] dreamt that he was a butterfly and during that dream he was not Chuang Tzu, but a butterfly. How, with space and self abolished, shall we link those moments to his waking moments and to the feudal period of Chinese history?" (*Labyrinths* 231)

[7]"Each moment is autonomous . . . each moment that we live exists, but not their imaginary combination." (*Labyrinths* 223)

only be joined to another, not by means of any law of causality but by an "association of ideas."[8]

Wheelock's observation about Borges's narrative system being based on a notion of mental processes is correct, but the critic illogically infers from this that every character, color, object in Borges's tales stands for a mental concept. It is this type of allegorical or symbolical intepretation (so popular during the 1960s) that more easily avoids dealing with the historical context of a literary text. Wheelock never looks for the ideological or historical reasons behind Borges's theory of mental processes. And yet it is another of Wheelock's observations that will allow us to do exactly that. I am referring to a comment that Wheelock makes in passing, in the first pages of his book, about the relationship between the idea of literature as a mental process and Borges's style. Wheelock says that Borges's interest in representing mental processes is the reason why he "is rightly called a Baroque writer." He then adds:

> The Baroque is, essentially, a time and a circumstance in which the creative intellect ceases to find value in the results of thought and turns to contemplating the forms of its own activity. (8)

It is a remarkable but isolated statement. It seems to come out of nowhere and it is not developed further. However, Wheelock's observation reveals an ingenious Borgesian practice: the union of a seventeenth-century philosophical theory and a seventeenth-century literary style. But before explaining the connection that Borges sees between the baroque style and philosophical idealism, I have to explain a few things about Borges's use of the baroque style. Most critics have called "baroque" the style in which Borges wrote his first books of essays (see Alazraki, "Introduction" 1-2), but, with a few exceptions, they have

---

[8]Borges apparently borrows the expression "association of ideas" from the British Empiricists' writings. See, for instance, Hume 14.

consistently failed to see the strong baroque elements of his mature prose.[9] Critics have chosen to ignore the author's well-known remarks about the baroque character of his major writings. In a 1954 "Preface" to a new edition of *A Universal History of Infamy*, Borges says about his style in that book:

> Yo diría que barroco es aquel estilo que deliberadamente agota (o quiere agotar) sus posibilidades y que linda con su propia caricatura... "*Barroco* (Baroco) es el nombre de uno de los modos del silogismo; el siglo XVIII lo aplicó a determinados abusos de la arquitectura y de la pintura del siglo XVII; yo diría que es barroca la etapa final de todo arte, cuando este exhibe y dilapida sus medios. El barroquismo es intelectual y Bernard Shaw ha declarado que toda labor intelectual es humorística. Este humorismo es involuntario en la obra de Baltasar Gracián; voluntario o consentido, en la de John Donne. Ya el excesivo título de estas páginas proclama su naturaleza barroca. (*Obras* 1.288)[10]

---

[9] Irby is one of the few who talks about the baroque characteristics of Borges's fictional writings. He points out devices and patterns in Borges's prose that "serve to dramatize the process of thought in the apprehension of truth." (*Structure* 157)

[10] "I should define as baroque that style which deliberately exhausts (or tries to exhaust) all its possibilities and which borders on its own parody. . . . "Baroque" is the name of one of the forms of syllogism; the eighteenth century applied it to certain excesses in the architecture and painting of the century before. I would say that the final stage of all styles is baroque when that style only too obviously exhibits or overdoes its own tricks. The baroque is intellectual, and Bernard Shaw has stated that all intellectual labor is essentially humorous. Such humor is not deliberate in the work of Baltasar Gracián, but is deliberate, or self-conscious, in John Donne's. The title of these pages [*A Universal History of Infamy*] flaunts their baroque character." (11)

No doubt Borges felt in 1954 that this baroque style that he started to use for narrative writing in *A Universal History of Infamy* and later used in his fantastic stories, was going to be the *final stage* of his always-evolving style. But in 1970, in *Doctor Brodie's Report* he tried to change again. In the preface to that book, Borges again mentions the baroque nature of his fantastic writings: "I have given up the surprises inherent in a baroque style as well as the surprises that lead to an unforeseen end" (11; *Obras* 2: 400).[11] That most critics have failed to recognize the baroque character of his *ficciones* can only be explained by their ignorance of the subtle difference between the two most commonly used styles of that period: *style coupé* and the "loose" style.

Both styles possess an anti-Ciceronian character. In other words, the original purpose of the baroque style is to avoid the completeness, the roundness of the Classical style. In the Classical or Ciceronian style the position of every part of the sentence had to be logically justified. The baroque style of writing was a reaction to the classical rules of writing. The two baroque styles, the loose style and the *style coupé*, emphasize in different ways spontaneity and lack of logical sequence. The curt style or *style coupé* is characterized by the brief members of its periods, the absence of syntactic connectives between the

---

[11]Contradicting himself, as he liked to do so often, Borges says in his "Autobiographical Essay" about his first book of essays (*Inquisiciones* [1925]):

> When I wrote these pieces, I was trying to play the sedulous ape to two Spanish baroque writers seventeenth-century writers, Quevedo and Saavedra Fajardo, who stood in their stiff, arid Spanish way for the same kind of writing as Sir Thomas Browne in "Urn-Burial." I was doing my best to write Latin in Spanish, and the book collapses under the sheer weight of its involutions and sententious judgements. (231)

The truth is that he never abandoned his project of updating the baroque style.

members, and the overuse of semicolons and colons. This example is from Thomas Browne's *Religio Medici*:

> To see ourselves again, we need not to look for Plato's year: every man is not only himself; there have been many Diogeneses, and as many Timons, though but few of that name; men are lived over again; the world is now as it was in ages pasts; there was none then, but there hath been some one since, that parallels him, and is, as it were, his revived self. (qtd. in Croll 95)

The baroque loose style possesses syntactic links like the Ciceronian style; these, however, do not connect "logically" the different parts of the sentence. Its conjunctions, for example, "do not necessarily refer back to any particular point in the preceding member; nor do they commit the following member to a predetermined form" (Croll 98). Croll uses this example from Bacon's writings in his article "The Baroque Style in Prose":

> For as knowledges are now delivered, there is a kind of contract of error between the deliverer and the receiver: for he that delivereth knowledge desireth to deliver it in such form as may be best believed, and not as may be best examined; and he that receiveth knowledge desireth rather present satisfaction than expectant inquiry; and so rather not to doubt than not to err: glory making the author not to lay open his weakness, and sloth making the disciple not to know his strength. (qtd. in Croll 97)

Notice the use of "loose" conjunctions such as "and," "and so" to link sentences to each other. Together these two baroque styles form what modern grammarians call *parataxis*. The loose style is clearly the style Borges tried to imitate in his early prose works. As an example, I can quote a paragraph from one of Borges's early books of essays, *Inquisiciones* (1925):

Haber conocido en la inmediación soldadesca tierras de Rusia y Austria, y Francia y Polonia, haber sido partícipe de las primeras victorias, terribles como derrotas, cuando la infantería en persecución de cielos y ejércitos atravesaba campos desvaídos donde mostrábase saciada la muerte y universal la injuria de las armas, es casi codiciadero pero indubitable sufrir. (*Inquisiciones* 147-48)[12]

By the early thirties his famous change of style takes place. Borges is supposed to have abandoned his early baroque style (Alazraki, *La prosa* 148-69). But as one can notice in the following example, Borges has simply replaced the "loose" style with his version of the *style coupé*:

> Limitar lo que padeció [Cristo] a la agonía de una tarde en la cruz es blasfematorio. Afirmar que fue hombre y que fue incapaz de pecado encierra contradicción; los atributos de *impeccabilitas* y de *humanitas* no son compatibles. (*Obras* 1.516-17)[13]

As in the example from Browne's *Religio Medici*, all the causative connectives are missing. They have been replaced by semicolons and periods. No doubt the reason that attracted Borges to the baroque style—to both variations of it—was the baroque writers' intention behind their paratactical way of writing:

---

[12]"To have known in the soldier's immediate experience the lands of Russia and Austria and France and Poland; to have participated in the first victories, as terrible as defeats, when the infantries in pursuit of skies and armies crossed dull fields where death looked satiated and the injury caused by arms was universal, is a desirable but certain suffering." (Rodríguez Monegal's translation of the paragraph, *Literary Biography* 146)

[13]"To limit all that happened [to Christ] to the agony of one afternoon on the cross is blasphemous. To affirm that he was a man and that he was incapable of sin contains a contradiction; the attributes of *impeccabilitas* and of *humanitas* are not compatible." (*Ficciones* 155)

Their purpose was to portray not a thought, but a mind thinking, or in Pascal's words, *la peinture de la pensée*. They knew that an idea separated from the act of experiencing it is not the idea that was experience. The ardor of its conception in the mind is a necessary part of its truth; and unless it can be conveyed to another mind in something of the form of its occurrence, either it has changed into some other idea or it has ceased to be an idea. . . . They deliberately chose as the moment of expression that in which the idea clearly objectifies itself in the mind, in which, therefore, each of its parts still preserves its own peculiar emphasis and independent vigor of its own—in brief, the moment in which truth is still *imagined*. (Croll 87)[14]

Because the mind's reasoning process is not necessarily coherent or logical, the baroque style omits links between the sentences in order to "portray thinking" or it uses "loose" connectives, which do not give the appearance of a logical sequence to the text. Borges's inge-

---

[14]Compare the similarity of Croll's definition of the baroque style with what Borges was already saying in 1925 about Quevedo's style:
El conceptismo...es una serie de latidos cortos e intensos marcando el ritmo del pensar. En vez de la visión abarcadora que difunde Cervantes sobre el ancho decurso de una idea, Quevedo pluraliza las vislumbres en una suerte de fusilería de miradas parciales... El quevedismo es psicológico: es el empeño en restituir a todas las ideas el arriscado y brusco carácter que las hizo asombrosas al presentarse por primera vez al espíritu. (Borges, *Inquisiciones* 44-45)

(Quevedo's "conceptismo" . . . is a series of short and intense heartbeats simulating the rhythm of thinking. Instead of the single and all-encompassing view of a topic that one finds in Cervantes, Quevedo looks at an idea from multiple points of view. . . . "Quevedism" is psychological; it is the attempt to restore to all ideas the tentative and unfinished character that they had when the mind first encountered them).

nious next step, after rediscovering the aesthetic possibilities of this style, was to bring together, to juxtapose, the idealist notion of the working of the mind as a mental process and the baroque writers' project of portraying thinking. Borges's idea was to use a style that was created with the intention of reproducing the workings of the human mind to represent artistically idealism's notion of mental processes. Borges's preference for the curt style might be better appreciated if one remembers his conclusion about the consequences that the Empiricist world-view has for the notion of time. Time, Borges says in "New Refutation of Time," is broken into autonomous instants, and, as a consequence, each mental process exists by itself, without any connection (causative or otherwise) to the others. Such independence of all world and mental events is best conveyed by the short members and the absence of syntactic links of the curt period (De Man, "Modern Master" 61). The absence of causative links and the use of loose conjunctions was for the baroque writers a way of representing the nonlogical manner in which the mind goes from one idea to the next. For Borges, however, the same device has become a way of representing the absolute autonomy of each mental process. Borges's extremely paratactical style divides every paragraph, every sentence, into small sections. Sections are separated from each other by a comma, period, colon, or semicolon (or, less often, a loose conjunction). Each one of these small parts is supposed to stand for an autonomous mental process. Borges wants to give us the impression that they are linked together, in the form of sentences and paragraphs, not by any causative relation among them but by an "association of ideas."[15]

---

[15]Jacobo Woscoboinik quotes from an interview that Borges apparently gave to a magazine entitled *Cabral*. There Borges talks about how much his "writing" style changed after he became blind and had to dictate instead of write:

> Thus, I discovered, just as Henry James did, that dictation is easy because one feels more irresponsible. [In contrast], before, for many years, I used to write one sentence at a time, and then move from one sentence to the next. Of course the text

No doubt the baroque writers' interest in mental processes reflects their historical situation. Not only were they under the influence of the modern concept of the mind created by Descartes (see Rorty 17-69), but the mind/body division only continued to increase after that cultural period. In several of Fredric Jameson's books and essays, he has argued that the initial mind/body split was followed in later centuries by a further "autonomization" of the different body parts as well as an autonomization of the brain functions. Dowling summarizes Jameson's theory as follows:

> [T]he fall from primitive communism into alienated or stranged individuality is accompanied for Jameson by an *interior* fragmentation, a process through which the senses become estranged from one another and begin to function autonomously . . . and through which, as well, the various functions or levels of the mind become similarly estranged and independent in their working, with the purely abstract or rational level splitting off from the emotional, the empirical or descriptive faculty alienated from the perception of meaning or value and so on. (24-25)

I have already explained that the exaggerated paratactic nature of Borges's style is intended to represent the subdivision of the mind's

---

> would lack continuity because each phrase was isolated. Emerson used the same procedure; that is why one can read several pages by Emerson, full of admirable sentences, but one cannot read an entire article, because every new sentence is not logically connected to the preceding one nor does it prepare the reader for the next one. Everything remains as a series of phrases or aphorisms. (*El secreto* 67)

If one compares Borges's comments here to what María Esther Vázquez has said about his way of dictating (35-36), one has to conclude, as Woscoboinik does, that Borges style did not really change after he became blind.

perception of the world into mental processes. Following Jameson one could also suggest that it reflects the effects of an increasing atomization and compartmentalization of the human world in modern times. This theory allows us to see the unique style of writing that Borges has created not only as the result of a personal choice but also as a reaction to a historical situation. If this is the case, Borges's extreme parataxis does not simply represent the "movement" of thought but also something else that he is trying very hard to push away from his texts: that is, his own situation as a subject affected by the changes brought about by modernization. About Borges's aesthetic strategy to escape the alienating effects of modernity I will talk extensively later. Suffice it to say, for now, that his "escape" takes place at the level of content, not of form, which, on the contrary, reveals the true relation of his texts to the historical period in which they were produced.

Rationalization and reification are here the key words for understanding how Jameson applies his theory to literature. The effect of the reification process on literature was to turn the "book" into an object and remove it from its original communicative function. The process of reification in Modernism goes even further as the different parts and chapters and even the sentences of the already autonomous work of art become autonomous themselves (Jameson, *Signatures* 205-206). In Borges's case reification affects the composition of the sentences and even reaches down to the members of every period. It is possible to suggest not that each sentence but that *each member of a sentence* represents for Borges a "mental process." Just as each moment in time is autonomous, there are no links that tie an individual sentence to others. Sentences can be "quoted," they can be transported to or repeated in another text, as Borges often does.[16] Each sentence in Borges's texts is an object that can be consumed independently. Put another way, each sentence becomes an object of pleasure in itself.

---

[16]The best-known example of a text repeated in another is the sentence about mirrors and fatherhood that appears in "The Masked Dyer, Hakim of Merv" and in "Tlön, Uqbar, Orbis Tertius."

The rationalization process, on the other hand, consists in segmentalizing traditional ways of doing things to achieve greater efficiency or to create products that perhaps could have never been produced in a precapitalist social system. In Borges's case, the aim of his fragmentation of reality could be said to have an analogous purpose. As the events of the external world become autonomous or semi-autonomous "mental processes," these fragments of a previous unity can be reorganized (by means of an "association of ideas") aesthetically by the author. The raw materials from the outside world are thus dissected and carefully put together again into those nice-looking new objects that are Borges's perfectly geometrical stories.

In this reading I present Borges's writings as being determined in their form by an individualistic ideology and an exaggerated emphasis on certain privileged faculties of the mind. Such reading is obviously in conflict with an equally justifiable postmodern interpretation of Borges's stories. In a hypothetical postmodernist reading of Borges, one could interpret his frequent use of the topic of pantheism in his short stories as somehow foreshadowing the end of man or the death of the subject. For Borges the consequence of a pantheist philosophy is that human individuality is lost: all "men," Borges frequently writes, become one "man." Borges often links this interpretation of pantheism to his belief about the impossibility of originality in literature. In "Pierre Menard," for example, a fictional French Symbolist writer rewrites word by word Cervantes's *Don Quixote*. Menard is, so to speak, a "dead" author: he can only repeat what others have already written. But the story also talks about the "death" of Cervantes as an author. Cervantes or any other writer can no longer hold a "copyright" over any idea or text. As the story hints, since "all men are one man," all "men" could have the same ideas, come up with the same inventions or write exactly the same books (see Foucault, "What Is an Author?"; also Borges's interview with Charbonier 74-78).

On the other hand, we have Borges's desire to create a distinctive style of writing. The idea that the style of a writer must be as unique as his/her own signature, belongs not to Postmodernism but to Modernism. Its origins can be traced back as far as Flaubert, whose obsession with style Roland Barthes links to the birth of modern capitalism (44-48). Before Modernism we used to think of style as the expression of an entire cultural period (there was, for example, a *baroque* style). With Modernism there is not a predominant style. Each artist tries to create a style so original that it cannot be confused with others: think of the typical Faulknerian sentence, of Proust's distinctive use of the past tense, of Hemingway's bare-bone prose. The modernists' idea of a private style implies the existence of an individual subject whose "peculiar" inner world his/her style is supposed to express. Style for the modern writers was, like Henry James's use of the "point of view" (Jameson, *Political Unsconscious* 221), also a way of rewriting *within* the text the fiction of a centered subject that, in a real world affected by reification, was becoming more and more difficult to sustain.

In opposition to the modernist desire for holding on to the idea of a subject, even if it is a multiple or fragmented one, postmodern discourse proclaims the total dissolution of the rhetoric of the self. All the topics that were in one way or another connected to the concept of self have almost disappeared from postmodern literature. For example, "point of view," the problematics of time (which has been replaced by "space") and style are no longer central topics or concerns. Postmodernism, as it is known, replaces the use of a private style with pastiche and parody—an aesthetic position that is, of course, related to the contemporary attacks on the idea of an author controlling the structure of the text from outside and to the attacks on all kinds of "essentialism" in general. In short, for postmodern writers there is no longer a "personal" world-view to be expressed by means of some original way of writing (Jameson, *Postmodernism* 15-17).

Borges's project of creating a unique style (his "will to style"), an enterprise which includes not only the rescuing of a half-forgotten baroque style but also the latinization of his vocabulary as well as the careful adaptation of his Spanish to an English syntax, cannot be dismissed as a residue from an earlier cultural period (on the main characteristics of Borges's style, see Barrenechea, *La expresión* and Alazraki, *La prosa* 187-271 and "Génesis de un estilo"). There is an undeniable overlapping of modern and postmodern characteristics in Borges. To explain the presence of modernist features in a "postmodern" Borges by classifying him as a transitional writer remains a useless explanation if it does not tell us why certain characteristics—such as style—were preserved and others were not, or what is the function of those apparently archaic elements in his texts.

One cannot deal with the contradiction between Borges's will-to-style and his post-individualistic topics by ignoring the presence of modernist elements of his writings. Instead I wish to present a reinterpretation of Borges's post-individualistic fiction, his famous "decentering" of the subject, that will help us understand the style chosen by Borges. It must be clear that what is being attempted here is not a flat rejection of the existence of postmodern elements in Borges's texts. Even less a rereading of those postmodern characteristics as if they had their origin elsewhere and not in Borges's own Postmodernism. On the contrary, I am asserting Borges's postmodernity, but in the process I think that we should not forget that his texts are only partially postmodern. What was earlier mistaken for a postmodern characteristic might in fact be something else.

In my chapter "Thinking as Pleasure," I analyzed briefly Borges's resentment of the specialization of knowledge and his artistic and fictional attempt to achieve "universal knowledge," that is, to give the impression of being an erudite author who possesses a large amount of knowledge of diverse and difficult fields. I showed that Borges takes this position as a personal reaction to modernist aesthetics and that his attempt to overcome specialization brings him close to some postmodern textual practices. I will now return to the question of Borges's *erudition imaginaire* or pseudoerudition to analyze the origin of this position in what I will call Borges's nostalgia for a premodern time. Nostalgia appears in his writings in the form of an archaic perception of knowledge and literature that we will now explore.

The increasing specialization brought about by the modernizing impulse manifests itself in the separation of all fields of knowledge into specialized areas that are only accessible to experts. In Borges's texts it is easy to see the presence of a nostalgia for a "premodern" world when being a "man of knowledge" meant knowing about all disciplines that were "worth" learning, when there was no distinction between philosophy and literature nor between literature and history. Borges's attraction for the writings of Thomas Browne (and other baroque writers) and his texts full of learned quotations that Borges tries to imitate, is partly the consequence of his desire to recover an old view of knowledge and literature.

The concept of literature as we know it today includes mainly "imaginative" works like fiction and poetry. But this perception of literature did not emerge until the eighteenth century and it only became the dominant view as late as the nineteenth century. The pre-eighteenth century notion of literature included all printed books, "all knowledge," that is to say, philosophy, history, essays and, of course, poetry were considered literature. The shift from this earlier idea of literature to one in which imagination and originality are overvalued is related to the industrialization of Europe and to the process of specialization of human activities (Eagleton 17-22; Williams, *Marxism* 45-54). The specialization of literature was a reaction to industrialization. The purpose of that process of specialization was to promote a different perception of life from the one created by capitalism:

> The process of specialization of "literature" to "creative" or "imaginative" works . . . is in part a major affirmative response, in the name of an essentially general human "creativity," to the socially repressive and intellectually mechanical forms of a new social order: that of capitalism and especially industrial capitalism. The practical specialization of work to the wage-labour production of commodities: of "being" to "work" in these terms; of language to the passing of "rational" or "informative" "messages"; of social relations to functions within a systematic economic and political order: all these pressures and limits were challenged in the name of a full and liberating "imagination" or "creativity." The central Romantic assertions, which depend on these concepts, have a significantly absolute range, from politics and nature to work and art. (Williams, *Marxism* 49-50)

But Borges's reaction to the specialization of literature was radically different from the Romantic writers'. Faced with an increasing modernization and specialization of society, Borges feels a nostalgia for an idyllic premodern time. This nostalgia clearly expresses itself in Borges's return to a premodern notion of literature that Romantic writers had already abandoned. Unlike Romantic writers, who found in the idea of imagination and creative intellect an alternative to modern social relations, Borges only saw in that process of specialization of literature the damaging influence of modernity. In both cases there is a reaction against modernization, but the expression that this reaction takes is shaped by different historical circumstances. Borges's historical situation is that of post-romantic writer, "in the sense of being [a product] of that epoch rather than confidently posterior to it" (Eagleton 18). Precisely because he is a post-romantic writer, Borges cannot entirely go back to a premodern epoch and abandon his. Just as he does not really become anachronistically a baroque writer, he does not simply abandon the Romantic idea of literature as "imaginative" writing. What he does is in a sense very postmodern. Borges enlarges the concept of "imaginative" work so as to include philosophy and history and, of course, essays: they are all subsumed under the category of "fiction." In "Tlön, Uqbar, Orbis Tertius" the narrator states that "la metafísica es una rama de la literatura fantástica" (*Obras* 1.436),[17] and theology and historical studies receive the same treatment in other stories. This is one of Borges's fictional strategies to deal with the problem of specialization; another one, as we are about to see, is his interpretation of pantheism.

In another chapter I discussed how Borges's desire to overcome specialization of knowledge influences the form of his writings. Recapitulating briefly, specialization is the result of the modern redistribution of work in order to achieve greater efficiency. Specialists, because they are able to dedicate themselves exclusively to one branch of knowledge, have developed their disciplines into complex fields only accessible to experts. Since it is impossible to become an expert in several fields, Borges can only aspire to include different fields of knowledge in his stories if he reduces them to their most simplistic and superficial aspects. We have already seen how this influences the composition of his stories at the level of form. The same desire to overcome specialization

---

[17]"metaphysics is a branch of fantastic literature." (*Labyrinths* 10)

can be detected, at the level of content, in Borges's treatment of individualism.

Borges's dream of eliminating the effects of specialization and atomization of modernity can only be imaginarily achieved by a suppression of subjectivity. In Borges's pantheistic fantasies his characters discover, on the one hand, that individual subjectivity does not exist and that all subjects are essentially "one." On the other hand, the same subject can in theory be anyone, do anything. This idea is perhaps best represented in the story "The Immortal." This is the story of a man who becomes immortal after drinking from a sacred river. In his immortal life he does almost everything, from composing the *Iliad* (he is Homer; all men are Homer in Borges's pantheist fantasies) to being the owner of an antique shop in early twentieth-century England:

> Recorrí nuevos reinos, nuevos imperios. En el otoño de 1066 milité en el puente de Stamford... En el séptimo siglo de la Héjira, en el arrabal de Bulaq, transcribí con pausada caligrafía, en un idioma que he olvidado, en un alfabeto que ignoro, los siete viajes de Simbad y la historia de la Ciudad de Bronce. En un patio de la cárcel de Samarcanda he jugado muchísimo al ajedrez. En Bikanir he profesado la astrología y también en Bohemia. (*Obras* 1.542)[18]

Borges is fascinated with the idea of pantheism because it allows him to overcome the modern problem of specialization. A man who is all men is the ultimate fantasy of an alienated subject. If a man is able to be both an intellectual and a man of action, and if all knowl-

---

[18]"I traveled over new kingdoms, new empires. In the fall of 1066, I fought at Stamford Bridge.... In the seventh century of the Hegira in the suburb of Bulaq, I transcribed with measured calligraphy, in a language I have forgotten, in an alphabet I do not know, the seven adventures of Sinbad and the history of the City of Bronze. In a courtyard of a jail in Samarkand I played a great deal of chess. In Bikaner I professed the science of astrology and also in Bohemia." (*Labyrinths* 116)

edge is now available to a single mind (to anyone's mind), then there is no place for modern "anxieties" about the increasing compartmentalization and specialization of the world. Borges's "pantheism" could very well be interpreted as a postmodern attack on "essentialism," as a rejection of the idea of the subject as center and origin. But it is also the reflection of a nostalgic desire to go back to a premodern state of life. It is an imaginary solution to the modern problem of alienation.

Borges's texts oscillate between the fantasy of nonalienation just described above and a fierce protection of the individual subject. While the content of the stories tends toward the annihilation of individualism, the latter's existence is affirmed by the form of the texts. Borges's "will-to-style," his attempt to create a unique, individual style that cannot be imitated reveals a refusal to surrender completely his individualism. There is a passage from "Tlön, Uqbar, Orbis Tertius" that shows the importance that Borges attached to the individualism represented by his style. At the end of "Tlön, Uqbar, Orbis Tertius," the world is being taken over by a New Order: soon "El mundo será Tlön" (*Obras* 1.443)[19], says the narrator. Written in 1938, the story, as has been said many times, reflects Borges's concern about the spread of fascism throughout the world.[20] In fear of a State that begins to intrude into the lives of its members, "Borges," the narrator in the story, withdraws himself from the world and, without paying any attention to what is happening, goes on "[revisando] una indecisa traducción quevediana (que no pienso dar a la imprenta) del *Urn Burial* de Browne" (*Obras* 1.443).[21]

---

[19]"The world will be Tlön." (*Ficciones* 35)

[20]Borges was a member of the group of writers publishing the magazine *Sur* whose antifascist position during this period is well known. Borges wrote several short articles against the war and against fascism that were published there.

[21]"[revising] a tentative translation into Spanish, in the style of Quevedo, which [he does not] intend to see published, of Sir Thomas Browne's *Urn Burial*." (*Ficciones* 35)

Reading these lines one realizes that Borges is not one of those modern intellectuals "who are and always have been part and parcel of society, to which as a group they even owed their existence and prominence" (Arendt, *On Revolution* 118). Instead, he is closer in spirit to an older group of writers and thinkers that originated in prerevolutionary France: the *hommes de lettres*, whose attitude toward society, as Arendt describes it, could not be more similar to Borges's:

> In contrast to the later writers and *literati* . . . these men [i.e., the *hommes de lettres*], though they did live in the world of the written and printed word and were, above all, surrounded by books, were neither obliged nor willing to write and read professionally, in order to earn a living. Unlike the [modern] class of the intellectuals, who offer their services either to the state as experts, specialists, and officials, or to society for diversion and instruction, the *hommes de lettres* always strove to keep aloof from both the state and society. Their material existence was based on income without work, and their intellectual attitude rested upon their resolute refusal to be integrated politically or socially. (Arendt, "Introduction" 27-28).[22]

In a strikingly similar gesture, both Borges and the *hommes de lettres* withdraw from society to cultivate their mind in "freely chosen seclusion" (H. Arendt notes that at the bottom of these writers' contempt for society there is nothing but a reaction towards their own political powerlessness). However, it is important to stress again historical differences. While in the case of these men of letters—as well as in the other sixteenth- and seventeenth-century examples mentioned throughout this chapter—we are witnessing the emergence of the individual subject who is trying to affirm his right to act freely, in Borges's case we are

---

[22]The *Martin Fierro* group—to which Borges belonged as a young writer—rejected the idea of making money out of literature. Sarlo explains that this is related to the rejection of a class of writers with immigrant origins (and who obviously did not come from wealthy families). See Sarlo, *Jorge Luis Borges* 100-101.

witnessing a last and desperate attempt on the part of that subject to survive. In Borges's story, then, the individual subject must be protected from the modern state whose all-pervading influence he at times sees as unstoppable. That is why it is not surprising at all that, in that historical moment when Borges believes that individualism is being threatened by the "malignant forces" of the State, he remembers the writings and styles of two of his favorite baroque writers, Quevedo and Browne.

Borges's style reveals his ambiguous position toward Modernism. On the one hand, we have Borges's very modernist will-to-style. He sees in the creation of an individual, unique style a representation of the individuality of the self. Borges's need to hold on to the notion of individuality is obviously a reaction to the political situation of the time as he saw it: the spread of fascism and totalitarian governments that tried to control all aspects of the individual lives of their subjects. But Borges's writings also reveal his nostalgia for a premodern time, a time untouched by modern alienation. But in spite of this rejection of modernity, his style reproduces in its extremely paratactic form the atomization and fragmentation that Borges is trying to escape. Nowhere is the overlapping of elements from different cultural periods more evident than in his style.

THE OTHER FACE OF MODERNITY: BORGES AS AN ANTI-FASCIST

During the early 1970s Borges started making controversial political statements in his interviews. He became well known for praising dictators such as Franco, Pinochet, and Viola in Argentina, for showing a lack of faith in democratic processes and for his attacks on the massification of culture.[1] It is then understandable that the perception that the general public had of him was that he was a "fascist" in political matters and an "elitist" in cultural ones. Critics who tried to defend Borges from these accusations often followed two different paths: either they argued that his literary work should not (could not) be explained taking as point of reference his political ideology or they pointed out that Borges wrote several antifascist texts during the 1940s, showing this as proof of Borges's antitotalitarianism. Readers were then sometimes asked not to use politics to interpret Borges's writings or to make a distinction between Borges's political *opinions*, expressed in his interviews, and his real political position found in the literary texts that he wrote in the 1930s and 1940s. The critic Jaime Alzraki represents

---

[1] See, for example, several of the interviews recorded by María Esther Vázquez and collected in her book *Borges, sus días y su tiempo*, specifically those from between 1970 and 1975. One can easily find there Borges's statements about his support for dictatorships (280) and a few negative comments about liberal politics and democratic societies (119; 272-73), some of which are blatantly racist (247-48). Closely related to his criticism of democracy is his rejection of the massification of culture (254-55; 271-72). Among his most "famous" political comments there is one about the military leaders that ruled Argentina during the late 1970s and early 1980s: Borges called them the "only gentlemen capable of serving the country" (qtd. in Alazraki, *Kabbalah* 179). See also note 31.

the first position very well. For Alazraki, using politics or history to interpret Borges's work is useless since he only deals with philosophical or literary problems: "the typical Borgesian story aims not so much—like conventional fiction—at capturing a 'slice of life' as at advancing an *argumentum theologicum* or *philosophicus*" (*Kabbalah* 182; Alazraki's italics). On the other hand, in his article "Borges and Politics," Rodríguez Monegal differentiates between Borges's political opinions and the political ideas found in his literary work (54). The political opinions that Borges expressed in his interviews are not to be taken seriously, according to the critic, and they are mostly the result of Borges's humor: his desire to play the "deadly game of *vieillard terrible*" (56; Rodríguez Monegal's italics). In this chapter I will try to study the evolution of Borges's ideology from the late 1930s, when he wrote his first fantastic tales, to the mid-1970s, when he produced his last collection of stories. I hope to be able to show that those political "opinions" that Borges was so fond of pronouncing in the 1970s are not unrelated to the ideology present in his fictional work and in his antifascist writings from the 1940s. On the contrary, the controversial opinions that Borges expressed in interviews late in life must be seen as the last stage in the evolution of an ideology.

Toward the end of my previous chapter, I analyzed the relation between Borges's individualistic ideology and his reaction against fascism, but I am afraid that I did it in very general and even abstract terms. I wish to expand on that analysis and return to an investigation of the meaning of Borges's individualism through a close reading of his antifascist writings, whose importance most critics, with the exception of Rodríguez Monegal, have ignored.[2] Ultimately, as I explained above, my intention is to discover the origins of Borges's ideological position during the last decade and a half of his life. In my first chapter I tried to establish the importance that the socioeconomic changes that occurred in Argentina during the late 1920s had on shaping Borges's ideology and his perception of modernity. No less important—to understand the

---

[2] He has studied Borges's antifascist writings in "Borges and Politics" and in a section of *Literary Biography* (300-305).

shifts that will occur in his thinking—were the political events that took place during the 1930s and 1940s at both the local and international levels, especially the rise of fascism. Most of Borges's anti-Nazi texts were written between 1937 and 1944, but if we consider (as Borges himself did) his writings against the Perón regime as part of his antifascist literature, then, one can see that this antifascist period lasted for over a decade (until 1955, when Perón was overthrown) and that it roughly coincided with the same period during which he wrote his main fantastic tales.

Some of Borges's first anti-Nazi articles appeared in *El Hogar*, a magazine for which he was the editor of a literary section, and they mostly consist of brief notes denouncing antisemitism in Germany. Two general characteristics can be observed in these texts. The first one is that apparently Borges thought that it was going to be self-evident to his readers why antisemitism was wrong. In 1937, Borges published a review of a German school primer on racism, *Trau keinem Jud bei seinem Eid*, that according to him was already in its fourth printing and had sold over fifty thousand copies in Germany. In his review of the book, Borges limits himself to describe the book's illustrations ("El primer grabado ilustra la tesis: 'El Demonio es el padre de los judíos'" [*Textos cautivos* 136]),[3] but does not make any comments about the book or the illustrations and, after he has finished with his description, simply adds, "Dejo el estupor (o el aplauso) a cargo del lector."[4] In another review of the same book that he later wrote for *Sur*, Borges expressed his opinion more directly: "What can one say about a book like this? Personally, I find it repugnant, less for Israel's sake than for Germany's own; less for the insulted community than for the insulting nation. I do not know if the world can do without the German civilization. But I find it shameful that it should be corrupted with teachings of hatred.'"[5] Even

---

[3]"The first illustration is based on the thesis that 'Devil is the Jew's father.'" (qtd. in Rodríguez Monegal, *Literary Biography* 303)

[4]"I will leave the stupefaction (or the applause) to the reader."

[5]"Una pedagogía del odio." *Sur* 32 (1937): 81; qtd. in Rodríguez Monegal, "Politics" 61.

though Borges seems more concerned with the future of German civilization than with that of the Jewish community in Germany, there are many essays and literary texts that show the great admiration that he always had for the Jewish culture as well.[6] In any case, his preoccupation with the future of German civilization leads us to another predominant characteristic of his antifascist writings, which is the use of the opposition barbarism/civilization to analyze the political situation in Germany. One of Borges's main concerns is the "destruction" of the German culture (a culture that he greatly admired) by the Nazi government. Borges saw the emergence of fascist governments in Europe as the return of "barbarism," as a threat to Western civilization in general. It must be added that at the time it was not unusual, among critics of fascist politics, to refer to fascism as barbaric or irrational.[7]

The view that the German culture was in danger can be perceived in other reviews that he wrote for *El Hogar*. One of these was the review of a book catalogue from one of Germany's publishing houses, Insel-Verlag. The catalogue had obviously been reduced by the Nazi government censors and limited to literary works that were considered appropriate by them. Borges does not mention this, although from his

---

[6]The influence of the Jewish culture on Borges's writing has been amply documented by Sosnowski and Alazraki (*Borges and the Kabbalah*) among others. Borges had the tendency to judge the value of a culture in terms of its contribution to the Western cultural canon. On occasions, this practice allowed him to justify his own prejudiced views of other cultures/races: "I went to a congress . . . where translations problems were being discussed and there were [in that congress] some black poets who said that [blacks] belonged to a superior race. It was something like reverse Hitlerism, and less justifiable [*con menos razón*] because, let us face it, Germany has been more important to the world than Congo" (Vázquez 247).

[7]T. W. Adorno was one of the critics that dedicated several articles to study the connection between irrationality, fascism, and antisemitism. (See the last chapter of *Dialectic of Enlightenment*.) For a brief analysis of this aspect of Adorno's criticism, see Crook's "Introduction: Adorno and Authoritarian Irrationalism."

comments one is supposed to infer that the government is using the publishing house for propaganda purposes. Borges simply concludes that "Germany, literarily, is poor."[8] Once again the reader is left to infer the damaging effects of Nazism from the facts presented by Borges; this time he hopes that the reader will notice Nazism's debasement of the German culture. A similar textual strategy can be detected in a brief item (also published in *El Hogar*, on September 3, 1937) about a German magazine directed by Erich Ludendorff, a hero from the World War I. In this case, Borges wanted to denounce not only the ongoing destruction of the German culture by the fascist regime, but also the lack of logic or the "irrationalism" of the latter:

> La revista de Ludendorff "Desde el sagrado manantial de la fuerza alemana" prosigue en Munich su campaña implacable y quincenal contra los judíos, contra el papado, contra los budistas, contra la masonería, contra los teósofos, contra la Sociedad de Jesús, contra el comunismo, contra el doctor Martín Lutero, contra Inglaterra y contra la memoria de Goethe. (*Textos cautivos* 165)[9]

This disparate catalogue of everything that Nazism stands against is no different in content and intention from the equally illogical catalogues that Borges will later employ in his work. One that is well known because it is analyzed in the opening pages of Foucault's *The Order of*

---

[8]This review is mentioned by Rodríguez Monegal in his *Literary Biography* (303), which is where my quote comes from. According to Rodríguez Monegal the review was published in *El Hogar* on June 11, 1937. It is not included in *Textos cautivos*, which is a collection of some (not all) texts published by Borges in that magazine.

[9]"Ludendorff's magazine, *From the Sacred Source of German Strength*, continues from Munich its inexorable and fortnightly campaign against Jews, the Pope, the Buddhists, the masons, the theosophists, the Society of Jesus, communism, Dr. Martin Luther, England, and Goethe's memory." (Rodríguez Monegal's translation, *Literary Biography* 304)

Things, is the description of an imaginary Chinese encyclopedia in which animals appear divided into completely irrational—and often ridiculous—categories such as "embalmed ones," "innumerable ones" or "those that resemble flies from a distance." (*Obras* 2.84; *Other Inquisitions* 103). The same idea is present behind both catalogues: rationalization can be both the origin of a modern, more efficient society or of an irrational order.[10] In the description of Ludendorff's magazine, Borges's attack on Nazi ideology is more evident than in the examples previously quoted, but he does not yet express openly his point of view nor does he explain clearly why the Nazi ideology is unacceptable. It is possible to see a connection between Borges's timid position in his early antifascist texts, written around 1937, and the rejection of committed literature, which he also expressed in the pages of *El Hogar* (*Textos cautivos* 287-88). In relation to this, it is interesting to notice that Borges tried to find subjects that were somehow linked to literature (a review of a book for children, a book catalogue, a magazine) to justify his talking about politics in the literary section of the magazine. Expressing openly his political opinion there was against his view of literature as an entirely autonomous activity.

By 1940, Germany had invaded France and started the siege of England. Borges's literary section in *El Hogar* had been canceled, apparently because of lack of interest by the readers of the magazine. It appeared for the last time in July 1939. But in December 1940 an article is published by Borges in the first page of the magazine in which it is possible to see how much the success of Germany in World War II has forced him to change his writing strategy. If before, he wrote short texts about literary topics and rarely expressed directly his political opinions, now he is openly denouncing Nazism. In "Portrait of a Germanophile," Borges wants to show that those who in Argentina side with Hitler are even more irrational in their character than Nazi sup-

---

[10]See *Dialectic of Enlightenment*, in which Adorno and Horkheimer develop the theory that the rationalization of society "did not lead progressively to a rational social order, but instead to new structures of domination in the forms of monopoly capitalism and political totalitarianism" (Buck-Morss 61).

porters in Germany. The Germanophile, he explains, is a person who wants Germany to win the war, but does not know anything about German culture: "He tenido el candor de conversar con muchos germanófilos argentinos; he intentado hablar de Alemania y de lo indestructible alemán; he mencionado a Holderlin, a Lutero, a Shopenhauer o a Leibnitz; he comprobado que el interlocutor 'germanófilo' apenas identificaba esos nombres" (*Textos cautivos* 336).[11] The Germanophile does not know what Germany is and his hatred for England is the only reason why he is in favor of Hitler, concludes Borges, in allusion to the resentment against British imperialism that was predominant in Argentina during that time: "Al germanófilo le entristece muchísimo que las compañías de ferrocarriles de cierta república sudamericana tengan accionistas ingleses" (*Textos cautivos* 336).[12] Germanophiles are also antisemitic, which for Borges is only another proof of the irrationality of their ideology. For Borges it is a contradiction that "[el germanófilo] quiere expulsar de nuestro país a una comunidad eslavogermánica en la que predominan apellidos de origen alemán (Rosenblatt, Gruenberg, Nierenstein, Lilienthal) y que habla un dialecto alemán: el *yiddish* o *juedisch*" (*Textos cautivos* 336; *Reader* 336).[13] Borges concludes his article with a portrait of the psychology of those Argentines that support Nazism:

> Descubro, siempre, que mi interlocutor idolatra a Hitler, no a pesar de las bombas cenitales y de las invasiones fulmíneas, de las ametralladoras, de las delaciones y de los perjurios, sino a

---

[11]"I have tried to talk about Germany and German indestructibility; I have mentioned Hölderlin, Luther, Shopenhauer, and Leibniz; I have ascertained that the Germanophile interlocutor barely identified those names." (*Reader* 128)

[12]"The Germanophile is quite unhappy that the railroad companies of a certain South American republic have English stockholders." (*Reader* 128)

[13]"[the Germanophile] wishes to expel from our country a Slavo-Germanic community in which names of German origin predominates (Rosenblatt, Gruenberg, Nierenstein, Lilienthal) and which speaks a German dialect-Yiddish or Jüdish."

causa de esas costumbres y de esos instrumentos. Le alegra lo malvado, lo atroz. La victoria germánica no le importa; quieren la humillación de Inglaterra, el satisfactorio incendio de Londres. Admira a Hitler como ayer admiraba a sus precursores en el submundo criminal de Chicago... El hitlerista, siempre, es un rencoroso, un adorador secreto, y a veces público, de la "viveza" forajida y de la crueldad. Es, por penuria imaginativa, un hombre que postula que el porvenir no puede diferir del presente, y que Alemania, victoriosa hasta ahora, no puede empezar a perder. Es el hombre ladino que anhela estar de parte de los que vencen. (*Textos cautivos* 337)[14]

The change in Borges's discourse that can be detected in this article (his first direct attack on Nazi ideology) suggests that he began to recognize that his earlier textual strategy for dealing with this political problem, that is, showing the facts and letting the reader use common sense to see the "truth" about fascism, was not effective. Not only did the Germanophiles, as Borges describes them in his 1940 essay, lack common sense (and therefore were not able to see the "irrationality" of fascism that was so clear to Borges), but also they could not understand how Nazism was "destroying" the German culture since they did not know anything about that culture to begin with.

---

[14]"I always discover that my interlocutor idolizes Hitler, not in spite of the zenithal bombs and the fulminous invasions, the machine guns, accusations, and perjuries, but because of those customs and those instruments. He is cheered by wickedness and atrocity. Germanic victory does not matter to him; he wants the humiliation of England, the satisfactory burning of London. He admires Hitler as yesterday he admired his precursors in Chicago's criminal underworld. . . . The Hitlerist is a spiteful man, and a secret and sometimes public admirer of vicious cleverness and cruelty. Because of his imaginative penury, he is a man who postulates that the future cannot differ from the present, and that Germany, victorious until now, cannot begin to lose. He is a cunning man who longs to be on the winners' side." (*Reader* 129)

If anything, this short piece records Borges's thoughts about one of the major mysteries of the period: the popularity of fascism. The rapid spread of this ideology throughout the world and the support that fascist political movements found among the masses as well as from many artists and intellectuals is a phenomenon that has been amply studied. Needless to say that many theories have been developed as an attempt to explain the rise of fascism, especially the coming to power of Nazism in Germany.[15] Borges was definitely not alone in trying to understand the powerful attraction of fascism. Understanding this ideology, for example, and antisemitism as an expression of it, became one of the major concerns of the Frankfurt School during the 1940s. Of the many studies on the subject that were made by the members of the group perhaps the most important one was *The Authoritarian Personality* (1950), which consisted of a social study of the psychology of fascist and antifascist personalities. According to this study, the authoritarian personality type is characterized by "conformism, sexual repression, false projection, authoritarian submission which [alternate] with aggressive domination, a lack of critical reflection and stereotypy" (Buck-Morss 181). Like Borges's Germanophiles, they are susceptible to political-authoritarian manipulation. Those who like Borges were antifascist, were described in the study as critical and nonconforming individuals. It is interesting to compare Borges's conclusions at the end of "Portrait of a Germanophile" with one of the techniques of fascist propaganda analyzed by Adorno and called *fait accompli*. In his introduction to a recent collection of articles by Adorno, the critic Stephen Crook gives an explanation of this technique:

> In fascist propaganda the movement has unstoppable momentum, the leader has unconquerable strength, and a final blood thirsty settling of accounts with the enemy is inevitable. The technique has many superficial attractions: people want to be associated with a successful concern and are likely to think

---

[15]See Kershaw's brief summary of some of these theories and the problems related to the concept of fascism (*Nazi Dictatorship* 22-39).

twice before opposing it. However, the technique has an objective basis in the fact that "to most people their life actually is decided in advance." By resonating with this experience "the fait accompli technique . . . touches upon one of the central mechanisms of the mass psychology of fascism: the transformation of one's feeling of one's own impotence into a feeling of strength." That feeling arises "mysteriously and irrationally" from the acknowledgment of weakness and identification with the victor. ("Introduction" 11)

These are exactly the ideological traits that Borges identified in the Germanophiles. He too noticed in the Argentine fascists' thinking a desire to be "on the winner's side" and the view that Germany's victory was inevitable. Borges was obviously not engaged in a serious sociological research about the nature of fascism, but like everybody else at the time he was trying to understand it. In "Portrait of a Germanophile" as well as in later texts, he presents those who favor fascism as largely uneducated people (they do not know any of the German literature that he values so highly), irrational (there is no logic in their arguments), and extremely nationalistic.[16] On the other hand, those who like Bor-

---

[16]In the story "A Celebration of the Monster," which I will analyze later on in this chapter, the main character fits perfectly this description. Even though the character is not a "Nazi" in the strict sense of the term, he exhibits all the characteristics that Borges attributes to the Germanophiles in this essay; like them, he shows fascist tendencies in his behavior. In "*Deutsches Requiem*" (*Obras* 1.576-81), on the other hand, Borges writes about an extremely well-educated man, who is also a Nazi. One should not overlook the fact that whereas the latter is European, the former is South American. Even though any type of antisemitism seemed ridiculous to Borges, he "understood" the origin of European antisemitism, but not of the Argentine one. In a 1940 preface to the book of poetry *Mester de Judería* by Carlos M. Grünberg, Borges compares both versions of antisemitism:

En Alemania cuya lengua literaria se basa en la versión de textos hebreos que ha legado Lutero, Hitler no hace otra cosa

ges and his friends from the *Sur* group oppose fascism, are very well educated and appreciate foreign cultures. Borges was, of course, very well aware that there were intellectuals who were also attracted to fascism, but he rarely mentioned them.[17] The opposition antifascism/fascism had become one of culture/barbarism and internationalism/nationalism in his discourse.

I want to argue that one of the effects that the events during this historical period had on Borges was that of distancing him from democratic political positions. Since by making this statement I am one step away from repeating the common accusations of "elitism" that were often leveled against Borges, it is important to avoid this by reconstructing the different stages that his political thinking went through. Besides the controversial opinions that Borges expressed in the numerous interviews that he gave since the early 1970s, another justification for these accusations of "elitism"—in this case one related to the structure of his writings—is the presence of an extreme individualism that shapes his fantastic short stories. This aspect of Borges's work is more

---

que exacerbar un odio preexistente; el antisemitismo argentino viene a ser un facsímil atolondrado que ignora lo étnico y lo histórico. (*Prólogos* 77)

(In Germany, whose literary language is based on Luther's version of some Hebrew texts, Hitler is only exacerbating a preexisting hatred; Argentine antisemitism is only a bad imitation of the German one and ignores ethnic and historical facts).

Then he goes on to suggest that most Argentines have Jewish ancestors.

[17]Borges ridiculed Marinetti's inventions in the pages of *El Hogar* (*Textos cautivos* 212-13) but did not mention anything about his politics. An interesting case is his evaluation of Carlyle. Even though this was a writer that Borges admired and who greatly influenced his work, in his prologue to a 1949 Spanish translation of Carlyle's *On Heroes and Hero Worship*, Borges criticized the author's proto-fascism (*Prólogos* 34-39).

evident in his creation of an original private style that emphasizes the individuality of the subject and imitates the way a person's mind understands reality, but it can be seen as well in other components of his fictional work. For example, it has been noticed that his fantastic tales are constructed around a single view of reality and that all of Borges's characters seem to "speak" in the same tone of voice (they all use Borges's exaggerated paratactic style) without taking into account their cultural background or social class (Marcos, "Reseña" 707). One could say Borges's voice predominates over all the others; he does not allow anyone else to speak. "Borges," comments Alfred Kazin, "has built his work, and I suspect his life itself, out of the same effort to make himself a home in his own mind" (129). Describing Borges's fantastic short stories as solipsistic is perhaps not an exaggeration.

Borges's extreme individualism is interpreted too often as an example of his rejection of the masses and popular culture in general. However, if one looks back at Borges's early writings, it is possible to see that his individualism always coexisted with an interest in mass culture and popular politics. The origin of his individualism can be traced back to the influence that Expressionism, with its subjective view of art and the world, had on him as a young artist in Europe. But even for the young Borges the emphasis on subjectivity went hand in hand with the idea of a "brotherhood of men" and by no means was a monad-like individualism. Once he was back in Buenos Aires, Borges continued to be preoccupied with the concept of the self as a philosophical problem in essays like "The Nothingness of Personality," which he included in his first book of prose, *Inquisiciones* (84-95). At the same time, during that period he wrote books of essays and poetry about topics that he associated with the Argentine popular culture of the 1920s: the tango, slums, hoodlums. And in 1930 he wrote a book about a popular poet, Evaristo Carriego. More importantly, he supported the popular politics of Hipólito Irigoyen and praised in his writings the charismatic leader Juan Manuel de Rosas, Argentina's nineteenth-century *caudillo*, calling him "our greatest man" (Borges, *El tamaño de mi esperanza* 8; qtd. in Rodríguez Monegal, *Literary Biography* 206). The important place that, after working for *Crítica* in the early 1930s, Borges started to give to popular forms of fictions (e.g., detective stories, adventure tales) as well as his desire to erase the boundaries between high brow/low brow literature, show that his individualism was not a reflection of any type of "elitist" position during the first part of his career as a writer. In 1933 it was possible for Borges to write a story like "Street Corner Man" in which he seems to be suggesting that some sort of collective action must be taken by the people at a moment of political and economic crisis in Argentina, because he did not see a conflict between his individualism and his interest in popular (cultural and political) movements. No doubt there is an individualistic element in Borges that was part of his ideology from the very beginning of his career, and perhaps one could analyze his writings as the result of a conflict between that aspect of his thought and his interest for popular culture. One could even argue that in his early work Borges remained unconscious of the conflict between his individualistic ideology and the popular culture that he was promoting with his writings. It will not be until after experiencing the "fascist decade" of the 1940s that Borges begins to distance himself from "mass" culture. And one can see the conflict surfacing in a short essay that Borges wrote after the liberation of Paris, entitled "A Comment on August 23, 1944," when in the middle of a massive celebration, he mentions how he has discovered for the first time that "una emoción colectiva puede no ser innoble" (*Obras* 2.105).[18] The distinction that he made between the intellectual's and the masses' reaction to fascism is another example of this unconscious problem manifesting itself. I wish to show that even during this period, which is when Borges's individualism becomes the predominant characteristic of his fictional writing, Borges *still* believed in the possibility of collective political action.

The defeat of Nazism in Europe did not mean the end of Borges's fight against fascism. By 1945, in Argentina, Juan Domingo Perón had become an extremely popular political leader who counted on the support of thousands of workers. Borges compared these developments in local politics to the situation that preceded the rise of Nazism in

---

[18]"a collective emotion can be noble." (*Other Inquisitions* 134)

Germany. In an interview given that year to an Uruguayan newspaper, he expressed his concerns about the changes going on in Argentina:

> The [political] situation in Argentina is very serious, so serious that a great number of Argentines are becoming Nazis without being aware of it. Tempted by promises of social reform—in a society that undoubtedly needs a better organization than the one it now has—many people are letting themselves be seduced by an outside wave of hatred that is sweeping the country. It is a terrible thing, similar to what happened at the beginning of fascism and Nazism [in Europe]. But I must add that Argentine intellectuals are against it. . . . Nevertheless, I am pessimistic about a more or less speedy return of the Argentine government to democracy. (*La plata*, Montevideo, October 31, 1945. qtd. in Rodríguez Monegal, *Literary Biography* 391)

The difference between the intellectuals' and the masses' reaction to fascism, which Borges had already mentioned in "Portrait of a Germanophile," is again highlighted in this paragraph: while the masses are being seduced by the figure of Perón and his "fascist" politics, intellectuals are against him. But, as we are going to see, this does not yet mean that Borges has lost "faith" in the Argentine people. When the next year Perón is predictably elected president (1946), Borges is forced to resign from his job as a library clerk, probably as a result of having written articles like "Portrait of a Germanophile." In order to humiliate him, the new government "promoted" him from librarian to inspector of poultry and rabbits in a public market. As a sort of reparation, his friends in The Argentine Society of Letters organized a dinner in his honor. There Borges read a short text, "Hurry, Hurry!," in which he again interpreted the current regime in Argentina as a continuation of European Nazism: "el nazismo, arrojado de Berlín, buscó nuevas regiones" (*Ficcionario* 223).[19] And he asked Argentines to oppose the government:

> las dictaduras fomentan la opresión, las dictaduras fomentan el servilismo, las dictaduras fomentan la crueldad; más abominable es el hecho de que fomentan la idiotez. Botones que balbucean imperativos, efigies de caudillos, vivas y mueras prefijados, muros exornados de nombres, ceremonias unánimes, la mera disciplina usurpando el lugar de la lucidez... Combatir esas tristes monotonías es uno de los muchos deberes del escritor. ¿Habré de recordar a los lectores de *Martín Fierro* y de *Don Segundo [Sombra]* que el individualismo es una vieja virtud argentina? (*Ficcionario* 224)[20]

When asserting that a writer has the "duty" to fight against fascism, Borges was accepting that a writer has a social responsibility. It is a remarkable statement if one considers that only a few years before he was attacking Breton and Diego Rivera's manifesto for a revolutionary art (*Textos cautivos* 287-88). More important than his acceptance that there is a link between society and art is that Borges is proposing a strategy to combat fascism: to remember what he calls traditional Argentine individualism. The proposal, which is one that Borges had been trying to put in practice in his fantastic tales, is that a defense of individualism is the best resistance to fascism. The idea of using individualism as a "collective action" against fascism is developed further in another essay

---

[19]"Nazis, driven out of Berlin, sought refuge elsewhere." (*Reader* 173)

[20]"[D]ictatorships foster oppression, dictatorships foster servitude, dictatorships foster cruelty; more abominable is the fact that they foster idiocy. Hotel clerks mumbling orders, effigies of caudillos, prearranged 'long live's' and 'down with's,' walls embellished with names, unanimous ceremonies, mere discipline substituting for lucidity. . . . To combat such monotonies is among the writer's many duties. Do I have to remind readers of *Martín Fierro* and *Don Segundo [Sombra]* that individuality is an old Argentine virtue?" (*Reader* 173).

written later that year, "Our Poor Individualism" (1946). In this essay Borges explains that by tradition the Argentine does not identify himself (or herself) with the State. But instead of seeing this as a negative trait that can lead to social chaos, he sees it (under the circumstances) as a positive one:

> Se dirá que los rasgos que he señalado son meramente negativos o anárquicos; se añadirá que no son capaces de explicación política. Me atrevo a sugerir lo contrario. El más urgente de los problemas de nuestra época (ya denunciado con profética lucidez por el casi olvidado Spencer) es la gradual intromisión del Estado en los actos del individuo; en la lucha con ese mal, cuyos nombres son comunismo y nazismo, el individualismo argentino, acaso inútil o perjudicial hasta ahora, encontrará justificación y deberes. (*Obras* 2.37)[21]

Curiously, Borges is once again appealing to his countrymen's nationalistic feelings as he did in "Street Corner Man," because for him individualism is the most typical Argentine trait. It should be pointed out that two views of nationalism are set against one another here: there is a "bad" nationalism that results in the fascist ideology that brought Perón to power and a "good" one that encourages individualism, therefore, antifascism. Paradoxically, to be against the State is to be nationalistic. This double view of nationalism explains to a certain point the two irreconcilable interpretations of the gaucho figure that we find around

---

[21]Perhaps someone will say that the qualities I have mentioned here [i.e., Argentine individualism] are merely negative or anarchical ones, and will add that they are not capable of political application. I venture to suggest that the opposite is true. The most urgent problem of our time (already proclaimed with prophetical clarity by the almost forgotten Spencer) is the gradual interference of the State in the acts of the individual; in the struggle against evil—called communism or fascism—Argentine individualism, which has perhaps been useless or even harmful up to now, would find justification and positive value (*Other Inquisitions* 34-35).

the mid-1940s in Borges's work. While in "Hurry, Hurry!" he saw the gaucho as an example of Argentine individualism, a couple of years earlier, in 1943, he had written "Conjectural poem," in which he narrates the story of one of his ancestors, Francisco Narciso Laprida, who participated in Argentina's civil war. In the poem the victory of the gauchos over Laprida symbolizes the victory of barbarism over civilization:

> Vencen los bárbaros, los gauchos vencen.
> Yo, que estudié las leyes y los cánones,
> yo, Francisco Narciso de Laprida,
> cuya voz declaró la independencia
> de estas crueles provincias, derrotado,
> de sangre y de sudor manchado en el rostro,
> sin esperanza ni temor, perdido,
> huyo hacia en Sur por arrabales últimos. (*Obras* 2.245)[22]

Here the gaucho is seen by Borges as a symbol of the "bad" nationalism that was leading the country towards fascism (for related interpretations of this poem, see Rodríguez-Luis 173-74 and Rodríguez Monegal, *Literary Biography* 376-77). The gaucho then could be used to represent the two options that Argentina had at that moment: fascism or liberalism.

Perhaps Borges did not realize that one of the sources of fascism's popularity was the same anti-individualism that he was criticizing. As the critic Howard Williams explains, fascism was able to attract massive support because it offered certainty and economic stability in an increasingly chaotic modern world. It must be remembered that the

---

[22]"The gauchos have won: / victory is theirs, the barbarians'. / I, Francisco Narciso Laprida, / who studied both canon law and civil / and whose voice declared the independence / of this untamed territory, / in defeat, my face marked by blood and sweat, / holding neither hope nor fear, the way lost, / strike out for the South through the back country." (*Poems* 83)

economic progress brought about by modernization also had as a result a dislocation in the social life of the Western world. The anonymity and impersonalization of life caused by the process of urbanization had disastrous consequences for those individuals who were not able to adjust to it. "Fascist ideology," says Williams, "was able to give the individual a sense of purpose and belonging in a troubled world" (60). Fascists were opposed

> to the atomism of modern society. They resented the individualist and competitive nature of modern industrial society and wanted to hark back to feudal times where the individual was integrated through his job into the system of states and, therefore, the state itself. Fascists wanted to re-create that organic connection between the individual and the state in modern society. Thus corporate rather than individual representation was integral to their nationalism. (68)

Fascism was in many ways the result of the impact of modernization on the European society.[23] And at a moment of economic unbalance it certainly represented for many an alternative to the capitalist and socialist models of modernization, but this was not a modernization project that Borges could support. Borges was defending the classical liberal position that the state should not interfere with a citizen's private life. For the liberal, the role of the state is that of resolving and regulating conflicts that may arise from the clash of individual interests. Fascists, however, could not accept this liberal dichotomy between the private and the public, which for them only lead to a denigration of the state (Williams, *Concepts* 70).

---

[23]"Apart from the nation and the state," argues Howard Williams, "the Fascists put everything else in doubt. They were prepared to wipe the slate clean. Unlike all the other political parties and movements, they were wholly modernist. If necessary, they were prepared to sunder all connection with the past" (60). For a summary and a critique of the theories that see Nazism in particular as originating in the problems of modernization in Germany, see Kershaw 131-49.

One should notice that Perón's rise to power was for Borges a second moment of crisis in Argentina's contemporary history, similar in his mind to the one that took place in 1929. And just as in 1933 with the writing of "Street Corner Man," Borges reacted to the crisis by suggesting that some sort of collective action needed to be taken by the Argentine people, he was in 1946, once again, issuing a "call" to the Argentine people to act and help the country get out of the crisis. He was going as far as saying (in "Hurry, Hurry!") that Argentine writers have the responsibility to take a stand against totalitarian governments. But the political strategy that Borges was proposing to combat fascism was, to say the least, a very paradoxical one. The "collective" action to be taken was that of behaving "individualistically."

For Borges, developing this political strategy was an important step in solving an artistic/ideological contradiction. The commitment to a collective political objective that he was requesting from Argentine writers was in conflict with the individualism that had always been present in his writings but that began to acquire prominence in the fantastic fiction that he started to write around 1939, as a response to the emergence of European fascism. The action of withdrawing into one's private world as a rejection of totalitarianism, which is what the narrator of "Tlön, Uqbar, Orbis Tertius" suggests at the end of the story, can hardly be seen as an effective way of combating it. On the contrary, it could be criticized as leading to political quietism. In 1946, feeling the presence of "fascism" now at home, it became obvious to Borges that something more than a personal reaction and a defense of one's individualism were needed. How could Borges as a writer advocate any type of collective political action against the Peronist regime without renouncing his individualist ideology? Would he have to start writing a different type of literature? One would think that in a moment like this Borges would become aware of the limitations of his ideology. However, instead of facing the contradiction of his way of thinking, he looks for a way to "solve" it. Thus, Borges found a *political* strategy that allowed him to become a committed writer and fight against fascism without renouncing the *textual* strategy that he had been employing in his fiction. The view that if everyone embraces that "old Argentine virtue" that is individualism they will be free from fascism is for Borges a justification of his ideological and aesthetic thinking. It solves the contradiction between his individualism and his desire to become a committed writer who promotes collective action in a moment of social crisis. He can be both solipsistic and politically engaged at the same time without perceiving any problems in adopting this position.

One of the reasons why he was able to find this aesthetic/political solution to his conflict was because he had already redefined the concept of "commitment" or "social responsibility" in literature. What should an Argentine writer do in this moment of crisis? Borges was certainly not saying in "Hurry, Hurry!" that they had to start criticizing the Perón regime and writing political pamphlets. Borges's writings are an example of the type of commitment that he was requesting from other writers. All he asked—and practiced in his own work—was a defense of the individualism that "fascism" was trying to destroy in Argentina. I have already mentioned that one of the ways in which Borges creates this sense of individuality is by placing himself, his own subjective view of reality at the center of his stories. Another aspect of his literary practice that contributes to create the impression of individuality is one whose political meaning is very often misunderstood: the creation of fictional texts that apparently are completely autonomous from the real world. Autonomous art is art that is free from religious, political, commercial, or any other social roles (Bürger 35-54). For Borges, an author's individuality is asserted by the invention of an entirely self-sufficient, monad-like world. A narrative technique employed by Borges in the creation of autonomous art consists in writing fantastic short stories. The fantastic nature of the events in these stories distances them from the real world. And they must have seemed even more unreal to Borges's countrymen when they were published because most of these fictions are set in exotic or faraway places. It is the combination of unreal events and "exotic" places that disconnects Borges's fictional world from that of everyday life. More than any other aspect of his work, Borges's conception of literature as an autonomous task has helped create the impression that his writings are devoid of political meaning. "Borges's work is a prodigious artifice," says the critic Jaime Alazraki, repeating the common perception of these writings, "an iridescent language, a self-contained form severed from historical reality"

(*Kabbalah* 187). The content of his fantastic short stories may not have anything to do with Argentina's social reality but their form carries a definite political meaning. A fictional representation of Borges's understanding of the complex relationship between the autonomous artwork and society can be found in "The Secret Miracle." This is the story of Jaromir Hladík, a Jewish writer and translator, who is arrested when the Third Reich invades Czechoslovakia in 1939. Hladík has only written one fictional work, a play entitled *The Enemies*, which he has left unfinished. While waiting in his cell to be executed by the Nazi army, Hladík asks God for another year of life to finish his play. Moments before he is executed, he is granted his wish. Time stands still but continues to pass in Hladík's mind. Nothing moves, but he can think. Thus, he has a year, in his mind, to finish his play. He "rewrites" in his mind the play, adding or changing words and dialogues. As soon as he finishes, he is killed by the firing squad which has suddenly regained movement. Hladík's play is the most perfect example of literary autonomy: he was not "writing" for anyone but himself; his play will never be printed and will have no readers. It is a purposeless work of art. But at the same time the act of composing this play is an individual's rebellion against a fascist government. The social reality that is altering Jaromir Hladík's life cannot interfere with the completely autonomous work of art that he has created inside his mind. The story is, if you like, an allegory of Borges's own writing practice. In 1946 Borges was suggesting to Argentine writers that they should follow a similar writing strategy to the one that he had been using for several years: that is, the creation of a literary work that in its content does not directly criticize the social changes taking place but whose mere autonomous existence is a critique of society. It is in the form of Borges's stories, not in their content, where social criticism makes its appearance. What Adorno said about autonomous literary works in another context can easily be applied here to Borges: "Even in the most sublimated work of art there is a hidden 'it should be otherwise.' [The moment of true volition] is mediated through nothing other than the form of the work itself, whose crystallization becomes an analogy of that other condition which should be" ("Commitment" 194). By attempting to be free, independent in a world that was suppressing individual freedom, Borges's stories were showing how the world should be.

But, then, was Borges putting in doubt the political efficacy of this aesthetic theory when a year later he wrote "A Celebration of the Monster" (1947)? This story, which circulated anonymously around Buenos Aires during Perón's government, is about a man who is going to participate in a demonstration in honor of the president: "All the story's sordid details," comments Rodríguez Monegal, "bare out Perón's demagogic arrangement of 'spontaneous' demonstrations in support of his regime" ("Politics" 68). The climax of the narration occurs when the demonstrators kill a young Jewish intellectual, not before forcing him into singing Peronist slogans. Unlike the other stories that Borges wrote during this period, there is nothing fantastic about this one. It is written in a realistic style and with the sole intention of criticizing the government in power. It is, in fact, almost a political pamphlet. "A Celebration" is an example of the kind of political literature that Borges was always criticizing, which leads us back to the question of why he decided to show his political position with this type of literary text. This story must be compared to the essay "Portrait of a Germanophile" in both their intentions and the events that surrounded their geneses. In both cases Borges breaks away from his traditional idea that a literary text should allude to a political position rather than express it directly. We saw this idea at work in his antifascist writings and in his fantastic short stories. Like "Portrait of a Germanophile," the anonymous story about Perón's supporters was produced at a moment of "despair," when fascism was apparently having a dangerous success. When he writes "Portrait" the Nazi army seemed unstoppable. Similarly, he writes "A Celebration" at a moment in his life when he feels personally persecuted by the new (to him fascist) government.[24]

---

[24]Rodríguez Monegal gives an impressive description of this period of Borges's life (1946-49) and his paranoid behavior. So convinced was Borges of the fascist nature of Perón's government that Rodríguez Monegal did not dare to disagree with him: "[I wanted] to argue that Perón was more than a mediocre tyrant," says Rodríguez Monegal remembering their conversations, "that he represented something com-

When did Borges's political thinking begin to change? It is difficult to say. Up to 1949, one can find texts in which he sees democracy as the alternative to fascism. In his preface to the Spanish translation of Carlyle's *On Heroes*, Borges lists among those aspects of Carlyle's thought that he finds unacceptable because he considers them an anticipation of fascism is Carlyle's rejection of democratic governments (*Prólogos* 36). By 1955, when Perón is no longer in power, Borges is not writing fiction any more, and he is beginning to write poetry again (his last fantastic short story from this period was "The South" [1953]. He will not return to fiction again until 1967 when he writes "The Intruder"). He had also become almost totally blind by then. Not only did he change from fiction to poetry during these years but he also changed, in his poetry, from free verse to regular verse. Borges has explained these changes as a consequence of his blindness (poetry written in classical metrics is easier to remember ["Autobiographical Essay" 250]). But when in 1970 he published a new volume of fiction (*Dr. Brodie's Report*), he also went back to a classic realist style and wrote a preface to it in which he attacked nationalist political parties. This new change in the form of his writings, that is, the return to more traditional styles in prose and poetry, is a sign of the transformation that his political thinking underwent during the years after the end of the Peronist government.

In 1974, a year after Perón returned to power, Borges wrote an "Epilogue" to the edition of his *Complete Works* published by Emecé. This short text is an entry for an imaginary encyclopedia that, Borges explains, will be published in Buenos Aires in the year 2074. The entry is about Borges himself and, in a way, it is a condensed autobiography:

---

pletely different for the workers and the poor, that he introduced new and necessary social laws, that he was trying (perhaps unsuccessfully) to liberate Argentina from foreign powers. I wanted to tell him that the sinister Buenos Aires of his tales and nightmares hardly existed in reality. . . . But how can one establish a dialogue with a dreamer?" (*Literary Biography* 397)

[Borges] pensaba que el valor es una de las pocas virtudes de que son capaces los hombres, pero su culto lo llevó, como tantos otros, a la veneración atolondrada de los hombres del hampa. Así, el más leído de sus cuentos fue "Hombre de la esquina rosada", cuyo narrador es un asesino... Su secreto y acaso inconsciente afán fue tramar la mitología de un Buenos Aires, que jamás existió. Así, a lo largo de los años, contribuyó sin saberlo y sin sospecharlo a esa exaltación de la barbarie que culminó en el culto del gaucho, de Artigas y de Rosas. (*Obras* 3.506)[25]

The name of Perón should be added to the list since Borges saw in his never-ending battle against the Peronist government a continuation of his forefathers' resistance to the government of Rosas in the nineteenth century. It is not surprising that the only one of his stories that is mentioned is "Street Corner Man," given the symbolic meaning that it has for him. In fact, he indirectly mentions most of his prose and poetry from the 1920s up to *Evaristo Carriego*, but none of the work for which he was already well known in 1974. What is surprising, however, is the sense of guilt with which Borges talks about this story ("Street Corner Man") and his pre-1930 production. His mention of the criminal underworld as one of the topics that he felt attracted to when he was a young man should remind us his own description of the Germanophile: "[El gemanófilo] admira a Hitler como ayer admiraba a sus

---

[25]"[Borges] used to think that courage was one of the few virtues of which men are capable, but his worship of courage led him, and many others, to the thoughtless adoration of the underworld [*hombres del hampa*]. Thus, the most popular of his short stories was "Street Corner Man," whose narrator is a murderer. . . . His secret and perhaps unconscious desire was to create a mythology for a Buenos Aires that never existed. Thus, throughout the years, without knowing or suspecting it, he contributed to that praising of barbarism that in the end resulted in the cult of the gaucho, the cult of Artigas and that of Rosas."

precursores en el submundo criminal de Chicago" (*Textos cautivos* 337).[26] When Borges admits having contributed through his pre-1930 writings to foster barbarism, he is also expressing his guilt about having contributed—without knowing about it—to the rise of fascism. In the poem "Nineteen Hundred and Twenty-Odd" (published in *Dreamtigers* [1960]), Borges was already seeing a connection between his literary projects of the 1920s and the "fascist" government of the 1940s in Argentina:

> La rueda de los astros no es infinita
> Y el tigre es una de las formas que vuelven,
> Pero nosotros, lejos del azar y de la aventura,
> Nos creíamos desterrados a un tiempo exhausto,
> El tiempo en el que nada puede ocurrir.
> El universo, el trágico universo, no estaba aquí
> Y fuerza era buscarlo en los ayeres;
> Yo tramaba una humilde mitología de tapias y cuchillos
> Y Ricardo pensaba en sus reseros.
> No sabíamos que el porvenir encerraba el rayo,
> No presentimos el oprobio, el incendio y la tremenda noche de la Alianza;
> Nada nos dijo que la historia argentina echaría a andar por las calles,
> La historia, la indignación, el amor,
> Las muchedumbres como el mar, el nombre de Córdoba,
> El sabor de lo real y de lo increíble, el horror y la gloria. (*Obras* 2.211)[27]

---

[26] "[The Germanophile] admires Hitler as yesterday he admired his precursors in Chicago's criminal underworld." (*Reader* 129)

[27] "The wheeling of the stars is not infinite / And the tiger is one of the forms that return, / But we, remote from chance or hazard, / Believed we were exiles in a time outworn, / Time when nothing can hap-

The poem contrasts his innocence as a young artist with the political events of decades later (Perón coming to power and later being overthrown by a "revolution" that started in the city of Córdoba). Here too his desire to create a "mythology" for Buenos Aires based on popular culture is presented as somehow linked to the emergence of totalitarian regimes. In the same book he included a brief text ("The Sham") about a man in a small town who stages a sort of play in which he represents a Perón grieving for the death of Eva Duarte, who, in turn, is represented by a blond doll in a cardboard box. The people from the town come to see "Perón" and pay their respects. Borges comments:

> El enlutado no era Perón y la muñeca rubia no era la mujer Eva Duarte, pero tampoco Perón era Perón ni Eva era Eva sino desconocidos o anónimos (cuyo nombre secreto y cuyo rostro verdadero ignoramos) que figuraron, para el crédulo amor de los arrabales, una crasa mitología. (*Obras* 2.167)[28]

Perón and Eva became part of Argentina's mythology, and, of course, these were developments that Borges could not foresee in the 1920s. These examples show that many of the ideas that we find Borges's

---

pen. / The universe, the tragic universe, was not here / And maybe should be looked for somewhere else; / I hatched a humble mythology of fencing walls and knives / And Ricardo thought of his drovers. / We did not know that time came to held a lightning bolt; / We did not foresee the shame, the fire, and the fearful night of the Alliance; / Nothing told us that Argentine history would be thrust out to walk the streets, / History, indignation, love, / The multitudes like the sea, the name of Córdoba, / The flavor of the real and the incredible, the horror and the glory." (*Dreamtigers* 79)

[28]"The mourner was not Perón and the blond doll was not the woman Eva Duarte, but neither was Perón Perón, nor was Eva Eva. They were, rather, unknown individuals—or anonymous ones whose secret names and true faces we do not know—who acted out, for the credulous love of the lower middle classes, a crass mythology." (*Dreamtigers* 31)

expressing in the 1970s were developed much earlier and as a reaction to the government of Perón (these two texts that I have mentioned above were probably written in the late 1950s. It is clear that after experiencing the Perón regime Borges no longer tried to distinguish between a "good" type of nationalism and a "bad" one. In the 1940s fascism was barbaric and so it was a certain kind of nationalism that supported fascist governments. By the early 1970s, Borges classifies any type of nationalism as barbarism. Once again his view of nationalism is symbolically represented through his interpretation of one of Argentina's national symbols: the gaucho. When in 1946 Borges analyzed the gaucho figure, he saw it as either representing barbarism or as a positive symbol of Argentine individualism. The gaucho embodied the two different paths that Argentina could follow: totalitarianism (barbarism) or liberalism (individualism). By 1974, in the "Epilogue" to his *Complete Works*, on the other hand, the gaucho appears next to the name of Rosas, two figures in which Borges tried to see positive values in the past, and both of them have now become symbols of barbarism.[29] Within the logic of this 1974 text, Borges's earlier appreciation of popular culture led to nationalism and nationalism, in turn, led to barbarism. Borges can thus unfairly equate popular culture (and politics) to nationalism and fascism. For him leaving political decisions in the hands of the people could only lead to totalitarian regimes. Only a Borges whose political thinking had become so narrow could say in the "Preface" to *La moneda de hierro* (1976): "Me sé del todo indigno de opinar en materia política, pero tal vez me sea perdonado añadir que descreo de la democracia, ese curioso abuso de la estadís-

---

[29]Borges had already returned in his short story "The South" (*Obras* 1.525-30) from 1953 to the same interpretation of the gaucho as representing barbarism that he used in "Conjectural Poem" (1943). It is not surprising that he went back to a pessimistic attitude around this time, since 1953 was witness to some of the most repressive acts by the Peronist regime, including the incarceration of Victoria Ocampo, editor of the magazine *Sur* and a friend of Borges (Rodríguez Luis 173).

tica" (*Obras* 3.122-23).³⁰ His support of dictatorships during his later years can be understood as the result of his fear that popular movements and democratic processes only lead to fascism.³¹

Another event that influenced this ideological change was Borges's final acknowledgment of the incompatibility of his individualism and popular culture/politics. The conflict, as we have seen, had been present in his work from the very beginning of his career, but Borges's ideology managed to hide all the contradictions that could have forced him to recognize it. Even in moments of crisis when it was evident that his individualistic position was at odds with any type of collective action, Borges found a way to avoid accepting this. In his stories and interviews from the 1970s it is clear the path that he has chosen. In "The Other" (*The Book of Sand* [1975]), a Borges of over seventy years of age imagines a conversation with a much younger Borges, probably around twenty years old. With the depiction of the improbable conversation between these "two" characters, Borges wants to show us how much his artistic and political ideas have changed. The young Borges mentions that he is writing a book that will be called *Red Hymns* or *Red Rhythms*:

> [M]e aclaró que su libro cantaría la fraternidad de todos los hombres. El poeta de nuestro tiempo no puede darle la espalda a su época. Me quedé pensando y le pregunté si verdaderamente se sentía hermano de todos. Por ejemplo, de todos los empresarios de pompas fúnebres, de todos los carteros, de todos los buzos, de todos los que viven en la acera de los nú-

---

³⁰"I know I am not qualified to talk about politics, but perhaps you will allow me to say that I do not believe in democracy, that strange abuse of statistics."

³¹After Argentina's defeat in the Falkland Islands war, the military dictatorship was replaced by a new democratic government. In 1985 Borges gave one of his last interviews to María Esther Vázquez, and in it he admitted being mistaken when he praised the military government. He also said that after seeing the Argentine people electing Alfonsín as president he recovered his faith in democracy (Vázquez 229-42).

meros pares, de todos los afónicos, etcétera. Me dijo que su libro se refería a la gran masa de los oprimidos y parias. (*Obras* 3:14)[32]

But the Borges of the seventies can no longer support popular movements or politics. He has come to realize the incompatibility of this political position with his individualistic ideology: "Tu masa de oprimidos y de parias...no es más que una abstracción. Sólo individuos existen, si es que existe alguien" (*Obras* 3.14).[33] This rejection of mass culture and popular political movements becomes a rejection of democracy, which for Borges, by putting political power in the hands of the people, may in the end help (or lead to) fascism. In the 1970s he saw the fascist ideology represented by the Soviet Union. It was no longer Tlön (or Germany) that was taking over the planet, but the Soviets and it was not with democratic ideas that they could be stopped: "Rusia está apoderándose del planeta; América, trabada por la superstición de la democracia, no se resuelve a ser un imperio" (*Obras* 3.13).[34]

Although it received less attention than his statements in support of dictatorships, Borges also started to mention frequently during this epoch anarchism as another political option to which he felt attract-

---

[32]"[He] explained that his book would celebrate the brotherhood of man. The poet of our time could not turn his back on his own age, he went on to say. I [i.e., the older Borges] thought for a while and asked if he truly felt himself a brother to everyone—to all funeral directors, for example, to all postmen, to all deep-sea divers, to all those who lived on the even numbered street, to all those who were aphonic, and so on. He answered that his book referred to the great mass of the oppressed and alienated." (*Sand* 16)

[33]"Your mass of oppressed and alienated," he answers the young Borges, "is no more than an abstraction. . . . Only individuals exist—if it can be said that anyone exists." (*Sand* 16)

[34]"Russia is taking over the world; America, hampered by the superstition of democracy, can't make up his mind to become an empire." (*Sand* 15)

ed (Vázquez 251). Borges's utopian conception of anarchism is that of a "state" in which his individualism will never be threatened by the government. Even though Borges attributes his interest in anarchism to the influence of his father ("Autobiographical Essay" 206) and even says that he always believed in this ideology, the truth is that this is a political idea that only begins to appear in his work after he has abandoned any hope that a liberal government can be effectively established in Argentina.[35] This does not mean that one cannot find in Borges's earlier work moments in which he seems to be attracted to radical individualistic positions. In "Our Poor Individualism," for example, he fantasizes about having a government that would be the exact opposite of fascism: "Sin esperanza y con nostalgia, pienso en la abstracta posibilidad de un partido que tuviera alguna afinidad con los argentinos; un partido que nos prometiera (digamos) un severo mínimo de gobierno" (*Obras* 2.37).[36] In Borges's case, anarchism is the next logical stage in the development of his individualistic ideology.[37] It sounds paradoxical but Borges was attracted to anarchism for the same reason that he supported dictatorships. What these two extreme positions have in common, in Borges's view, is that they both take the power away from the masses, thus preventing the return of fascism. Whereas dictatorships impose the will of a minority on the people, in the perfect anarchical society the "people" would have no power because no "society" or "community" would exist, only individuals.

---

[35]Two short stories from the 1970s that are directly influenced by Borges's concept of anarchism are "Avelino Arredondo" and "Utopia of a Tired Man" (both from *The Book of Sand*).

[36]"Without hope and with nostalgia, I think of the abstract possibility of a political party that has some affinity with the Argentine character; a party that would promise us, say, a rigorous minimum of government." (*Other Inquisitions* 35)

[37]On the differences and similarities between liberal individualism and anarchism, see Brown, *The Politics of Individualism*.

I have tried to show that the fact that Borges's fantastic tales are constructed around a form that privileges the individuality of the subject does not necessarily imply an "elitist" view of culture and a lack of political commitment by the author. No doubt part of Borges's thinking from the beginning of his career is an emphasis on individualism that at different times and by different means he tried to harmonize with collective political action. He saw the defense of individualism as a way of combating fascist politics. Even at crucial moments when it was obvious that only collective and not individual actions could affect the political scene of the country, he still held on to his individualistic ideology. The antidemocratic position that Borges adopted after the 1970s must be seen as a logical result of that ideology.

WORKS CITED

Accaria-Zavala, Diane. "Grasping Shadows in the Flickering Light: Film and the Re-Definition of Literature in Latin America." Diss. New York University, 1992.

Adorno, Theodor W. *Aesthetic Theory*. London: Routledge and Kegan Paul, 1982.

—. *The Culture Industry. Selected Essays on mass culture*. Edited with an Introduction by J.M. Bernstein. London: Routledge, 1991.

—. "Commitment." *Aesthetics and Politics*. Ed. by Ronald Taylor. London: New Left Books, 1977. 177-95.

Adorno, Theodor W., et al. *The Authoritarian Personality*. New York: Harper, 1950.

Adorno, Theodor W., and Max Horkeimer. *Dialectic of Enlightenment*. New York: Herder and Herder, 1972.

Alazraki, Jaime. *Borges and the Kabbalah. And Other Essays on His Fiction and Poetry*. New York: Cambridge UP, 1988.

—. "Génesis de un estilo: *Historia universal de la infamia*," *Revista ibero-americana* 123-24 (1983): 247-61.

—. "Introduction" to *Critical Essays on Jorge Luis Borges*. Ed. Jaime Alazraki. Boston: G.K. Hall, 1987. 1-20.

—. *Jorge Luis Borges*. New York: Columbia UP, 1971.

—. *La prosa Narrativa de Jorge Luis Borges*. 3rd. ed. Madrid: Gredos, 1983.

Alonso, Amado. "Borges, narrador." *Materia y forma en poesía*. 3rd. ed. Madrid: Gredos, 1965. 434-49.

Alonso, Carlos J. *The Spanish Regional Novel. Modernity and Autochthony*. Cambridge: Cambridge UP, 1990.

Anderson, Perry. "Modernity and Revolution." *New Left Review* 144 (1984): 96-113.

Andrew, J. Dudley. *The Major Film Theories*. London: Oxford UP, 1976.

Anzieu, Didier. "Le corps et le code dans les contes de J.L. Borges." *Nouvelle Revue de psychanalyse*. 3 (1971): 177-210.
Arendt, Hannah. "Introduction." *Illuminations*. By Walter Benjamin. Ed. Hannah Arendt. New York: Schocken Books, 1985. 1-55.
—. *On Revolution*. New York: Viking P, 1963.
Balderston, Daniel. *El precursor velado: R.L. Stevenson en la obra de Borges*. Buenos Aires: Editorial Sudamericana, 1985.
Barradas, Efraín. *Para leer en puertorriqueño: acercamiento a la obra de Luis Rafael Sánchez*. Río Piedras, PR: Editorial Cultural, 1981.
Barrenechea, Ana María. *La expresión de la irrealidad en la obra de Borges*. 2nd. ed. Buenos Aires: Paidós, 1967.
Barthes, Roland. *Writing Degree Zero*. New York: Hill and Wang, 1977.
Bazin, André. *Orson Welles*. New York: Harper and Row, 1978.
—. *What Is Cinema?* Vols. 1 and 2. Berkeley: U of California P, 1971.
Bell-Villada, Gene. *Borges and His Fiction. A Guide to His Art and Mind*. Chapel Hill: U of North Carolina P, 1981.
Benjamin, Walter. *Reflections. Essays, Aphorisms, Autobiographical Writings*. New York: Harcourt Brace Jovanovich, 1978.
Berman, Marshall. *All That Is Solid Melts into Air. The Experience of Modernity*. New York: Simon and Schuster, 1982.
Bernès, Jean Pierre. "Notes et variantes. L'Homme au coin du mur rose." 1497-1505. *Oeuvres complètes*. By Jorge Luis Borges. Paris: Gallimard, 1993.
Bloch, Ernst. "Discussing Expressionism." *Aesthetics and Politics*. Ed. Ronald Taylor. London: New Left Books, 1977. 16-27.
Bordwell, David, and Kristin Thompson. *Film Art: An Introduction*. New York: Knopf, 1986.
Bordwell, David, Janet Satiger, and Kristin Thompson. *The Classical Hollywood Cinema. Film Style and Mode of Production to 1960*. New York: Columbia UP, 1985.
Borges, Jorge Luis. *The Aleph and Other Stories*. New York: Dutton, 1970.
—. *Antología personal*. Buenos Aires: Sur, 1964.

—. "Autobiographical Essay." *Critical Essays on Jorge Luis Borges.* Ed. Jaime Alazraki. Boston: G.K. Hall, 1987. 22-55.
—. *The Book of Sand.* New York: Dutton, 1977.
—. *Borges: A Reader.* Ed. Emir Rodríguez Monegal. New York: Dutton, 1981.
—. *Borges en Revista Multicolor.* Ed. Irma Zangara. Buenos Aires: Atlántida, 1995.
—. *Doctor Brodie's Report.* New York: Dutton, 1972.
—. *Dreamtigers.* Austin: U of Texas P, 1964.
—. *Evaristo Carriego.* New York: Dutton, 1984.
—. *Ficcionario. Una Antología de sus textos.* Ed. Emir Rodríguez Monegal. México, D.F.: Fondo de Cultura Económica, 1985.
—. *Ficciones.* New York: Grove P, 1962.
—. *Inquisiciones.* Buenos Aires: Proa, 1925.
—. *Labyrinths. Selected Stories and Other Writings.* New York: Modern Library, 1983.
—. *Obras completas.* 3 vols. Buenos Aires: Emecé, 1989.
—. *Oeuvres complètes.* Paris: Gallimard, 1993.
—. *Other Inquisitions.* Austin: U of Texas P, 1964.
—. *A Personal Anthology.* New York: Grove P, 1967.
—. *Poesía juvenil de Jorge Luis Borges.* Ed. Carlos Meneses. Pequeña Biblioteca Calamus Scriptorious 18. Barcelona: José J. de Olañeta Editor, 1978.
—. *Prólogos.* Buenos Aires: Torres Agüero, 1975.
—. *Selected Poems, 1923-1967.* New York, Delacorte P, 1972.
—. "Sobre la descripción literaria." *Sur* 97 (1942): 100-102.
—. *Textos cautivos. Ensayos y reseñas en "El Hogar" (1936-1939).* Ed. by Enrique Sacerio-Garí y Emir Rodríguez Monegal. Barcelona: Tusquets, 1986.
—. *A Universal History of Infamy.* New York: Dutton, 1972.
Borges, Jorge Luis, and Delia Ingenieros. *Antiguas literaturas germánicas.* México: Fondo de Cultura Económica, 1951.
Bradbury, Malcolm and James McFarlane. "The Name and Nature of Modernism." *Modernism, 1890-1930.* Ed. Malcolm Bradbury and James McFarlane. Sussex: The Harvester P, 1978. 19-55.

Brown, Susan L. *The Politics of Individualism.* New York: Black Rose Books, 1993.
Buck-Morss, Susan. *The Origin of Negative Dialectics.* London: Free P, 1977.
Burgin, Richard. *Conversations with Jorge Luis Borges.* New York: Holt, Rinehart and Winston, 1969.
Bürger, Peter. "The Decline of the Modern Age." *Telos* 62 (1984-85): 117-30.
—. *Theory of the Avant-Garde.* Minneapolis: U of Minnesota P, 1984.
Campra, Rosalba. *América Latina: la identidad y la máscara.* México, D.F.: Siglo Veintiuno, 1987.
Carpentier, Alejo. *Tientos, diferencias y otros ensayos.* Barcelona: Plaza y Janés, 1987.
Charbonier, Georges. *El escritor y su obra. Entrevistas con Jorge Luis Borges.* México, D.F.: Siglo Veintiuno, 1970.
Christ, Ronald. *The Narrow Act.* New York: New York UP, 1969.
Clark, Michael. "Political Nominalism and Critical Performance." *Literary Theory's Future(s).* Ed. Joseph Natoli. Chicago: U of Illinois P, 1989.
Cozarinsky, Edgardo. *Borges en/y/sobre cine.* Madrid: Fundamentos, 1981.
—. *Borges in/and/on Film.* New York: Lumen Books, 1988.
Croll, Morris W. "The Baroque Style in Prose." *Literary English Since Shakespeare.* Ed. by George Watson. London, Oxford, New York: Oxford UP, 1970. 84-110.
Crook, Stephen. "Introduction: Adorno and Authoritarian Irrationalism." *Adorno: The Stars Down to Earth and Other Essays on the Irrational in Culture.* Ed. Stephen Crook. London: Routledge, 1994.
D'Alembert, Jean Le Rond. *Preliminary Discourse to the Encyclopedia of Diderot.* Trans. Richard N. Schwab. Indianapolis: Bobbs-Merrill Company, 1963.
Deleuze, Gilles. *Cinema 1.The Movement Image.* London: The Athlone P, 1986.
De Man, Paul. *Blindness and Insight.* Minneapolis: U of Minnesota P, 1983.

—. "A Modern Master." *Critical Essays on Jorge Luis Borges.* Ed. Jaime Alazraki. Boston: G.K. Hall. 1987. 55-62.
Dowling, William C. *Jameson, Althusser, Marx: An Introduction to The Political Unconscious.* Ithaca: Cornell UP, 1984.
Eagleton, Terry. *Literary Theory.* Minneapolis: U of Minnesota P, 1983.
Eisenstein, Sergei. *Film Form.* New York: Harcourt, 1949.
Ferreira-Pinto, Cristina. "La narrativa cinematográfica de Borges." *Revista iberoamericana* 155-56 (1991): 495-505.
Fló, Juan. *Contra Borges.* Buenos Aires: Ed. Galerna, 1978.
Foucault, Michel. *The Order of Things.* New York: Vintage Books, 1973.
—. "What Is an Author?" *Contemporary Literary Criticism.* Ed. Robert Davis and Ronald Schleifer. New York: Longman, 1989. 262-75.
Franco, Jean. "Dependency Theory and Literary History: The Case of Latin America." *The Minnesota Review* 5 (Fall 1975): 65-80.
—. "The Utopia of a Tired Man: Jorge Luis Borges." *Social Text* 4 (1981): 52-78.
Frisby, David. *Fragments of Modernity: Theories of Modernity in the Works of Simmer, Kracauer and Benjamin.* Cambridge, Massachusetts: MIT P, 1985.
Frye, Northrop. *The Anatomy of Criticism.* Princeton: Princeton UP, 1957.
Furness, R.S. *Expressionism.* London: Methuen, 1973.
Furtado, Celso. *Economic Development of Latin America. A Survey from Colonial Times to the Cuban Revolution.* Trans. Suzette Macedo. Cambridge: Cambridge UP, 1970.
González Echevarría, Roberto. *Myth and Archive. A Theory of Latin American Literature.* Cambridge: Cambridge UP, 1990.
—. *The Voice of the Masters.* Austin: U of T P, 1985.
Green, Martin. *Seven Types of Adventure Tale. An Etiology of a Major Genre.* University Park: The Pennsylvania State UP, 1991.
Habermas, Jurgen. *The Philosophical Discourse of Modernity.* Cambridge: MIT P, 1987.

Harvey, David. *The Condition of Postmodernity. An Enquiry into the Origins of Cultural Change.* Oxford: Blackwell, 1990.

Heidegger, Martin. *Basic Writings.* New York: Harper and Row, 1977.

Hume, David. *An Enquiry Concerning Human Understanding.* Indianapolis: Hackett, 1977.

Hutcheon, Linda. *A Poetics of Postmodernism. History, Theory, Fiction.* New York: Routledge, 1988.

Irby, James. "Borges and the Idea of Utopia." *The Cardinal Points of Borges.* Ed. by Lowell Dunham and Ivar Ivask. Norman, Oklahoma: U of Oklahoma P, 1971. 35-45.

—. "Introduction." *Labyrinths. Selected Stories and Other Writings.* By Jorge Luis Borges. New York: Modern Library, 1983. xv-xxiii.

—. *The Structure of the Stories of Jorge Luis Borges.* Ph.D. Dissertation, University of Michigan, 1962. Ann Arbor: UNMI, 1972.

Jameson, Fredric. *Late Marxism. Adorno, or, the Persistence of the Dialectic.* London: Verso, 1990

—. *The Political Unconscious.* Ithaca: Cornell UP, 1981.

—. *Postmodernism or the Cultural Logic of Late Capitalism.* Durham: Duke UP, 1991.

—. *Signatures of the Visible.* New York, London: Routledge, 1990.

Kazin, Alfred. "Meeting Borges." *Critical Essays on Jorge Luis Borges.* Ed. Jaime Alazraki. Boston: G.K. Hall, 1987. 127-30.

Kellner, Douglas. *Critical Theory, Marxism and Modernity.* Cambridge: Polity P, 1989.

Kershaw, Ian. *The Nazi Dictatorship. Problems and Perspectives of Interpretation.* New York: Edward Arnold, 1985.

Knapp, James F. *Literary Modernism and the Transformation of Work.* Evanston: Northwestern UP, 1988.

Lapidot, Emma. *Borges y la inteligencia artificial.* Madrid: Pliegos, 1990.

Lukács, Georg. *The Meaning of Contemporary Realism.* London: Merlin P, 1962.

—. "Realism in the Balance." *Aesthetics and Politics.* Ed. Ronald Taylor. London: New Left Books, 1977. 28-59.

Lyotard, Jean-François. *The Postmodern Condition: A Report on Knowledge*. Minneapolis: U of Minnesota P, 1988.
Mandel, Ernest. *Delightful Murder. A Social History of the Crime Story*. London: Pluto P, 1984.
Marcos, Juan Manuel. "Reseña de *Critical Essays on Jorge Luis Borges*." *Revista iberoamericana* 153 (1987): 706-707.
Martin, Jay. *Adorno*. Cambridge: Harvard UP, 1984.
Martínez, Carlos Dámaso. "Horacio Quiroga: la industria editorial, el cine y sus relatos fantásticos." *Todos los cuentos*. Por Horacio Quiroga. España: Archivos, 1993
Matamoro, Blas. *Jorge Luis Borges o el juego trascendente*. Buenos Aires: A. Peña Lillo, 1971.
Merrell, Floyd. *Unthinking Thinking: Jorge Luis Borges, Mathematics and the New Physics*. West Lafayette, Ind.: Purdue UP, 1991.
Molloy, Silvia. *Signs of Borges*. Durham: Duke UP, 1994.
Nicoll, Allardyce. *Film and Theatre*. New York: Thomas Y. Crowell, 1936.
Panek, Leroy Lad. *An Introduction to the Detective Story*. Bowling Green: Bowling Green State U Popular Culture P, 1987.
Priest, Stephen. *The British Empiricists*. London: Penguin, 1990.
Priestman, Martin. *Detective Fiction and Literature. The Figure on the Carpet*. New York: St. Martin's P, 1991.
Quiroga, Horacio. *Todos los cuentos*. España: Archivos, 1993.
Rama, Angel. *La ciudad letrada*. Hanover, NH: Ediciones del Norte, 1984.
—. *La novela en América Latina. Panoramas 1920-1980*. Bogotá: Procultura, 1982.
Rodríguez-Luis, Julio. "La intención política en la obra de Borges: hacia una visión de conjunto." *Cuadernos hispanoamericanos* 361-62 (1980): 170-98.
Rodríguez Monegal, Emir. "Borges and Politics." *Diacritics* 8.4 (1978): 55-69.
—. *Jorge Luis Borges. A Literary Biography*. New York: Paragon House, 1988.
Rorty, Richard. *Philosophy and the Mirror of Nature*. Princeton: Princeton UP, 1979.

Ruffinelli, Jorge. "Borges y el ultraísmo: un caso de estética y política." *Cuadernos americanos* 3.9 (1988): 155-74.
Sabato, Ernesto. *Obras. Ensayos.* Buenos Aires: Losada, 1970.
Sarlo, Beatriz. *La imaginación técnica: sueños modernos de la cultura argentina.* Buenos Aires: Nueva Visión, 1992.
Sarlo, Beatriz. *Una modernidad periférica: Buenos Aires 1920 y 1930.* Buenos Aires: Nueva Visión, 1988.
—. *Jorge Luis Borges: A Writer on the Edge.* London: Verso, 1993.
Savater, Fernando. *La infancia recuperada.* Madrid: Taurus, 1977.
Sorrentino, Fernando. *Seven Conversations with Jorge Luis Borges.* Troy, N.Y.: The Whitston Publishing Company, 1982.
Sosnowski, Saúl. *Borges y la cábala.* Buenos Aires: Hispamérica, 1976.
Sturrock, John. *Paper Tigers. The Ideal Fictions of Jorge Luis Borges.* Oxford: Clarendon P, 1977.
Tadié, Jean-Yves. *Le roman d'aventures.* Paris: Presses Universitaires de France, 1982.
Taylor, Ronald. Ed. *Aesthetics and Politics.* London: New Left Books, 1977.
Todorov, Tzvetan. *The Fantastic. A Structural Approach to a Literary Genre.* Cleveland: Case Western Reserve UP, 1973.
Torre Borges, Miguel de. "Jorge Luis Borges: A Day in the Life." *The New Yorker* (June 1993): 90-92.
Vázquez, María Esther. *Borges, sus días y su tiempo.* Buenos Aires: Javier Vergara Editor, 1984.
Wheelock, Carter. *The Mythmaker.* Austin: U of Texas P, 1969.
Whelan, Frederick G. *Order and Artifice in Hume's Political Philosophy.* Princeton: Princeton UP, 1985.
Williams, Howard. *Concepts of Ideology.* New York: St. Martin P, 1988.
Williams, Raymond. *Marxism and Literature.* Oxford: Oxford UP, 1977.
Woolhouse, R.S. *The Empiricists.* Oxford: Oxford UP, 1988.
Woscoboinik, Julio. *El secreto de Borges. Indagación psicoanalítica de su obra.* Buenos Aires: Grupo Editor Latinoamericano, 1991.
Zuidervaart, Lambert. *Adorno's Aesthetic Theory. The Redemption of Illusion.* Cambridge, Mass: MIT P, 1991.

INDEX

Accaria-Zavala, Daniel 105, 106, 107, 113, 128
Adorno, T.W. 32-33, 57, 177, 189
Alazraki, Jaime 89, 143, 144, 169, 170, 188
Alonso, Amado 29, 143
Alonso, Carlos J. 46
Anderson, Perry 12, 14, 20
antitotalitarianism 169
Anzieu, Didier 81
Apollinaire, Guillaume 16, 105
April March 79
Arabian culture 46
Arabian Nights 60
Argos Film 100
Atlántida 97
auteur theory 133
The Authoritarian Personality 177
autonomization 157
autonomous art 188

barbarism 39-40, 54-55, 56, 172, 179, 185, 193, 195
Baroque writers 22
Barthes, Roland 74, 75, 76, 159; *Writing Degree Zero* 74
Battleship Potemkin 121

Bazin, André 118, 119, 126, 127, 128, 133
Berman, Marshall 5-6, 12
Bioy Casares, Adolfo 60, 130, 132, 134; *La invención de Morel*, 60, 63
Borges, Jorge Luis, *El Aleph*, 52; "The Approach to al-Mu'tasim" 31; "The Argentine Writer and Tradition" 43-44, 121; "El arte narrativo y la magia" 79; "Autobiographical Essay" 30, 82, 85; "A Celebration of the Monster" 190; "A Comment on August 23" 181; *Complete Works*, 191, 195; "Conjectural Poem" 185; *Crítica*, 30, 83, 84, 87, 180; "The Dead Man" 134, 147; "Death and the Compass" 93, 141, 147; *Discusión*, 23, 30, 35, 38, 76, 102; *Doctor Brodie's Report*, 28, 53, 152; "Emma Zunz" 38; *Evaristo Carriego*, 30, 60, 101, 102, 103, 104, 180, 192; *Ficciones*, 31, 52, 78, 111; "Flaubert y su destino ejemplar" 76; "Fragmento sobre Joyce"

78; "The Garden of Forking Paths" 36, 38; *Historia de la eternidad* 109; "Hurry, Hurry" 182, 185, 187, 188; "The Immortal" 164; *Inquisiciones*, 16, 153, 180; "El jardín de senderos que se bifurcan" 79; "The Lottery in Babylon" 36, 69; *La moneda de hierro*, 195; "Narrative Art and Magic" 64, 79, 116, 135; "New Refutation of Time" 156; "Nineteen Hundred and Twenty-Odd" 192; "The Nothingness of Personality" 180; *Los orilleros*, 130; "Our Poor Individualism" 184, 198; "El paraíso de los creyentes" 130; *Personal Anthology*, 145; "Pierre Menard, Author of the Quixote" 30, 80, 84, 111, 159; "Portrait of a Germanophile" 174, 177, 178, 182, 190; "The Postulation of Reality" 106, 128; "Red Hymns" 196; "Rosendo's Tale" 25, 28, 53; "The Secret Miracle" 189; "The Shape of the Sword" 38; "The South" 80, 129, 137, 138, 191; "Story of the Warrior and the Captive" 54, 69, 94; "Street Corner Man" 23-25, 27-35, 38, 53, 84, 181, 184, 187, 192; "The Theologians" 138, 140; "Tlön, Uqbar, Orbis Tertius" 30, 84, 163, 165, 187; "Trau keinem Jud bei seinem Eid" 171; "Ulysses" 68, 78, 79; *A Universal History of Infamy*, 23, 24, 29, 30, 31, 80, 84, 101, 103, 105, 110, 151, 152; "Vindicación de Bouvard y Pécuchet" 76; "The Zahir" 40, 42; anarchism in Borges 197, 198; Byzantinism in Borges 3; modern aesthetics in Borges 16; modernity in Borges 32; nationalism in Borges 9, 27, 34, 35, 39, 51, 54, 179, 184, 185, 186, 194, 195; nostalgia in Borges 18, 161, 162, 163, 167, 198; pessimism in Borges 50, 51, 53, 54; postmodern characteristics in Borges 160, 161; solipsism in Borges 145

Bordwell, David 119, 123, 124, 133, 136, 137, 138
Breton, André 183
British Imperialism 175
Browne, Thomas 153, 154, 161, 165, 167
Buenos Aires 16, 17-19, 24, 27, 82, 85, 97, 100, 180, 190, 191, 192, 194
Bürger, Peter 32, 33

Cahiers du cinéma 133
Campra, Rosalba 55
Caras y caretas 97
Carlyle, Thomas, *On Heroes* 191
Carpentier, Alejo 46, 47, 48, 55
Casa Rosada 25
Cervantes y Saavedra, Miguel de, *Don Quixote* 62, 159
Chaplin, Charles 121, 125, 138, 139, 140
Chesterton, G.K. 64, 101
Cinema Chat 100
Citizen Kane 106, 107, 108, 112, 133
Clarté 97
Collins, Wilkie 67
committed art 4, 14

Dadaism 7
D'Alembert, Jean, *Preliminary Discourse* 90-91
Darío, Rubén 48-49
De Quincey, Thomas 62
découpage 126, 127, 128, 129, 133, 134
Descartes, René 157
Diderot, Denis 90, 91
Dostoyevsky, Fyodor, *Crime and Punishment* 115
Duarte, Eva 194

Eisenstein, Sergei 106, 116, 117, 118, 125, 126, 127, 133

Eliot, T.S., *Waste Land, The* 89, 139
Elizabethan theater 100
empiricism, British 9, 148
encyclopedia, concept of 89-90, 91, 111, 174, 191
Expressionism 14-15, 105, 180
expressionist cinema 105, 106

fantastic fiction 23, 29, 35, 38, 52, 69, 187
fascism 10, 165, 167, 170, 171, 172, 176, 177, 178, 179, 181, 182, 183, 184, 185, 186, 187, 188, 190, 191, 193, 195, 196, 197, 198
Faulkner, William 160; *Wild Palms*, 85
Film revista 100
Flaubert, Gustave 40, 74, 75, 76, 77, 159
Foucault, Michel 111, 112; *The Order of Things* 111, 173
Franco, Francisco 169
Franco, Jean 48
La fuga 113, 116
Futurism 15

Gallegos, Rómulo 39
gaucho 39, 45, 138, 184, 185, 195
geometrization 29, 65, 67-68
German expressionist cinema 113, 124
Gide, André, *Persephone* 85
Gilbert, Stuart 79

The Golden Ass 62
Greek tragedy 120
Griffith, D.W., *Intolerance* 136, 137, 138
Güiraldes, Ricardo 39

haiku 125
Heidegger, Martin, *Letter on Humanism* 94
Los héroes del cine 100
Hitchcock, Alfred 124
El hogar 84, 86, 87, 97, 171, 172, 173, 174
Hogar y cine 100
Hollywood films 68, 98, 113, 114, 116, 117, 118, 120, 121, 123, 124, 125, 126, 127, 128, 129-37, 140
Homer, *Iliad* 164

Icelandic sagas 37, 38, 126
individualism 164, 165, 167, 170, 179, 180, 181, 183, 184, 185, 187, 188, 195, 196, 198, 199
Irby, James 19, 143, 144
Irigoyen, Hipólito 26, 27, 180

Jameson, Fredric 157, 158
Joyce, James 68, 75, 78

Kabbala, Jewish 93
Kafka, Franz 62, 85
Kazin, Alfred 180
Krazy Kat 121

Lukács, Georg 34
Lyotard, Jean-François 72-73, 89

Mandel, Ernest, *Delightful Murder* 92
Mayo, Archie 139
Mexico 18
Miró Gabriel 108, 109, 110, 112, 140
Modernism 6-9, 11-13, 20, 21, 23, 29, 32, 34, 35, 39, 41, 42, 43, 51, 52, 57, 70, 72, 73, 80, 88, 106, 122, 158, 159, 160, 167
modernity 6, 8, 11, 12, 15, 21, 32, 38, 41, 50, 63, 158, 163, 164, 167, 170
Molloy, Sylvia 30, 36, 108, 109, 110, 111, 113, 139; *Signs of Borges* 108
Moore, Thomas, *Lalla Rookh* 60

La nación 97
Nazism 173, 174, 175, 176, 177, 181, 182, 184
neologisms 22
Nicoll, Allardyce 99, 100
Njal Saga 38

Panek, Leroy 66-67
pantheism 134, 138, 159, 163, 164, 165
parataxis 29, 102, 153, 158

Perón, Juan Domingo 53, 107, 171, 181, 182, 184, 187, 188, 190, 191, 192, 194, 195
Petit de Murat, Ulyses 98
Picasso, Pablo 32, 33
Pinochet, Augusto 169
Postmodernism 10, 57, 72, 95, 144, 159, 160, 161
Pound, Ezra 74
Prisma 97
Proust, Marcel 75, 88, 160
Psycho 124

Quevedo, Francisco de 167
Quiroga, Horacio 55, 97, 98, 99, 121

Rama, Angel 46-48, 49
Realism 9, 28, 32, 33, 34, 35, 37, 38, 39, 50, 51, 52, 53, 54, 56, 61, 106, 127
regionalism 45
Rilke, Rainer Maria, *Notebooks* 89
Rio de Janeiro 18
Rivera, Diego 183
Rodríguez Monegal, Emir 14, 76, 80, 81, 82, 83, 85, 89, 170, 190; *Literary Biography* 82
Roman Empire 54
Romantic writers 163
Rosas, Juan Manuel 27, 180, 192, 195
Ruffinelli, Jorge 15

Russian Revolution 13

Sabato, Ernesto 65
Sarlo, Beatriz 100, 114; *La imaginación técnica* 114
Seven Voyages of Sindbad 62
Soviet cinema 116, 117, 121, 124, 128, 131, 134
Staiger, Janet 119
Stevenson, Robert Louis 58, 101; *Treasure Island* 60
Stravinsky, Igor 33
style coupé 22-23, 152, 154
Sur 85, 86, 98, 108, 171, 179
surrealism 7, 8

Tadié, Jean-Yves 62-63, 67
Thompson, Kristin 118, 119, 136, 137, 138

Ultraism, 13, 15, 16

Vargas Llosa, Mario 55
Vázquez, María Esther 28
Viola, Roberto Eduardo 169

Welles, Orson 106, 108, 112, 133
Wheelock, Carter 69, 144, 145, 146, 147, 149, 150
Williams, Howard 185
The Wizard of Oz 137-38, 140
Woolf, Virginia; *Orlando* 85; *A Room of One's Own* 85
Woscoboinik, Julio, *El secreto de Borges* 81